Elvis Presley, Reluctant Rebel

Elvis Presley, Reluctant Rebel

HIS LIFE AND OUR TIMES

Glen Jeansonne, David Luhrssen, and Dan Sokolovic

PRAEGER

AN IMPRINT OF ABC-CLIO, LLC
Santa Barbara, California • Denver, Colorado • Oxford, England

Library of Congress Cataloging-in-Publication Data

Jeansonne, Glen, 1946–
   Elvis Presley, reluctant rebel : his life and our times / Glen Jeansonne, David Luhrssen, and Dan Sokolovic.
     p. cm.
   Includes bibliographical references and index.
   ISBN 978-0-313-35904-0 (hard copy : alk. paper)—ISBN 978-0-313-35905-7 (ebook)
   1. Presley, Elvis, 1935–1977. 2. Rock musicians—United States—Biography. I. Luhrssen, David. II. Sokolovic, Dan. III. Title.
   ML420.P96J36   2011
   782.4166092—dc22 [B]   2010040863

ISBN: 978-0-313-35904-0
EISBN: 978-0-313-35905-7

15 14 13 12 11   1 2 3 4 5

This book is also available on the World Wide Web as an eBook.
Visit www.abc-clio.com for details.

Praeger
An Imprint of ABC-CLIO, LLC

ABC-CLIO, LLC
130 Cremona Drive, P.O. Box 1911
Santa Barbara, California 93116-1911

This book is printed on acid-free paper ∞

Manufactured in the United States of America

Contents

Preface

Elvis came to me directly. I heard him on the radio, watched him on television, and saw him gyrate live. When I drove alone in my dad's '57 Chevy I often listened to country music with its sad lyrics and upbeat melody that registered in my mind, "keep humming even when things go badly. If the world ends, don't let it spoil your day."

But when I drove around with friends, or went to the ice cream drive-in, we played rock and roll. And most of all, when I danced, I danced to rock and roll. I lived in a small farm town in Louisiana, not far from the roiling Mississippi, and never took dancing lessons. But I had the natural moves of a broken-field runner. What I always liked most about Elvis songs, and what I think he liked best, were the romantic ballads made for slow dancing. They allowed you to hold your partner closer than the waltzes of my mom and dad's day. I could look into a girl's eyes—often up—because teenage girls were frequently taller than me.

Yet the fast dances offered the opportunity for something less patterned than most social dances, and it was an opportunity to really let go. If you were agile and athletic, it was, and is, the most enjoyable kind of dance. Instead of moving to patterns, I always preferred simply to move to the music. My partner, in these dances, was less relevant than in the slow dances. It was much the same as what Elvis did when he moved as he sang—he was doing something natural, moving to something inside him.

If you don't have that kind of internal rhythm, you can't buy it on Broadway. I did not need alcohol or anything else to achieve intoxication; I got high on the music. Because the music is still with us even though Elvis is not, it still makes me high. With that music, there is never any reason to be lonely. If I had to make a list of 100 things to do to pull out of a slump, I would begin with: Listen to a song you love. As many times as it takes. You can also listen with baby boomers, or with your children. Of course we boomers have the inside track because Elvis is in us and of us. And I agree with him that what the world needs is "A Little Less Talk, and a Lot More Action."

Glen Jeansonne

My parents never cared for Elvis Presley and, as I was growing into a teenager, neither did my peers. I came of age with Led Zeppelin and Pink Floyd, when the line connecting Elvis to what was current in rock music was blurry at best. To me, Elvis was an uncomfortable transitional figure between the swing era of my parents and the foundational rock of the 1960s, the star of movies everyone found laughable.

And then I heard "Heartbreak Hotel," with its anguished vocals, slightly surreal lyrics, and searing electric guitar. I began to wonder whether there might not be something about Elvis that remained valuable, that spoke beyond his particular place and time. Months later, Elvis died. Awash in tributes and retrospectives, I sought out his earliest music, recordings recently made available for the first time in many years on an LP called the *Sun Sessions*. What I heard was a revelation.

My story is not entirely unique. In many respects death gave Elvis's career a second lease on life, liberating him from the druggy isolation of his final years, his end game of Las Vegas glitz. In death Elvis became whatever anyone wanted to see in him. His demise also forced many people to listen with fresh ears and evaluate his place not only in American music but in the evolution of popular culture the world over. Rock and roll was already happening before Elvis set foot in the recording studio, but he became its great ambassador and embodiment. Elvis may have wanted nothing more than to become a pop singer, the new Dean Martin. Instead, he helped point the way to what seemed, to middle-class teenagers of the 1950s, a new world of possibility. It was the world inherited by generations to come.

David Luhrssen

In 1947, while Elvis was probably reading his treasured comic books in a two-room shotgun shack in East Tupelo, Mississippi, I was busy being born in a displaced persons camp in the British sector of Germany. My hometown, if you would like to call it that, was Grossenbrode, a former Luftwaffe/U-boat base. My parents, grandparents, aunts, and uncles had all fled from Yugoslavia across the border into

Trieste, Italy, one step ahead of the Communist regime of Josip Broz Tito. First they endured and fought as nationalistic freedom fighters against the Germans, and then they lost a second fight to the Communists. There was nothing left for them in Yugoslavia. Their flight led them on a year's trek through camps in Italy, Austria, and eventually, Germany. They were searching for a home they did not know; the only question was, where? Where exactly would this "promised land" be?

Arriving in the United States with nothing but the clothes on our backs, and one battered suitcase apiece, it was only much later that I would figure out that our parents took this perilous step into a new world, not for themselves, but for their children. Their lives and dreams were effectively over; they would spend their thoughts, wishes, and money on their children and that promise of their future. With the promise of sponsorship by my mom's uncle (that small part of the family had arrived in America a generation earlier), and a permanent job in a factory for my dad, we settled into my Uncle Peter's home. We had two rooms in the upstairs part of their house.

By 1954, as Elvis gathered up the nerve to enter the door of Sun Studios to cut a simple recording for "his mother," my entire family and I had found a home in West Allis, Wisconsin, a working-class suburb of Milwaukee. My Memphis consisted of a two-block stretch of 73rd Street. When Elvis had his first record released by a major label, RCA Victor, in 1956, I was fighting my way through early grade school. I was actually held back for half a year to concentrate on English, my second language.

It would not take long for me to have my first encounter with Elvis. American radio did not intrigue me at such a young age because I had difficulty with the language; the radio generally wasn't on in our house. But one late spring morning in 1956, when I came bounding down the stairs, my ear glued itself to the speaker of the living room radio. I had no idea who was singing, I had no idea why he was singing, and I certainly had no idea what he was singing about. But I was sure he was saying something.

When I saw Elvis for the first time on *The Ed Sullivan Show*, we had moved to our own house by then. Kids in school were talking about the upcoming performance, and we were lucky to have acquired a used, black-and-white television with a tiny screen, set in a large cabinet. I was one of those glued to a screen, four feet from the set, my chin braced on my arms.

I was mesmerized, and it only took a few days for me to talk my mom into getting me a small portable radio. Popular music—rock and roll in particular—quickly became a constant companion for me. The songs have served me as oral traditions are supposed to, as a remembrance of the past, and a window into other worlds.

To this day, the sounds of "Well, since my baby left me . . ." set me off in search of a cheap, white, plastic Japanese radio with one ear plug. That one evening of television helped to liberate and transform me.

Dan Sokolovic

Acknowledgments

The authors thank Elizabeth Demers, who approved our proposal for this book before leaving her position as acquisitions editor at Praeger. We appreciate the enthusiasm and perceptive comments of our new editor, Mariah Gumpert, who supported the project from onset through publication.

Research for *Elvis Presley, Reluctant Rebel* was assisted by Bruce Cole of Marquette University's Raynor Memorial Libraries, a music fan whose expertise with interlibrary loan made a world of information accessible; Meredith Vnuk of the Milwaukee Public Library System, whose tireless search for books was invaluable; and Martin Jack Rosenblum of the University of Wisconsin–Milwaukee, who provided many helpful leads.

The authors also appreciate Mary Manion for searching the archives for photos of Elvis, and Hannah Jeansonne for her work as research assistant. Glen Jeansonne would also like to thank his wife, Lauren, for her constant, loving support.

1

Love Me Tender

The state of Mississippi may not have been the only place where the blues was born, given the music's unchronicled origins in the work songs and field hollers of African Americans across the South, but it was the state where the blues received its most distinctive and influential form. Mississippi blues became the building stone for American music in the 20th century. The spontaneous invention of the blues and its ability to transmute anguish into joy was vital to the development of jazz, born down river in the port city of New Orleans. The crying notes of the blues found their way into country music; its search for transient pleasure in the midst of poverty became a cornerstone of rhythm and blues. Rock and roll as we know it would not have existed without the blues.

The Mississippi River, which is Mississippi's western border, enthroned cotton as king of the state's economic and social life. The kingdom of cotton was the ideal catalyst for the blues. Through the middle years of the 20th century, the flat delta country was carved into sprawling cotton plantations employing many hundreds of African American field hands and the labor of sharecroppers. White sharecroppers, including the Presley family, also engaged in cotton picking. Elvis's mother, Gladys, returned to the cotton fields soon after his birth, laying the boy on a cotton sack to watch as she labored.

Given the enormous demand for cheap labor in the cotton fields, black hands outnumbered white hands in many districts where racism reached a terrible pitch. Fearing unrest, white Mississippi enacted repressive Jim Crow legislation and tolerated lynch laws to keep blacks at the bottom of the social system. More recorded lynchings—534 in all—occurred in Mississippi from 1882 through 1952 than in any other state. The total number of victims will never be known.[1]

The tensions of everyday life for African Americans in rural Mississippi found release in gospel music and its estranged, earthier brother, the blues. Not unlike the churches attended by poor whites, the black churches empowered their members with a sense of dignity and worth, while tending to defer fulfillment to the afterlife or the Day of Judgment. The blues focused instead on temporal reality and represented a way of transcending the hardship of being black in a racist society.

By definition, there were no white blues singers in the music's early decades, yet the echo of the blues could be heard with increasing clarity in swing jazz, country, and popular music. By the time Elvis Presley entered the recording studio to cut his first commercial release, a version of Arthur Crudup's blues song "That's All Right," he already stood at the end of a long line of white singers who learned how to invest earthy emotion into their music from the example of blues. Although Crudup began recording after his move to Chicago, he was born and raised, like most significant blues musicians, in the Mississippi Delta.[2]

As the artery of American commerce, the river of dreams, the Mississippi River and its tributaries formed nature's grid work for the nation's transportation hubs, linked in the 20th century by railroads and highways as much as riverboats, which became stepping stones and channels for the Great Migration of African Americans seeking opportunities in the North. The condition of blacks in Mississippi molded the blues and encouraged many musicians to migrate northward in search of greater freedom and opportunity. Likewise, many of the state's poor whites were on the move as the 20th century progressed, including the Presley family, who followed the direction of the Mississippi River to the crossroads city of Memphis, Tennessee.

After he assumed his role as King of Rock and Roll, Elvis Presley held court from rented houses and suites in Hollywood and Las Vegas, where he made the movies that encumbered his career in the 1960s and staged the shows that sustained him through the 1970s. Hollywood and Las Vegas were looming paradoxes in the imagination of most Americans in the 1950s, symbols of the country's corruption and enterprise, places where dreams could be played out. Elvis eagerly chased those dreams, but was never more than a sojourner in dreamland. With the exception of his two years of military service, and a few childhood months in Pascagoula, Mississippi, where his father found work in the shipyards, Presley traveled little aside from what was necessary for his career as an entertainer. He knew only two hometowns: his birthplace, Tupelo, Mississippi; and the city where the Presleys found work, Memphis, Tennessee.

Tupelo Childhood

Tupelo is tucked into the northeast corner of the Tennessee Hills, a spur of the Appalachian range, a wooded countryside rich in game and fertile black soil. By the 20th century, land that had once been used for hunting, trapping, and grazing had been enclosed by wealthy landowners; the district's rural inhabitants became perennially indebted to planters and storekeepers and increasingly reliant on Mississippi's principal cash crop, cotton, whose value was subject to the speculation of world markets. At the time of Elvis Aaron Presley's birth on January 8, 1935, there were two Tupelos. Elvis entered the world in East Tupelo, the smaller, ramshackle town on the wrong side of the tracks from the more metropolitan Tupelo. The St. Louis-San Francisco and Gulf Mobile and Ohio railroads, which converged in Tupelo, marked the boundary. The city fathers of Tupelo, the seat of Lee County with some 6,000 inhabitants at the time of Elvis's birth, promoted their community as a bustling center of the New South. Tupelo was home to several cotton mills and benefited from the Tennessee Valley Authority's ambitious program to light the rural South with electricity. It was a small town with the amenities of city life, including a department store, cinemas, restaurants, and a radio station. East Tupelo was the bad neighbor with a rough reputation as a den of bootleggers and prostitutes, a shallow breeding pond for all the vices associated with the Old South.[3]

Born Gladys Smith, Elvis's mother was one of eight children, the daughter of a tenant farmer who maintained a precarious life in the face of drought, cyclones, and insects. After her father's death, she moved to East Tupelo to be closer to her job sewing work shirts at the Tupelo Garment Company in the Mill Town district, where the county's cotton mill was located. Elvis's father, Vernon, and grandfather, Jessie, had also been sharecroppers tending farm fields for landowners. The spelling of the family name was uncertain. It often appeared as Pressley in official records. Many of the Presley men had been known as hellions or ne'er-do-wells, while the women, as was often true in the rural South, tended to keep the ends together. The unhurried routine of the Old South, where the Yankee work ethic had not fully taken hold and incentives for hard work in a sharecropping economy were slim to nonexistent, continued into the time of Elvis's youth.

Vernon had completed fifth grade, which represented an advance over the formal education of his ancestors in a state where the reach of public schools extended slowly to the lower classes. Despite a reputation for being shiftless, Vernon "always worked at somethin'," in the words of Elvis's cousin, Harold Lloyd. He would periodically snatch the crumbs of economic opportunity modernity brought to East Tupelo. Vernon worked as a carpenter for the Works Progress Administration, the New Deal agency charged with putting America back to work during the Great Depression. At the time Elvis was born, Vernon was a milkman driving a delivery route.[4]

The Presley family stares at an uncertain future during the Great Depression. (Corbis)

Elvis's parents took part in the rapid shift from rural to urban, from agriculture to blue collar work, which began to transform the South in the 1920s and 1930s. The Presleys, like many thousands of sharecroppers and tenant farmers across the South, desperately clung to their rural folkways as the economic basis of their life was transformed by tractors and federal agriculture policies and the spread of manufacturing and service jobs. "Even if rural, white Southerners no longer physically resided in the backwoods, down a country road, or on a small farm, they continued to live there in their memories."[5] This cultural phenomenon explains much of the imagery and audience for country music, which was transformed from folk music into a branch of the entertainment industry in the years preceding Elvis's birth.

Poverty and family, religion and race, were the primary facts of life for a rural Southerner of Elvis's time regardless of the Great Depression. Vernon and Gladys met at a church social. He was regarded as handsome, a natty dresser within his means, and she was a vivacious dark-haired beauty. According to rumor, Gladys was partially of American Indian heritage. "Elvis knew that he had Indian blood in him. He liked that. He said that's where he got his high cheekbones," said his cousin Billy Smith.[6] Vernon had to borrow the three dollars for the marriage license on their wedding day (1933).

The Presleys nailed together the two-room shotgun shack with a covered porch where Elvis was born with money advanced from the planter Orville Bean. "He financed the house and then rented it to them. He did that a lot in the neighborhood," recalled Gladys's coworker at Tupelo Garments, Faye Harris.[7] The house had no running water or electricity. An outhouse and water pump answered for plumbing and the interior was lit by kerosene lamps. Gladys, Vernon, and Elvis often slept together in one bed, the only one they owned. After Elvis became a star, the city of Tupelo refurbished the shack into a tourist attraction furnished with amenities the Presleys could never have afforded. Money was always scarce and credit, aside from whatever was extended by local shopkeepers, was unknown.[8]

The emotional bonds prevailing within extended families were reinforced by economic necessity. Kinfolk were expected to feed, clothe, and shelter one another in hard times. To accept "commodities" from the county was considered shameful, but in the hardship of the Great Depression, the Presleys were sometimes forced to seek handouts. Not all of the Presleys were as hard put as Vernon. His uncle Noah was East Tupelo's mayor and grocer; another uncle, Jessie, owned a house. The Smiths and the Presleys were bound tightly together in a network of mutual support. Vernon's brother, Vester, was married to Gladys's sister, Clettes. Most of the townsfolk subsisted on little meat aside from pork and lived on cornbread, okra, and other garden vegetables along with canned and dried fruit in the winter. Cousin Harold Lloyd, whose parents owned a farm, recalled giving the Presleys sausages and beans. "We shared," he said.[9]

The Power of Faith

Religion provided an explanation for life in a literal reading of the Bible, with moments of joy in the present and the promise of a better world to come. The heartfelt singing of the congregation at the Sunday services of the First Assembly of God Church in East Tupelo, where Gladys's uncles Sims and Gains were co-pastors, afforded emotional release and the opportunity to perform before sympathetic listeners. The long sermons and the words to the hymns made deep impressions in a society where communication remained largely oral.

The church had sprung up as a tent on a vacant field only a few years before Elvis's birth and grew quickly into a simple clapboard edifice. Although Baptists and members of more established denominations branded them as "holy rollers," the Assembly of God was the public face of respectable social life in East Tupelo, in opposition to the bootleggers who plied their trade in the face of Prohibition (which lasted in Mississippi until 1966) and a bordello district called Goosehollow. Church life reinforced a sense of community among members and endowed their existence with meaning.[10]

The perspective shared by the taciturn Vernon and the socially gregarious Gladys was shaped on the hard wooden pews of Southern Protestantism. Vernon recounted saving Elvis from a dangerous fever through the power of faith. "My wife and I turned in prayer to the greatest healer of all, God. I do believe in miracles, so that day I prayed to God that he would miraculously heal our child."[11]

It should be no surprise, however, that its members often ignored many of the church's restrictions on personal behavior. Whiskey bootlegging was pervasive through much of the South, and as suggested in the lyrics of many country songs, Southerners often lionized bootleggers as rebels against federal authorities who were still viewed as an occupying power as the centenary of the Civil War approached. Vernon never distilled his own whiskey but apparently worked for one of the local bootleggers, using the delivery truck he drove for L. P. McCarty to haul illegal whiskey to customers. Some Tupelo residents claimed the Presleys fled Tupelo for Memphis because Vernon's moonlighting in the hidden economy of bootlegging, along with other shady activities, was about to land him in trouble.[12]

The Assembly of God also had a profound impact on Elvis, but not only on his sense of place in the world. "When Elvis was a little fellow, not more than two years old, he would slide down off my lap, run into the aisle and scramble up to the platform. There he would stand looking at the choir and trying to sing with them," Gladys recalled.[13]

Contrary to some published accounts, the congregational singing of the Assembly of God was tame in contrast to the black gospel churches. "I sang some with my folks in the Assembly of God church choir, it was a small church, so you couldn't sing too loud," Elvis said.[14] The wife of his church's pastor, Corene Randle Smith, had this to say about worship: "There was a few people that got so happy they called it 'shouting,' but about all they did was stand there and move their feet up and down real fast . . . dancing was taught against."[15] Elvis's love of singing was instilled early in life at his parents' church, but the true sources of his adult style are found elsewhere.

The slaves of the antebellum South had long before discovered a subversive message within Christianity. The religion taught them by their masters contained an inspiring legacy from Judaism in the evocative imagery of the Hebrews who escaped bondage under Pharaoh and followed Moses to the Promised Land. For African Americans the imagery of the Children of Israel and their flight from slavery remained consoling after subjugation continued under other forms after the abolition of slavery.

Before the civil rights movement, many poor whites took comfort in the racist hierarchy of the United States because it ensured they were not lowest in the land of opportunity. For the economically and socially marginalized white underclass, "whiteness was the only advantage that most could muster."[16] Violence against blacks by impoverished whites stemmed from "their own social and economic frustrations in white society."[17] As one contemporary writer noted, the South "not only likes the Negro 'in his place' but likes every man in his place and thinks there is a certain place providentially provided for him."[18]

The nation's blacks occupied a lesser station, and because of the indelible mark of complexion, could never rise higher, even if they could become doctors or teachers. However, some white Christians considered the meaning of St. Paul's message in 1 Corinthians 12:13, and found it unseemly to denigrate coreligionists of a different race:

"For by one Spirit we are all baptized into one body, whether we be Jews or Gentiles, whether we be bond or free; and have all been made to drink into one Spirit." The Presleys took that message to heart, raising Elvis without the racial bigotry endemic at the time in American society, in the North and South. "We never had any prejudice. We never put anybody down. Neither did Elvis," Vernon recalled.[19] The Assembly of God and other Pentecostal churches may have been more racially tolerant than other Southern denominations. Modern Pentecostalism came into being in 1904 out of a series of fiery prayer meetings at Los Angeles's Azusa Street Mission conducted by a black preacher, W. J. Seymour. Congregants claimed that the Holy Spirit descended and caused speaking and singing in tongues along with professions of prophecy. Gladys and Vernon may not have intended for Elvis to embrace black culture, yet their tolerance left him empathetic to the cry of the blues. In the context of the South on the cusp of federally mandated desegregation, this positioned him as a rebel against one aspect of the status quo.

Child of Destiny

Gladys earned two dollars a day for a 12-hour shift at the Tupelo Garment Company to supplement Vernon's meager wages; she quit in the final months of her pregnancy but was unable to afford the luxury of staying at home for long. Elvis was preceded in the early morning hours on the day he was born by a stillborn twin, Jesse Garon. Jesse was laid out in a tiny coffin in the Presley home before burial in an unmarked grave but lived on in the family's imagination. Elvis was raised as if set apart from his extended family, a child of destiny treated with unusual deference for a poor Southern boy of his day. Miraculous portents accompanied his birth in Presley family lore, including a dazzling blue light that shone in the sky.[20]

Elvis accepted Gladys's belief that at Jesse's death, he received the strength that would have belonged to his twin. This loss prompted Gladys to become protective and indulgent of Elvis, who was unusually tied to his mother, dependent on her love and direction. "She worshipped him from the day he was born," a neighbor recalled.[21]

Elvis was also deeply attached to Vernon, and the trauma of his father's imprisonment weighed heavily in boyhood memories and marked his childhood with the fear of losing him again. On November 11, 1937, Vernon, Gladys's brother, Travis Smith, and a companion were charged with adding a zero to a four-dollar check written to Vernon by Orville Bean in payment for a hog. "Vernon always wanted more of things, and they got this bright idea," recalled Travis's son, Billy.[22] They spent time awaiting trial in the county jail and were sentenced on May 25, 1938, to three years at Parchman Farm, the sprawling Mississippi prison camp infamous as the setting for many blues songs. It was a place were prisoners in striped garb labored in cotton fields from sunrise to sunset under the hot sun and the lash of their guards. Gladys and Elvis were despondent. Every Sunday, the day set aside for conjugal visits, mother and child rode the Greyhound bus to the prison with money scrimped from her new job at a Tupelo laundry. Only three years old, Elvis played outside the "Red House" set aside for Sunday visitations with the children of other mothers. The ride lasted five hours each way.[23]

Vernon and his companions were released from Parchman Farm on February 6, 1939, after serving only eight months of their sentences, following a request by Orville Bean for their early release. Bean was responding to the prevailing sentiment around East Tupelo that the sentence was too harsh. The Presleys suffered during Vernon's imprisonment; they lost their shack and were forced to seek shelter in the home of one relative after another while Gladys struggled to make do on her wages from the laundry. The absence of his beloved father at an impressionable age only strengthened Elvis's dependence on his mother.

Afterward, the coming of World War II provided an economic boon to Vernon, as it did for millions of other Americans. In 1940, Vernon and his cousin Sales were recruited by the WPA to work on the expansion of the Pascagoula shipyard. Later he worked in the construction gang that erected "Japtown," a POW camp in Como, Mississippi, originally intended for interned Japanese Americans, and then at a munitions plant in Memphis. He returned home to East Tupelo on weekends.[24]

Despite the privations of his family, Elvis was pampered with attention and toys, as much as their meager finances allowed, including a red wagon that made him the envy of the neighborhood boys. All summer he went barefoot, like most children and many adults in the neighborhood. In the fall, he wore a pair of hand-me-down shoes from his cousins.

Every day beginning in the fall of 1941, when Elvis started first grade at East Tupelo Consolidated School, Gladys walked her son to school across a dirt road called "the levee," hand in hand, anxious that no harm should come to him on the roadside. It was a half-hour walk each way. One imagines Gladys scrubbing her boy's face and behind his ears each morning with a rough bar of homemade soap to make him shine like the sun. The school, with a cafeteria operated by the WPA, was a source of pride for the local community. It was modern with electricity and central heating, amenities that were lacking in the homes of many of its students. Discipline was firm but the environment was encouraging. Gladys fervently wished for her son to become the first member of his family to complete high school. She was animated by the promise of social mobility that many see as a particularly American characteristic, but was in reality a spirit that swept across the world in the first half of the 20th century. Vernon and Gladys may have reached as far as possible, but were determined that their son would travel further, even if the destination was unclear.[25]

Elvis went fishing with neighborhood boys, but averse to killing, he refused to hunt birds. Unable to afford a swimsuit, he swam naked with the neighborhood boys until, after he nearly drowned, Gladys put a stop to it. Gladys stood out in East Tupelo for her protective ways. "I'll tell you one thing, nobody run over Elvis down there," recalled Elvis's great aunt, Christine Roberts Presley. "One night I seen Gladys get a stick after this boy that lived out there, and that tickled me slap to death. That boy thought he was so smart. He said something about Elvis, and, boy, Gladys picked up a broomstick."[26]

Elvis's social links extended no further than his church and extended family, a community bound together by poverty and proximity, class and race. "Though we had friends and relatives, including my parents, the three of us formed our own private world," Vernon said.[27]

The Presleys were careful to teach Elvis his place in the larger world. Throughout his life he rose to his feet whenever an elder or authority figure entered the room. A narrow circle of wealthy families dominated the region around East Tupelo. Below them was a small middle class of shopkeepers; the much wider ranks of white sharecroppers and laborers; and at the bottom the black population, largely confined to sharecropping and menial jobs. Whatever anger the Presleys may have felt about their status was dampened into sullen resentment. Elvis was taught the unfailing politeness of a Southern gentleman, to address elders and anyone in authority as "sir" or "ma'am." The Presleys, painfully aware that they amounted to little in the eyes of the world, were determined to maintain their dignity and took comfort in the words of the gospel that those who are now last will be first in the coming kingdom.

Music had always been integral to life in the rural South, and East Tupelo was no exception. Elvis sang in church from the time he could raise his voice, and relatives later recounted that as a child he often sang to amuse himself and entertain his family. When he was 10, his teacher, Oleta Grimes, the daughter of Orville Bean, entered him in the children's talent contest at the Mississippi-Alabama Fair and Dairy Show held on October 3, 1945, at the Tupelo fairgrounds. It was a big event in Tupelo, broadcast on the local radio station, WELO. Area schools were closed and children were bussed to the fairgrounds to watch the competition. Elvis sang Red Foley's tearful country hit "Ole Shep." He later recalled the contest as his first performance before "a real audience" and that he took fifth place.[28] However, other research has concluded that Elvis probably won nothing on that day aside from the opportunity to sing before a large audience.[29]

A year later, Gladys bought Elvis a guitar for his birthday, a $7.75 model from the Tupelo Hardware Company. According to legend, Elvis was disappointed, hoping to receive a bicycle instead.[30] His uncle Vester, a sometime honky-tonk musician, taught him his first chords, and an Assembly of God preacher, Frank Smith, also gave him instruction.

Finally, Elvis found a mentor for any daydreams he may have entertained about being a professional entertainer in Mississippi Slim, a country singer and occasional recording artist who befriended him. Born Carvel Lee Ausborn, the East Tupelo native was as gaunt in photographs as Hank Williams; similarly, he strummed his guitar wearing suit and tie with only a white cowboy hat signifying his vocation as a country singer. Mississippi Slim blended country and blues in autobiographical songs that sounded close to rockabilly. He supposedly recorded at Sun Studio in 1952 but his songs were never issued by Sam Phillips.[31]

Elvis performed occasionally at the country music jamboree held Saturday afternoons outside the Tupelo courthouse and aired on Mississippi Slim's station, WELO. He may also have performed live on the radio. Like most locally owned radio stations in the 1940s, the programming was produced by hometown personalities and included music performed live in the studio by local talent.

Elvis "was crazy about music. That's all he talked about," said James Ausborn, a classmate at East Tupelo Consolidated.[32] With the end of both World War II and Vernon's defense job, the peripatetic Presleys were forced to stay one step ahead of the rent collectors. Elvis enrolled in Tupelo's Milam Junior High School, a modern

Art Deco structure with a strong academic reputation. Beginning in seventh grade, he brought his guitar to school every morning. In the Tupelo school, Elvis felt socially isolated from his relatively affluent classmates. Those schoolmates who remembered him at all described him as a "loner," "forgettable," and "sad, shy, not especially attractive." Kenneth Holdritch, a middle-class Tupelo classmate who went on to teach English at the University of New Orleans, recalled that his set "were not kind" to the trickle of East Tupelo children who enrolled in Milam. Some of the better-off children made fun of him as a country bumpkin for the overalls he wore to school and the hillbilly music he played on his guitar, but Elvis was undaunted by their taunting. Music was already deeply integral to his sense of identity, forged against the odds of poverty and social disadvantage.[33]

Like many white Southerners, Elvis was aware of the music of his black neighbors. Segregation was rigidly enforced at lunch counters, schools, and cinemas; on busses and trains; and even in restrooms and at drinking fountains. The races were separate but side by side. It was a short walk for Elvis to Shakerag, Tupelo's impoverished African American district, whose residents worked as domestic servants to the city's better-off whites and as unskilled laborers. Blues singers could be found on street corners, R&B jumped from the jukeboxes of social clubs, and the hard-driving sound of black gospel music wafted out of a sanctified church established inside a tent. For a time the Presleys even lived in a house set aside for whites on North Green Street in one of Tupelo's better "colored" neighborhoods. African American music was at Elvis's doorstep, enriching his already keen appreciation for music and his lack of prejudice against its diverse sources.[34]

Even before the Tennessee Valley Authority brought electricity to rural areas such as East Tupelo, the Presleys owned a radio, powered by the battery of their truck. They listened to the country stars on the *Grand Ole Opry* on Saturday nights. Like most white Southerners who developed an inclination for turning their love of music into a career, an option whose scope had considerably widened in the 1920s with the rise of radio and the recording industry, the *Opry* provided a forum for Elvis's dreams. Other radio programs filled the Presley home, including the more urbane sounds of Bing Crosby and the Metropolitan Opera, which also played a role in Elvis's musical education. Gladys even owned a copy of Enrico Caruso's "O Sole Mio," which she played on a wind-up gramophone. Her son would later enjoy a hit record with a rewritten version of that old Neapolitan melody, "It's Now or Never" (1960). Elvis would not have been able to hear African American music on the radio until Memphis station WDIA began broadcasting blues and R&B in 1948, the year the Presleys moved to Memphis.

National popular culture was increasingly penetrating the South, even places as remote as East Tupelo. The business of entertainment, which had always been a marginal activity, rapidly grew into a powerful industry in the early years of the 20th century. With New York and Hollywood as its principal meccas, the entertainment industry was spurred by the growth of an urban working class in need of leisure, a middle class with discretionary income, and new technologies such as sound recordings, motion pictures, radio, and the advent of high-speed printing presses permitting the proliferation of pulp fiction and comic books. The radio airwaves were a two-way street, beaming the *Opry* to the North where country music was unknown and bringing the high-tone performances of urban dance bands to the South. Although the Assembly of God frowned on movies, Vernon occasionally treated Elvis to a show at the Strand, a second-run cinema in Tupelo where they sat spellbound in darkness as a Hollywood dream world of Roy Rogers and Gene Autry, and Fred Astaire and Ginger Rogers, unfolded before their eyes. As soon as he was old enough to read, Elvis began to devour *Captain Marvel* and other comic books, whose baroquely costumed heroes, brave and unflinching in their crusade against wrongdoers, returned in later years to dominate the imagination of the King of Rock and Roll, not only in his sartorial choices but his attitude toward himself and the world.

Notes

1. James W. Loewen and Charles Sallis, *Mississippi: Conflict and Change* (New York: Pantheon, 1974), p. 180.

2. Arnold Shaw, *Black Popular Music in America* (New York: Schirmer, 1986), pp. 172–173.

3. Federal Writers Project, *Mississippi: The WPA Guide to the Magnolia State* (New York: Viking, 1938), pp. 261–266; Dale Dobbs, "A Brief History of East Tupelo, Mississippi," in *Elvis Presley Heights, Mississippi, Lee County, 1921–1984* (Tupelo, MS: Elvis Presley Heights Garden Club, 1984).

4. Rose Clayton and Dick Heard, eds., *Elvis Up Close: In the Words of Those Who Knew Him Best* (Atlanta: Turner, 1994), p. 8.

5.   Susan M. Doll, *Understanding Elvis: Southern Roots vs. Star Image* (New York: Garland Publishing, 1998), p. 12.

6.   Alanna Nash, *Elvis Aaron Presley: Revelations from the Memphis Mafia* (New York: HarperCollins, 1995), p. 2.

7.   Jerry Hopkins, *Elvis: A Biography* (New York: Simon & Schuster, 1971), pp. 19–20.

8.   Doll, p. 5.

9.   Clayton, p. 10.

10. Charles L. Ponce de Leon, *Fortunate Son: The Life of Elvis Presley* (New York: Hill & Wang, 2006), p. 16. For an overview of Southern Pentecostals, see Robert Mapes Anderson, *Vision of the Disinherited: The Making of American Pentecostalism* (New York: Oxford University Press, 1979).

11. "Elvis by His Father Vernon Presley," as told to Nancy Anderson. *Good Housekeeping*, January 1978, p. 157.

12. Elaine Dundy, *Elvis and Gladys* (New York: Macmillan, 1985), p. 145.

13. "Elvis Presley," *TV Radio Mirror* 1956, p. 8.

14. Robert Jennings, "There'll Always Be an Elvis," *Saturday Evening Post*, September 11, 1965, p. 78.

15. Clayton, p. 15.

16. Michael T. Bertrand, *Rock, Race, and Elvis* (Urbana: University of Illinois Press, 2000), p. 35.

17. Gunnar Myrdal, *An American Dilemma: The Negro Problem in a Modern Democracy* (New York: Harper & Row, 1962, 20th anniversary ed,), p. 582.

18. William T. Polk, *Southern Accent: From Uncle Remus to Oak Ridge* (New York: William Morrow, 1953), pp. 244–245.

19. *Good Housekeeping*, January 1978, p. 157.

20. Peter Harry Brown and Pat H. Broeski, *Down at the End of Lonely Street: The Life and Death of Elvis Presley* (New York: Dutton, 1997), p. 3.

21. Jerry Hopkins interview with Faye Harris, Mississippi Valley Collection, Memphis State University.

22. Nash, p. 15.

23. Dundy, pp. 82–84.

24. Dundy, p. 87.

25. Dundy, p. 99.

26. Clayton, p. 17.

27. *Good Housekeeping*, January 1978, p. 156.

28. Jerry Osborne, *Elvis Word for Word* (New York: Gramercy Books, 2006), p. 67.

29. Bill Burk, *Early Elvis: The Tupelo Years* (Memphis: Propwash Publishing, 1994), pp. 121–124, 135–136.

30. Nash, p. 19.

31. Dundy, pp. 94–96.

32. Peter Guralnick, *Last Train to Memphis: The Rise of Elvis Presley* (Boston: Little Brown, 1994), p. 21; Howard A. DeWitt, *Elvis the Sun Years: Elvis Presley in the Fifties* (Ann Arbor, MI: Popular Culture Ink, 1993), pp. 60–61.

33. Dundy, pp. 132–133, 136.

34. Guralnick, p. 25.

2

Memphis Blues

Memphis was distinct among Southern cities in the 1940s and 1950s, occupying a special place geographically and in the imagination of those who lived in the surrounding countryside. Protected from flood-waters on a bluff overlooking the Mississippi River, Memphis was a bustling place, one of the world's largest markets for cotton and hard-wood lumber; before the Civil War it was one of the largest slave markets in the United States.

Favored by geography, Memphis had long been a gateway between the natural resources of the South and the industry of the North. By the middle of the 20th century, it was the nexus of highways, railroads, and barge lines linking Pittsburgh, Chicago, and Sioux City with the Gulf of Mexico. Memphis represented prosperity in a sea of poverty, a city of light in a land that had just begun to know electricity. Memphis was an outpost of urbanity, the city where theater companies and divas stopped on their way from Chicago to New Orleans. Its daily newspaper, the *Commercial Appeal*, was the respected paper of record for much of Dixie and especially Mississippi. "People of the Magnolia State have always claimed the Tennessee town as their own. For trade and fun it, not Jackson, is their capital," wrote Southern writer Shields McIlwaine.[1]

The city had been a magnet since the Civil War for job seekers, black and white, on the docks and in the cotton and lumber mills. Later, Memphis became a way station, and sometimes the final stop, for African Americans traveling northward. The human tide of the Great Migration was spurred after World War I by the toll of racism, natural disasters such as flooding and the boll weevil, and the hope of greater freedom and opportunity outside the Southern backwaters. The vast majority of Memphis's black males toiled as day laborers and stevedores, delivery boys and bootblacks, elevator operators, and street vendors; large numbers of black women were employed as maids, cooks, and nannies for the city's wealthy and upper-middle class whites.

In the 1930s, white tenant farmers searching for work joined blacks on the northward trek. The introduction of tractors and mechanical reapers on the sprawling plantations of Mississippi, and New Deal farm policies instituted by the Agricultural Adjustment Act (1933), which paid planters for letting fields go fallow, left many tenant farmers and sharecroppers destitute.

In Memphis, however, the New Deal provided employment in the form of public works jobs. World War II brought additional prosperity from military bases and factories, including Ford Motors and Fisher Body Works, which converted to defense work.[2] Vernon Presley was one of many who benefited from wartime government spending as a worker at a Memphis munitions plant. The experience may have convinced him to move his family to the city, following a return to low wage jobs in Tupelo.

When they arrived in Memphis in 1948, the Presleys were much like thousands of rural Southerners described in a contemporary book on the city. The author wrote of country folk who "rode their first elevator, first street car, first Ferris wheel, or first anything of the industrial age" in Memphis.[3] For impoverished, dissatisfied Southerners, for whom pulling up stakes and moving up North was unimaginable, Memphis was the convenient terminus, the culturally comfortable final stop on the road to elsewhere. It would prove to be the end of the line for Vernon and Gladys Presley, and became in many respects the final home for Elvis, long before it became his last resting place.

Searching for a Better Life

For Elvis, only 13 years old upon arrival in Memphis, the crossroads city where North met South would become the turning point, the place where he lived through most of his formative experiences. His parents bore the anticipation and anxiety that colored the migration of rural families to cities, places painted in cautionary colors by preachers and country singers alike. Driven by the realization that opportunities at home had been exhausted, the Presleys moved from Tupelo to Memphis on November 6, 1948. "We were broke, man, broke, and we left Tupelo overnight," Elvis recalled. "We just headed for Memphis. Things had to be better."[4] Setting forth in a 1937 Plymouth, their few belongings in trunks strapped to the top of the car, the Presleys traveled along with Travis Smith, his wife Lorraine, and their children Bobby and Billy. To pay for the trip, Travis sold both of his cows.[5] They resembled the Joads from John Steinbeck's novel *The Grapes of Wrath* as they headed for an uncertain yet hopeful future.

At first, job opportunities proved disappointing and living conditions were worse than in Tupelo. The only rent the Presleys could afford was in rooming houses. In Memphis this usually meant faded Victorian homes that had been carved into one-room apartments with a single bathroom on each floor. The Presleys and the Smiths shared such quarters in the early months on Washington Street in North Memphis, a bad side of town. They slept, cooked, and ate in the same room, carrying water from the bathroom down the hall. Cousin Billy remembers scavenging through the trash of a nearby fruit stand to supplement their meager diet. Elvis's parents moved several times; their addresses have become an issue of dispute among his biographers.[6]

Plugging the holes in his shoes with strips of cardboard, Vernon walked the streets looking for work, finding a job at Precision Tools and later at United Paint, where he packed cans of house paint into boxes for shipping at 83 cents an hour. Gladys continued in the trade she had learned in Tupelo, taking part-time employment behind a sewing machine at Fashion Curtains.

It was an emotional as well as a spiritual release for the Presleys to attend evening services at the Poplar Street Mission, a low-slung brick storefront with plate glass windows, where the Rev. J. J. Denson played guitar and led the congregation in fervent hymn singing. Denson's delinquent son Jesse Lee, a name familiar to the juvenile courts, gave Elvis guitar lessons. A communal meal followed services, providing respite from the simple fare the Presleys prepared on the hot plate in their room.[7]

Despite all difficulties, Memphis offered greater promise than Tupelo. Soon other members of the family followed them to the big city, including Vernon's mother Minnie and brother Vester. In some respects life continued as it had been for the Presleys and other migrants from the rural South. Years would pass before the atomization of modern urban life would be felt. Elvis remained surrounded by a traditional extended family of uncles, aunts, and cousins. Networking began in the Assembly of God and extended little further. Elvis's grandmother Minnie, whom he called Dodger "because he threw a ball once and it missed her face by a fraction of an inch," often watched over him when Gladys was at work. Several years earlier, Minnie had been deserted by her husband, Jessie.[8]

What would prove different for Elvis was the extraordinarily diverse society that thrived in Memphis beyond the circles familiar to the Presley family. Elvis would explore this wider world soon enough.

Nearly a year after their journey to Memphis, on September 20, 1949, the Presleys experienced the first step up in their material circumstances. Because of their poverty and appearance of being "very nice and deserving," in the report of social worker Jane Richardson, they were allowed to rent an apartment in Lauderdale Courts. Years later, Richardson recalled the Presleys as "just poor people" and Elvis as "a very nice boy."[9]

A red brick, barracks-like complex grouped around grassy courtyards, Lauderdale Courts was a neatly kept public housing project abutting the city's downtown, only two blocks from the stores and cinemas of Main Street and an easy walk to Beale Street. It was built in the late 1930s as part of a federally funded slum clearance program. Although only whites were allowed to live there, the Courts sat on the site of a black neighborhood, and badly decayed shacks inhabited by blacks faced it from across the street. "In that neighborhood the fact that Elvis got through without serious trouble was an accomplishment," said one of his friends from the Courts.[10] The city's African American leaders objected to one of their districts being razed to make way for segregated housing projects, but their protests were swept aside. They were told to take solace in the relative security they enjoyed.[11]

Unlike blacks in Mississippi and many other regions of the South, the African Americans of Memphis had not endured lynchings or mob violence for decades. They were even allowed to vote, albeit their balloting was carefully manipulated by the political machine of Edward Hull Crump, who controlled Memphis from 1909 until his death in 1954, the year Elvis released his first recording.

The son of a Confederate officer, Crump was a Southern gentleman of the old school with a boutonniere always pinned to his lapel. He disliked being called "Boss Crump," because the word *boss* suggested big-city Yankee politics, but the title clung to him. Usually ruling from behind closed doors, dictating policy to elected officials in his capacity as local Democratic Party chairman in a region dominated by Democrats, Crump's agenda mixed reform with social conservatism. He reduced crime in a city that was once called "America's murder capital." He planted parks, constructed public buildings, improved public health programs, and sponsored the election of the South's first female judge, Camille Kelley.

Crump tolerated no unrest in his city and suppressed both the Ku Klux Klan and trade unions in a successful bid to make Memphis attractive to Northern industrialists and investors. On Election Day, Crump's political machine paid Tennessee's prohibitive $2.10 poll tax for African American voters and threw them a party afterward. Crump doled out municipal jobs to blacks, but his police kept a watchful eye on their political activity, and he warned black leaders to "keep in line" lest "overzealous" white racists take offense.[12]

The sometimes-benign paternalism of Crump's rule extended to the smallest details of the Presleys' life once the Housing Authority admitted them to Lauderdale Courts. The two-bedroom apartment with its own bathroom and kitchen was fully repaired before the Presleys moved in, and surprise inspections by the Memphis Housing Authority found that Gladys was a good housekeeper. Lauderdale represented unprecedented luxury for the Presleys. For the first time in his life, Elvis had his own bedroom.[13]

Lauderdale Courts was conceived as an incubator for middle-class life. Many of its residents had never previously enjoyed a bathtub or indoor plumbing, and many went on to become successful in business and the professions. Lauderdale was initiated during the New Deal, when a host of federal programs were launched with the goal of bettering the lives of impoverished Americans during the Great Depression. The New Deal was viewed with hostility by many Southerners, who were suspicious of the federal government and devoted to local autonomy and individual responsibility; yet Crump loyally supported Franklin D. Roosevelt, and understood that the New Deal would make unprecedented sums of money available to cities such as Memphis. Through funding of Lauderdale Courts and similar facilities, the New Deal gave the Presleys and thousands of other rural Southerners a taste of middle class life.

Despite the aspirations of many of its residents, Lauderdale Courts was still considered a rough district by Memphis's middle class. The specter of underclass violence was never long out of mind. Travis Smith and his brother John were "jumped" and "cut" by a gang of five white men.[14] The sheltered environment maintained by the Presleys resulted in an aloofness from the conflicts of their neighbors. Gladys's apron strings loosened a little in Memphis, but she remained closely tied to her son. Recollections by family members portray Elvis as a little prince, with a set of dishes and cutlery reserved for his use, and a collection of comic books neatly arrayed in his room. "Grandma Presley would tell my little boys, 'No, you can't look at them. Elvis will get mad at me,'" Gladys's sister Lillian remembered when asked about Elvis's prized comic book collection.[15]

School Days

Realizing that being walked to school would embarrass her son, Gladys at first brought Elvis as far as a street corner near L. C. Humes High School, 10 blocks away from the Courts. With 1,600 students, its enrollment was larger than the population of East Tupelo. Humes was neither a blackboard jungle nor the jewel of the Memphis school system. "It was a lower poverty-type school, one of the lowest in Memphis," according to Elvis's friend Buzzie Forbes.[16] Elvis caused no trouble for his teachers. "He was a gentle, obedient boy," remembered his ninth-grade homeroom teacher, Susie Johnson. His 12th-grade history teacher, Mildred Scrivener, recalled that he was shy, "more at ease with [the teachers] than with his fellow students."[17]

Elvis was neither a failure academically nor a standout. He received a C in music. According to Barbara Pittman, who in the wake of Elvis's success became a rockabilly singer for Sun Records, her older brother and his friends pelted Elvis with rotten fruit "because he was different, because he was quiet and he stuttered and he was a mama's boy."[18] Elvis made some efforts to socialize with classmates, playing football without much distinction for one year and joining the ROTC, wearing his cadet's uniform proudly. His high school yearbook also lists him as a member of the biology, English, history and speech clubs, academic activities that appear incongruous in the light of contemporary media coverage of Elvis and many of the memories collected by oral historians in search of his wellspring.[19] Elvis probably began to hide his intellectual interests under the peer pressure of a school system geared to produce blue-collar workers and a lower class society that distrusted the life of the mind.

"He seemed very lonely and had no real friends. He just didn't seem to be able to fit in," said Red West, the high school football star who befriended him and later became part of Elvis's entourage, the "Memphis Mafia." He added that Elvis's urban greaser hairdo, worn in defiance of the crew cut conformity surrounding him, "got him into all kinds of trouble."[20]

Another recollection by a schoolmate suggests that Elvis was developing a self-identity as a star, long before he starred in anything outside his own daydreams. "He would wear a coat and fashion a scarf like an ascot tie, as if he were a movie star. Of course he got a lot of flak for this, because he stood out like a sore thumb."[21] By the time he graduated, Elvis was already expressing his distinction from his peers, rebelling against surface appearances and their suggestion of narrow opportunities through choices in style, by turning up his shirt collar, growing sideburns, and cultivating a hairdo copied from the Northern urban street gangs in the Tony Curtis movie *City Across the River* (1949).

His rebellion did not extend to acting up in class. Elvis was never a juvenile delinquent. Carrying age-old rural expectations into the city, he contributed to his family's income with earnings from part-time jobs. The family remained an economic as well as an emotional unit. During the summer of 1951, Elvis operated a drill press at Precision Tool where Vernon had once worked, and where Vester Presley and uncles Travis and Johnny Smith were still employed.[22]

In comparison with high school, where he was often confronted by children of at least slightly more fortunate means, Elvis had better luck making friends in the Courts among boys from similar social backgrounds. He played football with them and began to explore the wider city in the company of Buzzy Forbes, Paul Dougher, and Farley Guy. Forbes remembered that the boys engaged in a football game against black youths at the waterworks.[23]

Finding Beale Street

Elvis discovered that Memphis—with its Italian fruit vendors, Greek grocers, and kosher butchers—was more ethnically diverse than the surrounding countryside.[24] He cautiously explored fabled Beale Street, "the Main Street of Negro America," celebrated in a familiar song by popular African American writer W. C. Handy. Handy was called "the father of the blues" for composing the first popular songs adapted from the blues in the opening decade of the 20th century. Among Handy's most popular tunes were "Memphis Blues," praising Boss Crump for his liberality, and "Beale Street Blues," which put the avenue on the map of American popular culture.

Beale Street was lined with pawnshops, drug stores selling hair-straightening products for African Americans, diners and theaters, and saloons and gambling dens with boogie-woogie and blues thumping loudly from inside. Down the side streets were houses of prostitution. The city's wealthiest African American, Robert Church Jr., owned

much of the real estate along Beale, but most businesses were owned
by Jews or other ethnics of Southern or Eastern European heritage.[25]
Beale Street thrived on Saturday nights as an entertainment magnet
for African Americans from Memphis and the surrounding country.
"On Beale you could forget for one shining moment the burden of
being black and celebrate being black." Along with numerous bars and
nightclubs came many opportunities for black musicians, for whom
Memphis was Mecca and Beale Street was paved in gold.[26]

Opportunities for the city's growing black population were also
increasing during the postwar years. Department stores along Main
Street began providing blacks-only lunch counters, which was a step
up from not being allowed to eat at all. The *Commercial Appeal* began
referring to blacks as "Negroes" and using the honorific of "Mrs." for
black women.[27]

Elvis became a familiar sight in Beale's bars and nightclubs only
after the release of his first record, when his local celebrity status was
already secured. Reports of a high-school age Elvis sneaking into the
clubs at night are apocryphal and suspect. Parts of the street were considered black turf and few whites ventured in without the assent of the
locals. Likely, Elvis visited the shops during daylight hours and never
ventured into the street at night until after the release of "That's All
Right."[28]

Through his high school years, Elvis played an eclectic grab bag of
songs that caught his ear. Although the Presleys were not a formal singing group, Elvis asserted that the family went "round together to sing
at camp meetings and revivals." He added that he "also dug the real
low-down Mississippi singers, mostly Big Bill Broonzy and Big Boy
Crudup, although they would scold me at home for listening to them."
The songs he learned also included country tunes mixed with numbers
by Bing Crosby and Perry Como, which he picked off of Memphis's
network broadcasters for the amusement of family and friends.[29]

Elvis was more reticent in the outside world. Unlike in Tupelo,
where he brought his guitar to school, his Humes classmates were
unaware of any musical interests until the final months of his senior
year. Even within the more familiar environs of the Courts, he sometimes played with the lights turned off, as if concealing his shyness
in the dark. He practiced guitar with several boys from church in the
basement laundry of Lauderdale Courts.[30]

Elvis became more aware than ever of blues and rhythm and blues,
even if the idea of adding such songs to his repertoire would not occur
to him for some time. African American music was audible on the

streets near Beale and permeated the local radio. WDIA ("the Mother Station of the Negroes"), which went to all-black musical, educational, and comedy programming in 1949, was the first station of its kind in America and began a national trend toward hiring more black DJs and targeting black audiences.[31] On-air personalities included blues legend B. B. King, who performed live and played records. Sunday nights brought live broadcasts from the East Trigg Baptist Church, whose preacher, Rev. W. Herbert Brewster, wrote Mahalia Jackson's gospel classic "Move On Up a Little Higher." Elvis was sometimes seen at East Trigg's ecstatic services along with other white hipsters who sought out black music.

WDIA's success coincided with the postwar rise in black assertiveness and the proliferation of personality disc jockeys as arbiters of taste. DJs were no longer simply radio announcers but became entertainers in their own right. Unlike the tightly scripted Top-40 radio formats that dominated the AM band after 1960, the first generation of disc jockeys chose the records they played and were eagerly courted by the record industry. Airplay from a popular DJ on a major radio station became crucial for record sales.[32]

WDIA was not the only local station Elvis listened to. With its low 250-watt signal and dawn-to-dusk license (entailing a 5:00 P.M. sign-off during the shortest days of winter), WDIA was vulnerable to competition for the African American audience. In 1949, WHBQ, which had experimented over the years with "race music" programming and live broadcasts of black gospel and choral music, began to seek black listeners after sundown with an evening rhythm and blues program hosted by a wild-mannered white man, Dewey Phillips. In keeping with the era's hipster jargon, he called himself Daddy-O-Dewey and his show *Red, Hot and Blue*. He apparently ad-libbed everything, including commercials; he often talked over records or replayed the same disc several times on a single show if the mood struck. Years before the better-known Alan Freed switched from classical music to rhythm and blues, Phillips was part of the rising postwar phenomenon of white DJs playing contemporary black music and finding, to the surprise of many observers, a substantial biracial audience.[33]

Before becoming the first disc jockey to spin Elvis's debut recording, Dewey's kinetic hipster delivery may have influenced Elvis as much as the records he played. *Red, Hot and Blue* featured blues and rhythm and blues by Lowell Fulson, Elmore James, Muddy Waters, and other black artists. American music had never been segregated but its presentation had been racially divided on bandstands, in record stores, and on radio. Phillips's program was one of many catalysts that shook up American culture in the 1950s. In Memphis, Boss Crump "might keep the streets and schools and public buildings segregated, but at night Dewey Phillips integrated the airwaves."[34] Black music also entered into Elvis's life from across the Mississippi River in West Memphis, Arkansas, where KWEM broadcast programs by blues stars such as Howlin' Wolf and Sonny Boy Williamson.

Forbidden Excitement

Along with the radio, Elvis completed his musical education by spending many hours listening to 78-rpm discs at Charlie's, a record store with a soda fountain only three blocks from the Courts. Elvis's growing taste for contemporary black music was part of a wider phenomenon noticed across America during the early 1950s. Many young whites, bored with the bland pop music of the day and the unadventurous expectations of middle class life, were turning to the combustible sounds of rhythm and blues for a taste of forbidden excitement.[35]

By some accounts young Southern whites were a step ahead of their Yankee peers. In 1954, Ahmet Ertegun and Jerry Wexler of Atlantic Records told a trade magazine that two years earlier, record distributors "began to report that white high school and college kids were picking up on rhythm and blues records, primarily to dance." They added: "From all accounts, the movement was initiated by youthful hillbilly fans rather than the pop bobby soxers and the latter group followed right along."[36]

In Memphis as elsewhere in the South, obstacles were in place to discourage cultural crossover between blacks and whites. In 1947, the year Jackie Robinson broke the color barrier in major league baseball, the city's notorious chairman of the censorship board, Lloyd T. Binford, banned the musical *Annie Get Your Gun* because its cast included a black railroad conductor. He also snipped footage of Lena Horne from local screenings of *Stormy Weather*.[37] One year later Memphis police commissioner Joe Boyle ordered his men to smash copies of blues recordings by Amos Milburn, Crown Prince Waterford, and Billy Hughes in one of the administration's periodic crackdowns on vice.[38]

In focusing on his outsider status at Humes High, many of Elvis's chroniclers have failed to perceive that his sartorial and musical tastes were not developed in isolation but as part of a wider phenomenon in the South and elsewhere. A subculture of hipness, drawing from

African American culture and especially by the aggressive, postwar bebop jazz with its jargon of cool cats, crazy grooves, and real gone daddies, began to seep into the consciousness of some young whites as a gesture of protest against an increasingly commercialized, homogenized America. Marion Keisker, the assistant to Sun Records's owner Sam Phillips, understood Elvis's direction when she described him as a "hillbilly cat" in an early interview.[39] "In an era that punished political dissent and distrusted new ideas, a little haberdashery could go a long way."[40]

Hipness found expression in styles of dress and manner. It was a wary attitude of cool detachment from Squaresville, the Protestant work ethic, and the phonies derided by Holden Caulfield in J. D. Salinger's *The Catcher in the Rye*, the great 1951 novel of restless youth. Hipness was not confined to black jazz musicians or the circles from which the Beat movement coalesced, but was broadcast widely through mass circulation magazines, pulp fiction, and film noir.

Robert Mitchum was the most popular embodiment of the new kind of postwar cool even before his arrest for marijuana possession (1948). His characters seemed to shrug off fancy talk and, like Elvis, smirked instead of smiled. His body language spoke the cool rhythms of jazz in movies such as *Out of the Past* (1947) and *His Kind of Woman* (1951), which found their way into neighborhood cinemas across the United States. With alienation as an increasingly prevalent theme, Hollywood had already laid the road for *The Wild One* (1954), in which Marlon Brando's motorcycle gang spoke in jive argot and listened to bebop on the jukebox.[41]

Brando's Johnnie, innocent of any political agenda, acted out an urge to upend the neatly planned bourgeois world of postwar America. A genuine outsider given his class status, Elvis wanted desperately to rise into the world of middle class success, but embraced the sense of hipness and cool represented by Brando's motorcycle, leather cap, and crooked sneer. In constructing his sense of identity, Elvis drew from gestures of hipness that found their way into Hollywood, along with other images from popular culture such as the Western hero and comic book superhero. By the 1970s, the bebop era hipster influence receded in favor of the more baroque pop culture fantasies that Elvis's wealth and isolation permitted him to enjoy.

As a young man he was at once conformist and nonconformist. Elvis behaved in many respects like mainstream teenagers of the time and adhered to a Norman Rockwell illustration of American life. Armed with a push lawnmower purchased by Vernon, Elvis went from yard to yard looking for grass to cut. He returned home with his pockets stuffed with spare change. As a sophomore in high school, he worked as an usher at Loew's State cinema. He contributed some of his earnings to his family, who used the money to buy their first television set. By 1951, with Gladys working as a nurse's aid six days a week and Minnie living in their apartment, the Presleys were able to purchase a 1941 Lincoln coupe, which became Elvis's car for dates. "My daddy was something wonderful to me," he later recounted.[42] His shyness seemed to abate in the company of women of all ages, on whom he exerted a reticent sexual appeal even as a teenager. "Elvis related to women more than he did men," according to cousin Billy Smith.[43] Music was his social lubricant. "He'd get out there at night with the girls and he just sang his head off," his aunt Lillian remembered. "He was different with the girls—I'm embarrassed to tell, but he'd rather have a whole bunch of girls around him than the boys."[44]

From around 1953 to 1955 he dated Dixie Locke, a girl three or four years his junior, often taking her to school dances.[45] The woman whom the Presleys hoped would become Elvis's wife kept in touch with the family for many years. "I thought maybe they would get married because Dixie was a mighty likable girl and Elvis thought the world of her," Vernon said.[46]

Dixie did not attend Humes. Elvis met her at his church, the First Assembly of God. Her family was working class but more economically stable than the Presleys were. Marrying her would have represented a small upward step for Elvis. She was an attractive, respectable companion in a relationship that included high school dances and evenings spent at the soda fountain and reflected the conventions of teenage American life in the 1950s. Dixie continued to date Elvis after his debut as a recording artist and professional singer but saw less and less of him, finally breaking off the long engagement by telling Gladys to pass her regrets to the boy she once loved.[47]

Elvis also escorted Regis Vaughan, four years his junior and a freshman at a Catholic school, to the senior prom. Elvis never danced with Regis because, as she claimed, he did not know how to dance. The story, like many tales from Elvis's youth, has been disputed.[48] Elvis apparently dated her through the spring of his final school year, taking her to All-Night Gospel Singings where he sang along fervently without admitting any musical aspirations of his own. She remembered that he repeatedly sang "My Happiness" to her, a pop hit from a few years earlier that featured in his first, tentative foray into the recording studio.

Whether it was the black music that poured from his radio or the sights and sounds of the city as he roamed through Memphis, Elvis's need to cut a distinct image among his peers brought him to a Jewish-owned Beale Street clothing store catering to African American men. Lansky's sold the bold fashions that would become associated with Elvis in his early years of stardom. The store's owners remembered that when they met Elvis, he was a shabbily dressed country boy, polite and diffident, saving his quarters from odd jobs to purchase the flashy clothing that would set him apart. Standing out for one's appearance was always dangerous in a conformist society, but identifying one's style with that of a despised underclass was judged foolhardy by some of Elvis's kin. Billy Smith remembers his parents worrying, "Somebody's going to beat the hell out of him and peel them nigger outfits right off his hide."[49]

However, at the All Night Gospel Singings where Elvis spent many nights, white Protestant spirituals were being presented with the flash of show business, a hint of R&B in the arrangements, and an echo of the black gospel churches. The groups who performed any given evening at the Gospel Singings in Ellis Auditorium were called quartets, regardless of the number of singers. Some of the gospel singers shook their legs as Elvis would later do and many engaged in crowd-pleasing choreography. Audiences, especially the women, screamed and jumped, reacting with emotional abandon to the performances. The tent revival fervor with which the performers were greeted was a foretaste of rock concerts to come. Although most rock critics chose to concentrate on the influence of blues on Elvis's music, he was always clear about gospel's impact on him. "Rock and roll is basically just gospel music, or gospel music mixed with rhythm and blues," he announced during his 1968 TV special.

The all-night singings were a feature of the postwar South, representing a transformation of gospel music from a cottage industry rooted in rural Southern Protestantism into a growing form of entertainment for urban audiences. During the late 1940s, gospel quartets found larger audiences through radio, concerts, and 78-rpm recordings. During this time, it was usual for black and white gospel quartets to travel separate circuits, playing before segregated audiences in large halls. The sound of gospel music was drawing closer to secular music and would in turn influence secular music; black quartets especially drew from the blues and were sometimes accompanied by electric guitar, while many white groups incorporated a rocking rhythm not unrelated to Pentecostal worship. In those Protestant denominations that frowned on motion pictures and popular music, gospel quartets became an acceptable form of "sanctified" entertainment.

Among Elvis's favorite quartets was the Statesmen. Formed in 1948, they were part of a new generation of professional gospel groups who recorded for major labels and hosted their own television show aired in many Southern towns. More than many others, the Statesmen incorporated songs of black origin and insisted on a dynamic, crowd-pleasing stage presence incorporating self-effacing humor. Their mark can be seen in Elvis's concerts in the latter part of his career.[50]

Another important gospel influence on Elvis was a quartet called the Blackwood Brothers. Their career paralleled Elvis's in some aspects. The Blackwoods moved from the rural South to Memphis in 1950 and released their earliest recordings on an independent label before being signed by RCA Victor. Like the Statesmen, they were lively yet respectable performers, setting a bar Elvis would reach for.

"I first met him when he was a kid in Memphis living in the projects. In fact, I used to sneak him in the back of the Ellis Auditorium so he could see our show," recalled singer J. D. Sumner. Sumner's account is probably correct, given the many links between the Blackwood Brothers and Elvis throughout the latter's career. The MC of the quartet's noontime show at WMPS, where Elvis reportedly spent many of his lunch hours, was Bob Neal. Neal would become Elvis's manager before Colonel Tom Parker took charge. In the uncertain months before his recording debut with Sun Records, Elvis auditioned for a spot in a quartet called the Songfellows, led by James Blackwood's nephew Cecil. Finally, Sumner became part of Elvis's backing group from 1972 through the star's death in 1977.[51]

Elvis also went by himself to classical orchestra concerts at Overton Park, where he would later perform. "I was fascinated by the fact that these guys could play for hours, you know, and most of the time the conductor wouldn't event look at his sheets," he recalled.[52]

In his senior year of high school, Elvis went to work for MARL Metal Products, a furniture plant. His shift, 3:00 to 11:30 P.M. five days a week, made going to school in the morning a difficult assignment. One of his teachers remembered Elvis wandering in and out of class "like a sleepwalker."[53] "He was so beat all the time, we made him quit," said Gladys, who returned to work at St. Joseph's Hospital to make up for the money Elvis would have earned at the plant.[54]

Her desire to give her son the opportunity to excel at school thrust the Presleys into the snare of bureaucracy. In November 1952, the Memphis Housing Authority determined that the Presleys' estimated annual income would rise to $4,133, which was over the limit allowed for residents of Lauderdale Courts. Although barely maintaining the appearance of lower-middle class life, they had become too prosperous for public housing. An eviction notice ordered the Presleys out of Lauderdale Courts by the end of February 1953.

They left a month early, on January 7, at first to a rooming house near Humes and then, in April, to a Victorian mansion across from Lauderdale Courts that had been divided into a duplex. The Presleys rented the lower apartment from Molly Dubrovner and her husband, Aaron, a kosher butcher. Minnie slept on a cot in the dining room. An Orthodox Jewish rabbi, Alfred Fruchter, and his wife, Jeanette, lived in the upstairs apartment.[55]

It was not Elvis's first encounter with Memphis's small Jewish community. The clothing store he frequented, Lansky's, was Jewish owned. One of his few male high school friends, George Klein, was Jewish. The Dubrovners treated the Presleys with great kindness. Rabbi Fruchter, prominent in the community, had recently co-founded the Memphis Hebrew Academy, the city's first Jewish day school. Elvis gladly served as the Fruchters' Shabbas goy, the Gentile who turned on their lights and gas oven on the Sabbath. The Fruchters reciprocated by lending Elvis their phonograph and letting the Presleys use their telephone at a time when many Americans still could not afford a monthly phone bill.

The Presleys' friendliness with their Jewish neighbors went beyond any desire to curry favor and is another example of the family's imperviousness to the prejudice of the surrounding culture. Shields McIlwaine represented the opinion of the city's elite toward immigrants who were not of white Anglo-Saxon Protestant stock when he wrote, "time and the absorbent ways of Memphis have put away this old rowdyism toward Jews as well as other white groups and bound all into the common life."[56] The Jews of Memphis prospered and had a role in Crump's machine. However, they were aware of their slightly precarious standing in a society rife with anti-Semitism and dominated by Protestant fundamentalism, and mindful that the Jews of Memphis had briefly been banished from the city during the Civil War by order of General Ulysses S. Grant.

Elvis's identification with the Jews continued once he became a star. When the Jewish Community Center was built in Memphis during the 1960s, he donated money for its construction. He had a Star of David engraved onto Gladys's tombstone, and often wore a Chai, the Jewish symbol for life, on a necklace.[57]

After his graduation on June 3, 1953, Elvis's parents proudly framed his diploma and displayed it prominently in their home. His high school yearbook referred to him and several classmates as "singing hillbillies." However, there was little in his outer life to indicate a musical career, much less the stardom he would soon attain. The only sign may have been his appearance in the "Annual Minstrel," a Humes student talent contest where he surprised the audience by singing "Till I Waltz Again with You" by pop jazz vocalist Teresa Brewer. Elvis later called the performance a turning point. "It was amazing how popular I became after that," he said of the reaction by his peers.[58]

Of his inner life we have only curious signals from a dream world constructed from Hollywood movies, comic books, and radio programs. "When he walked, the way he carried himself, it almost looked as if he was getting ready to draw a gun, he would spin around like a gunfighter. It was weird," a classmate said.[59] From the material of popular culture, principally comic books and Hollywood movies and the image of pop stars as conveyed on film and in the press, Elvis began, however uncertainly, to fashion an identity. He projected himself into the role of the hero. He had little idea of how to get there, but a vague determination to do something important beckoned on the horizon, beyond the job at M. B. Parker Machinists' Shop he started on the day after graduation from high school.

Notes

1. Shields McIlwaine, *Memphis Down in Dixie* (New York: E. P. Dutton, 1948), pp. 14–15.

2. George Brown Tindall, *The Emergence of the New South, 1913–1945* (Baton Rouge: Louisiana State University Press, 1967), pp. 354–432, 694–700.

3. McIlwaine, p. 14.

4. James Kingsley, "At Home with Elvis Presley," *Memphis Commercial Appeal, Mid-South Magazine*, March 7, 1965.

5. Alanna Nash, *Elvis Aaron Presley: Revelations from the Memphis Mafia* (New York: HarperCollins, 1995), p. 21.

6. Nash, p. 23.

7. Peter Guralnick, *Last Train to Memphis: The Rise of Elvis Presley* (Boston: Little Brown, 1994), p. 32.

8.   Nash, p. 4.

9.   Memphis Housing Authority records cited in Peter Guralnick, p. 33. Jerry Hopkins, *Elvis: A Biography* (New York: Simon & Schuster, 1971), p. 35.

10. Hopkins, *Elvis: A Biography*, p. 38.

11. Roger Biles, *Memphis in the Great Depression* (Knoxville: University of Tennessee Press, 1986), p. 95.

12. McIlwaine, pp. 354–386; William D. Miller, *Mr. Crump of Memphis* (Baton Rouge: Louisiana State University Press, 1964).

13. Jerry Hopkins interview with Memphis Housing Authority social worker Jane Richardson, Mississippi Valley Collection, Memphis State University.

14. Nash, pp. 7–8.

15. Guralnick, *Last Train*, p. 35.

16. Hopkins, *Elvis: A Biography*, p. 38.

17. Robert Johnson, *Elvis Presley Speaks!* (New York: Rave Publications, 1956), p. 18.

18. Guralnick, *Last Train*, p. 36.

19. *The Herald*, L. C. Humes High School 1953 yearbook.

20. Red West, Sonny West, and Dave Hebler, as told to Steve Dunleavy, *Elvis, What Happened?* (New York: Ballantine, 1977), p. 17.

21. Guralnick, *Last Train*, p. 50.

22. Guralnick, *Last Train*, p. 43.

23. Hopkins, *Elvis: A Biography*, pp. 38–39.

24. Guralnick, *Last Train*, pp. 36–37.

25. George W. Lee, *Beale Street: Where the Blues Began* (New York: Robert O. Ballou, 1934), p. 13.

26. Margaret McKee and Fred Chisenhall, *Beale Black and Blue* (Baton Rouge: Louisiana State University Press, 1981), pp. 13–21.

27. McKee and Chisenhall, p. 93.

28. Louis Cantor, *Dewey and Elvis: The Life and Times of a Rock'n'Roll Deejay* (Urbana: University of Illinois Press, 2005), pp. 47–50, 144–147.

29. *Hit Parade*, January 1957.

30. Guralnick, *Last Train*, p. 48.

31. Cantor, *Dewey and Elvis*, pp. 64–68.

32. R. Serge Denisoff, "The Evolution of Popular Music Broadcasting, 1920–1972," *Popular Music and Society* 2 (Spring 1973), pp. 202–226.

33. Cantor, *Dewey and Elvis*, pp. 2–3, 9–10, 60.

34. David Halberstam, *The Fifties* (New York: Villard Books, 1993), p. 460.

35. Arnold Shaw, *Black Popular Music in America* (New York: Schirmer, 1986), pp. 192–196.

36. From a 1954 issue of *Cashbox*, John Broven, *Rhythm and Blues in New Orleans* (New York: Pelican, 1978), p. 106.

37. David M. Tucker, *Lieutenant Lee of Beale Street* (Nashville: Vanderbilt University Press, 1971), pp. 145–146.

38. *Downbeat*, February 25, 1948.

39. *Memphis Press Scimitar*, February 5, 1955.

40. John Leland, *Hip: The History* (New York: HarperCollins, 2004), p. 118.

41. Martin Jack Rosenblum and David Luhrssen, *Searching for Rock and Roll* (Mason, OH: Thomson, 2007), pp. 29–32.

42. Edwin Miller, "Elvis the Innocent," *Memories*, May 1989, p. 13.

43. Nash, p. 17.

44. Guralnick, *Last Train*, p. 43.

45. Nash, pp. 25–26.

46. "Elvis by His Father Vernon Presley," as told to Nancy Anderson. *Good Housekeeping*, January 1978, p. 157.

47. Elaine Dundy, *Elvis and Gladys* (New York: Macmillan, 1985), pp. 171–173, 233.

48. Nash, p. 25.

49. Nash, p. 24.

50. James R. Goff Jr., *Close Harmony: A History of Southern Gospel* (Chapel Hill: University of North Carolina Press, 2002), pp. 57–174.

51. Charles Wolfe, "Presley and the Gospel Tradition," in *The Elvis Reader: Texts and Sources on the King of Rock'n'Roll*, ed. Kevin Quain (New York: St. Martin's, 1992), pp. 15–18.

52. Guralnick, *Last Train*, pp. 51–52.

53. Mildred Scrivener, "My Boy Elvis," *TV Radio Mirror*, March 1957.

54. Editors of *TV Radio Mirror, Elvis Presley* (1956), p. 10.

55. Nash, pp. 27–28.

56. McIlwaine, p. 27.

57. Selma S. Lewis, *A Biblical People in the Bible Belt: The Jewish Community of Memphis, Tennessee, 1840s–1960s* (Macon, GA: Mercer University Press, 1998), pp. 72, 149, 150, 185.

58. Guralnick, *Last Train*, p. 53.

59. Guralnick, *Last Train*, p. 50.

3

The Wonderful Wizard

A legendary artifact during his lifetime, Elvis Presley's first recording finally surfaced many years after his death.[1] The public was never intended to hear it. Elvis never convincingly explained the reason he recorded "My Happiness" and "That's When Your Heartaches Begin" one Saturday afternoon during the summer of 1953, probably in July. Elvis's story that he paid to make the record at the Memphis Recording Service "to surprise my mother" has entered the folklore surrounding Presley's life. He contradicted himself, however, by telling another interviewer that he recorded the songs because he "just wanted to hear what I sounded like."[2]

The first story is implausible, given that he had recently celebrated Gladys's birthday in April; the second is also unlikely. Elvis could have heard the sound of his own voice by making a disc for 25 cents at W. T. Grant's five-and-dime on Main Street. The Memphis Recording Service cost Elvis $3.98 plus tax, a significant sum for a poor boy earning $33 a week at the M. B. Parker Machinists Shop.

Elvis was greeted that Saturday in the modest storefront of Sun Records by Marion Keisker, the assistant to the label's owner, Sam Phillips. She recalled it as a busy afternoon with a line of guitar-carrying singers ahead of Elvis, waiting to make their own vanity records. According to her, Elvis apparently thought of his recording session as an audition for Sun, which had already released a string of recordings by regional performers. "If you know anybody that needs a singer . . ." he began. She understood his implication and interrupted by asking, "What kind of a singer are you?"

"I sing all kinds," he replied. When she demanded to know whom he sounded like, he famously answered, in the key of diffident defiance, "I don't sound like nobody."[3]

A 1948 hit for the pop duo Jon and Sandra, the sentimental "My Happiness" was a tune familiar to Elvis. He had sung it to entertain his neighbors during informal parties at Lauderdale Courts. On his recording debut, Elvis sounds yearning and vulnerable, already possessing the voice that was soon to become familiar the world over. There was no evident blues or country inflection from the singer who brought blues and country together on the singles he would record a year later for Sun Records; the intimate, soft-spoken tone suggested the influence of the crooners who became popular during his parents' youth. The accompaniment sounded spectral on the low-fidelity recording, nothing more than Elvis strumming the melody on his guitar. "My Happiness" was both a window onto his early performances at the Courts and a foretaste of things to come. Presley's assertion to Keisker was correct: he already sounded like no one else.

If an African American influence can be discerned, it was in his choice of the second song recorded that day. "That's When Your Heartaches Begin" was a 1941 release by the Ink Spots, a polished black vocal quartet popular with white audiences. Keisker remembers the story of that day a little differently than her boss. Beginning in the earliest years of Elvis's stardom, she maintained that Phillips was not in when Elvis first appeared and that she was the one who arranged the session by positioning him near a microphone, turning on the tape recorder, and operating the disc-cutting machine that produced a single copy of the recording. She also claimed that she kept a taped copy to play for Phillips, as if already understanding that the awkward boy who paid to sing was headed for greatness. "Now this is something we never did, but I wanted Sam to hear this," she said. In her rendition, Phillips arrived shortly before the session ended. "We might give you a call sometime," he told Elvis, whether out of politeness or genuine interest, and asked Keisker to keep the boy's name on file with the annotation, "Good ballad singer. Hold."

In other early accounts it was Phillips who took down Elvis's name. Many years later Phillips angrily insisted that he switched on the tape recorder and operated the lathe that cut the acetate.[4] The points in dispute are minor, but became a source of rancor between two old friends and evidence of the enormous cultural importance assigned to the particulars of Elvis's "discovery." There is no discrepancy over the essence of the narrative. Phillips and Keisker both insist the young, unknown Elvis was already memorable on that otherwise forgotten day in the summer of 1953.

"My Happiness" marks the tentative beginnings of a career that reverberated across the world. There had been pop stars before Elvis and there would be many after him, some selling more records in a world that has become saturated with recorded music. Elvis's distinction lies in the crucial role he played in popularizing a nascent form of music that had been given the name of rock and roll shortly before the Southern public heard his first recordings on Sun Records. More than simply the most popular early rock and roll singer, Elvis seemed to embody the restlessness of the rising generation of middle class teenagers whose emergence as consumers signaled the arrival of the baby boom. He was *theirs* and opposition from older generations only solidified his rebel image.

The Birth of Rock and Roll

Presley's association with Sun would lead, after the passage of many months, to a contract with the label and a string of 45-RPM singles. The Sun recordings were stepping-stones to Presley's unprecedented stardom and essential to the canon of rock and roll music. Elvis's time at Sun has been mythologized as a series of culture-altering epiphanies. Out of this has come the simplistic idea that Elvis, under Phillips's tutelage, invented rock and roll, or at least the Southern version called rockabilly, through a daring combination of country and blues. His debut single, the blues "That's All Right" backed with the bluegrass "Blue Moon of Kentucky," has been interpreted as a metaphor for crossing racial barriers at a time when the walls of segregation were first being breached by the civil rights movement.

The truth is more complicated, as tangled and thorny as the narrative of race relations in the United States. From the 19th century, the music that was understood as distinctly American usually resulted from creative interplay between Americans of West African and Northern European descent. The relationship became apparent with the minstrel shows and the songs of Stephen Foster. It continued in ragtime through Scott Joplin, in jazz from Louis Armstrong through Bix Beiderbecke and Duke Ellington, and in country music from Jimmie Rodgers through Elvis. Especially in the South, blacks and whites were seldom so far apart that they could not hear each other's music. Traditions of rhythm, harmony, vocalizing, and composition were carried to the New World by settlers and slaves and converged in countless intersections through everyday people entertaining their neighbors and, especially in the 20th century, entrepreneurs hoping to capitalize on expectations of novelty and the need for leisure in a society structured around work.

Even this interchange is not sufficient to fully explain the development of American music. Others in the nation's ethnic mosaic played their part. Jews formed a distinct group crucial to the process, especially as songwriters, producers, and owners of record labels catering to niche markets. Latin influences could be heard, not only from the absorption of Mexican lands and immigration but through centuries of commercial ties between Havana and New Orleans, one of the great birthplaces of American music.[5]

By the time Elvis released "That's All Right," rock and roll was already taking shape as the latest form of cross-cultural American music, a successor to ragtime, Dixieland jazz, and swing. The particular roots of rock and roll have been argued about by scholars and fans, many of them searching for an elusive first rock and roll record or at least recordings that pointed the way. Greil Marcus may have been the first to observe that several Robert Johnson blues songs recorded in 1936 and 1937 suggest the sound of rock and roll.[6] Critic Robert Palmer also found the prototype of rock and roll in "Run Old Jeremiah," a field recording made at a Southern black church made by Library of Congress folklorist Alan Lomax in 1934, along with a 1936 blues recording by the Mississippi Jook Band, "Dangerous Woman."[7] Other early candidates include Blind Willie McTell's "Statesboro Blues" (1928) and the Jazz at the Philharmonic performance of "Blues" (1944). The most popular contender is Jackie Brenston's "Rocket 88" (1951), recorded by Sam Phillips three years before his epochal sessions with Elvis. Contenders for the first rock and roll hit include a song Elvis would later cover, Roy Brown's "Good Rockin' Tonight" (1947); the Dominoes' "Sixty Minute Man" (1951); "Crazy Man, Crazy" by Bill Haley and his Comets (1953); the Chords' "Sh-Boom" (1954); and the Crows' "Gee" (1954). Despite the regional excitement they generated around Memphis and in the South, Elvis's early recordings for Sun are not in the running for first rock and roll record or first rock and roll hit.[8]

In seeking the origins of rock and roll, some critics have found musical elements present in earlier genres that became bedrock for the new sound. African American bandleader Jesse Stone has been credited with devising the bass line prevalent in rock and roll during the transitional period when swing shifted into rhythm and blues after World War II. The quick electric guitar arpeggio that became the basis for Chuck Berry's distinctive riffs has been traced to 1940s bluesman T-Bone Walker. The etymology of the phrase "rock and roll" has been followed at least as far as blues recordings of the 1920s, where it was used as a euphemism for sexual intercourse. By the 1930s, rock and roll assumed a double meaning in jazz and blues and often referred to upbeat rhythms. There was even a song called "Rock and Roll" by the Boswell Sisters, heard on the soundtrack of *Transatlantic Merry-Go-Round*, a film released in the fall of 1934 as Gladys was pregnant with Elvis.[9]

The meaning of rock and roll has also been understood sociologically as well as musically as "a quest for new sounds that amplified the quickening pace and changing texture of modern life . . . a trajectory by which the outsider moved into the mainstream."[10] The description fits Elvis's life as he moved up from the poor white underclass of the South into superstardom. Starting from the periphery of American life, Elvis rechanneled the mainstream in the direction of his own fantasies.

The music that Phillips and Presley worked out around "That's All Right," "Blue Moon of Kentucky," and the succeeding singles Elvis cut for Sun Records had been coalescing since at least the 1930s when Jimmie Rodgers recorded with Louis Armstrong and white country musicians began fusing their own music with black swing jazz in a genre called western swing. Bob Wills and the Texas Playboys helped set the stage for the rockabilly of the 1950s with their bluesy, rollicking country music. Wills's 1937 recording of "White Heat," a song originally performed by African American big band leader Jimmie Lunceford, featured searing electric guitar and a pounding drum kit. It rocked harder than most white rock and roll of two decades hence.

A more immediate predecessor was Bill Haley, who surfaced after World War II with western swing bands in Pennsylvania, a testimony to the popularity of rhythmic country music outside the South. In 1952 he changed his band's name from the Saddlemen to the Comets, shifting from rustic to a more modern, dynamic imagery. By this time Haley's combo was working out its own fusion of country and rhythm and blues, two years before Elvis. Haley scored a hit in New England with "Rock This Joint" (1952) and gained national attention with the hip-talking original "Crazy Man, Crazy" (1953) and a bowdlerized take of Big Joe Turner's sexually hungry rhythm and blues hit "Shake, Rattle, and Roll" (1954).

In April 1954, three months before Elvis recorded "That's All Right," producer Milt Gabler brought Haley into the studio to make "Rock Around the Clock." A Jew born in Harlem, New York City,

Gabler had already midwifed several important moments in American music. Gabler launched the jazz independent label Commodore, which released Billie Holiday's haunting "Strange Fruit" (1939), among the few jazz songs to directly address racism. Later, Gabler produced and cowrote the hit song "Choo Choo Ch'Boogie" (1946) by Louis Jordan and the Tympany Five, perhaps the most popular of the rhythm and blues combos to spin out of the swing era. Jordan sold records to white as well as black consumers.[11] "All the tricks I used with Louis Jordan, I used with Bill Haley," Gabler later said of the links between "Rock Around the Clock" and the music it came from. "The only difference was the way we did the rhythm. On Jordan we used a perfectly balanced rhythm section from the swing era . . . but Bill had the heavy backbeat."[12]

Despite the best efforts of the *Grand Ole Opry* to freeze the music and image in nostalgia for a time that never really was, country music was changing along with the country itself after World War II. The war ended with the use of atomic bombs, a weapon that emerged from the pages of pulp science fiction, and the discovery of terrible atrocities such as the Holocaust. During the war, women occupied many relatively well-paid jobs normally reserved for men. The return of millions of servicemen expecting to occupy those jobs and anxious over the implications of economically independent women lent a tense static to gender relations. America's racial status quo was left uncertain after a war fought in the name of human dignity and freedom. The unprecedented prosperity that flowed to the middle and lower classes as a result of wartime government spending threatened social mores.

Popular culture responded to the changes. Many Hollywood movies grew dark in form and content, coalescing into a genre called film noir. Music across all genres became nervous and jittery or tougher and harder in sound. Bebop pushed jazz to the sound barrier, blues musicians traded their acoustic guitars for electric models and cranked up the volume. Country music spawned a genre called "hillbilly boogie," yet another foretaste of the rockabilly sound of Elvis's Sun recordings. Swing orchestras broke up into small, hard-hitting rhythm and blues combos. Gospel singers such as Sister Rosetta Tharpe embraced electric guitars and blues rhythms. Even the new hillbilly genre called bluegrass, ostensibly a return to country's Appalachian roots, played out in hasty double speed.

Technology was altering the way music was made and heard. Recording tape, an innovation of Nazi Germany, was introduced in America and made the recording process less expensive and more accessible. Vinyl LPs and singles were more durable and easily carried around than their shellac predecessors. The transistor radio, introduced in 1947, also made music more portable and enabled members of a younger generation to escape into their own sonic universe.

Aside from the proliferation of professional recording facilities, none of these postwar developments, or even the ongoing dialogue between black and white in America, had much to do with Elvis's recording of "My Happiness." He probably was unaware that conservatives criticized the original generation of crooners when they emerged in the early 1930s, albeit without the vehemence that would be aimed at rock and roll.[13]

The crooning style of "My Happiness" would be less apparent on the recordings produced by Phillips for Sun Records. During his early years with RCA, the sway of the older generation of singers rebounded. To the dismay of most rock critics, troubled by the breadth of his music, Elvis never disowned any of his formative influences. "I like Crosby, Como, Sinatra, all the big ones. They had to be good to get there," he told an interviewer shortly after his own arrival at stardom.[14]

The Sun Sessions

According to Keisker, Elvis returned repeatedly in the months following his first visit to the studio, nervously making conversation and asking if she knew of a band that needed a singer. Hearing of a possible opening, he auditioned for a gospel quartet, the Songfellows. The member who had planned to leave the group decided to stay. "I think Elvis was disappointed, but he still sang with the boys from time to time, during rehearsals," recalled Memphis gospel singer J. D. Sumner.[15] After taking a job as a delivery driver for Crown Electric Company, he is said to have brought his guitar along with him in the Ford pickup truck.[16] Elvis seemed increasingly intent on pursuing music but had few ideas of how to chase his dream beyond persistence at Sun Studio. Maybe a glimmer of interest from Keisker or even Phillips himself on that first visit in the summer of 1953 sustained his dreams?

Sun Records may also have seemed a logical path for an aspiring singer from Memphis, even one uncertain of his direction, given the label's rise to regional prominence as it evolved out of the Memphis Recording Service. The careless legends that have grown up around Phillips should not be allowed to eclipse the man's contributions. He was not "one of the first white men to record black blues," as one otherwise authoritative work maintained.[17] White men had been recording the blues since the 1920s. Sun Records was part of a wave of small labels, usually sole proprietorships or partnerships, which began to proliferate during World War II in response to subtle seismic shifts in the jazz world. "Something new was going on beneath big-band swing," and after the war, this up-tempo small combo music would be named rhythm and blues.[18]

As the United States entered the war in 1942, three outlets for the new music were established: Savoy Records in Newark, founded by Herman Lubinsky; Beacon Records in New York, founded by Joe Davis; and Excelsior in Los Angeles, founded by Otis J. Rene Jr. Before long, new labels spread like mushrooms on a damp day in early spring. Apollo Records in Harlem and Premier and Exclusive in Los Angeles were both established in 1943. The following year Deluxe was founded in Linden, New Jersey, Gilt Edge in Los Angeles, National in New York, Gulf in Houston, and King in Cincinnati. In 1945, a plethora of rhythm and blues labels sprang up in Los Angeles, including Modern, Philo, and Bronze; and from the East Coast came Super Disc and Manor. A year later even Nashville, the center of country music, produced a label that released rhythm and blues records, Bullet Records. Its cofounder, Jim Bulleit, invested part of the money that allowed Phillips to launch Sun.

The most enduring name among these labels, Atlantic Records, was founded in New York in 1947. That same year Aristocrat, soon renamed Chess, began operating in Chicago and became home to many of the most important postwar blues singers. In 1949, Dot Records began in Gallatin, Tennessee, while Houston saw three new labels, Macy's, Freedom, and Peacock. In 1950 Trumpet Records began in Jackson, Mississippi, and in 1951 Nashboro in Nashville. In 1952, the year Sun Records began, two other labels were founded in Memphis, Duke Records and Meteor Records. By the time Phillips launched Sun, more than one hundred independent labels were in business, most of them devoting at least part of their catalog to rhythm and blues.[19]

Like all of the little labels, Sun was confined to the periphery of the music industry, shut out of national and international distribution and lacking a large budget for marketing and promotion. Its reach was largely regional, aided by localized networks of shopkeepers, disc jockeys, and jukebox operators. The performers recorded by Sun and most other independent labels were also usually local. These labels relied on niche markets not well catered to by the big corporate record companies. Little wonder Sun and dozens of similar postwar operations focused on the audience for African American popular music.

With only a few exceptions, the "indie labels," as they were already being called in the trade papers, were not managed by folklorists, aesthetes, or social activists, but by businessmen. Some of them enjoyed personal links to the audiences for their product and were nimbler than the major labels in their response to shifting trends. The ears of their owners were more perceptive to the music of minority interests while corporate labels focused on mass marketing. "I looked for an area neglected by the majors and in essence took the crumbs off the table of the record industry," said Art Rupe, founder of Specialty Records in Los Angeles.[20]

Independent labels were economically marginal for their owners. Consequently, recording artists were often cheated of their money or at least signed to contracts at unfavorable terms. Johnny Cash, whose career began at Sun in the wake of Elvis's success, recalled: "I'm not sure he [Phillips] treated me properly in a financial sense."[21] Roy Orbison, another post-Elvis graduate of Sun Records, recalled the label's now romanticized golden era as "hard times for all of us."[22] Phillips later referred to his artists as "my damn babies" and boasted of knowing "how to paddle their butt when they needed it."[23] One Southern historian has noted the affinity between 1950s record producers and the semi-feudal landlords who had long dominated the region.[24]

Sam Phillips claimed his boyhood dream had been to become a defense attorney, an advocate for the oppressed, but by the time the Alabama native arrived in Memphis (1945), he had compiled a resume in broadcasting. Working as an announcer and engineer for WREC, Phillips produced big band broadcasts from the rooftop ballroom of the elegant Hotel Peabody. There he met fellow WREC employee Marion Keisker. A cultured, articulate, and respected local talk show host with a "courtly Southern manner," she became his assistant when he opened the Memphis Recording Service in January 1950. She was a classic "Girl Friday" in the parlance of the time, running all aspects of the operation aside from the recordings themselves. Keisker called manufacturers and distributors and kept in touch with musicians. According to Elvis's friend Red West, the singer always acknowledged Keisker, not Phillips, as his primary benefactor, saying, "If it wasn't for that lady, I would never have got a start." The Recording Service barely made the rent on its compact studio in a brick storefront at 706 Union Avenue. By one account Keisker put her own money into the petty cash drawer to spare the depressive Phillips from financial anxiety. Although he was a married man, she fell in love with her boss.[25]

Phillips's recording studio was launched as a moneymaking venture. His business card read: "We record anything—anywhere—anytime. A complete service to fill every recording need." Phillips went on location with his suitcase-size Presto tape recorder to record political speeches and bar mitzvahs. He gladly opened the doors of his studio to amateurs like Elvis who paid to make vanity recordings.[26]

Phillips also recorded blues and rhythm and blues acts, leasing the master tapes to a pair of important independent labels, Chess and RPM, before founding his own record company. Those Northern labels considered Phillips an important source for black Southern talent. As a freelance producer and talent scout for other labels, Phillips was ideally situated geographically. Memphis had long been a magnet for African American talent, and the younger generation of regional black performers was making music that would appeal to the audience for rhythm and blues elsewhere in the country. Important blues singers such as B. B. King and Howlin' Wolf made some of their first recordings with Phillips in the salad days of his studio.[27] A music industry infrastructure that would be critical to Sun's success came into existence in Memphis after World War II, including a record pressing plant and a distribution company called Music Sales, which numbered Atlantic and Chess among its clients.[28]

One of Phillips's early sessions has been recognized as epochal, "Rocket 88," released by Chess Records (1951). Reaching number one on the R&B chart, it has often been called the first rock and roll record. The recording was credited to singer and saxophonist Jackie Brenston but was really the work of Brenston's teenage bandleader, Ike Turner. In the 1960s, Turner would gain fame for a string of hits with his wife, singer Tina Turner, and in the 1980s, infamy from Tina's tell-all post-divorce autobiography. He may have been a cruel husband but was a brilliant performer who took rhythm and blues into new territory.

The gestation of "Rocket 88" is almost as complicated as the roots of rock and roll. Turner rewrote it from a 1947 rhythm and blues recording, Jimmy Liggins's "Cadillac Boogie," which was derived in turn from Pete Johnson's 1946 instrumental, "Rocket 88 Boogie." The lyric's message would become a touchstone in 1950s teenage culture. The Oldsmobile Rocket 88 was a fast car promising freedom to its driver and hinting at sexual opportunity. The theme, however, was not new. Robert Johnson had already driven a fast car as a metaphor of male sexuality in "Terraplane Blues" (1936).

Epiphanies are rare. Most of what is called originality involves creative rearrangement of material already produced by others. The lyrics, strong rock beat, and fervid vocals of "Rocket 88" were not entirely unprecedented. Separating the recording from other rhythm and blues tracks of the period was the inspired use of an accident. When Turner and band arrived at Phillips's studio with a broken guitar amplifier, the producer decided to run with the distorted sound. Turner was game. The unique properties of amplification were becoming more and more prevalent, especially as blues guitarists exploited electricity to sustain pitches and create sounds that had been impossible and unknown to earlier generations. With "Rocket 88" and Turner's broken speaker cone, Phillips pushed sound recording further into a red zone whose harsh tone and texture echoed the sonic rush of modernity with greater force than any modernist experiment by academically trained "serious" musicians.

"The first thing to remember about Sam Phillips is that he was a great audio man. . . . And what made Sam great, Sam was not afraid to experiment," said Stan Kesler, who played bass and steel guitar for Sun Records's sessions and wrote "I Forgot to Remember to Forget" for Elvis. Phillips's willingness to try new things would come to its fullest fruition in the early records he made with Elvis for Sun.[29]

After Elvis's success Phillips often claimed that his choice of black recording artists reflected his desire to work for civil rights in the field of popular culture. "I thought to myself: suppose that I had been born black. Suppose that I would have been born a little bit more down on the economic ladder. I think I felt from the beginning the total inequity of man's inhumanity to his brother." He added that he never wanted to preach on the subject but to address injustice through practical action.[30]

There is no reason to doubt his good intentions or his respect for the humanity of the black performers he worked with. However, the notion of a Southern white man working with black entertainers was not unprecedented, as witnessed by other white-owned labels in the region. Phillips's earliest efforts were marketed to black audiences, despite a growing appetite among whites for rhythm and blues, and were not understood at the moment of their release as a call for cultural desegregation. The work by Phillips and other indie label owners was not unlike the campaign mounted by Pepsi Cola, then a relatively small beverage company in comparison to the giant Coca-Cola, to sell its product to a black market that Coke had ignored.[31]

Understandably, Phillips was concerned with money. He was supporting a wife and two small boys and, through June 1951, working fulltime for WREC in addition to this recording business. He also seemed to have larger ambitions than to just get by. His most famous quote speaks not only to the scope of the rhythm and blues audience, limited by the size of the black population and widespread cultural prejudice, but to a growing awareness on Phillips's part of a cultural shift manifesting itself in music.[32] "If I could find a white man who had the Negro sound and the Negro feel, I could make a billion dollars."[33] The man he found was called Elvis, and although the profit Phillips made from his investment was relatively modest, Elvis would become a billion-dollar industry.

Phillips was not alone in sensing that the tectonic plates of American culture were beginning to move. The older generation hoped for the return of the big bands but this was financially untenable. Popular music in the years following the war was increasingly dominated by balladry, but Tin Pan Alley, as the New York songwriting industry was called, was in an imaginative slump. While many members of the generation who had grown up in the Great Depression and into World War II sought the tranquility of quiet suburban subdivisions and found comfort in the soothing tones of singers such as Perry Como, younger people increasingly found Tin Pan Alley pop to be disconnected from their aspirations, from the thrill of excitement they sought, and the emotional catharsis of dance. One must be careful not to confuse the pleasure taken by many young whites in adopting black music or cultural gestures with a progressive social agenda. For many teenagers in the 1950s, the rise of rhythm and blues was more a matter of a new generation seeking to erect their own culture and searching for building materials in places declared off-limits by their parents.

There were signs that the major record labels were searching cautiously for new sources and new audiences. Cover versions of country and rhythm and blues songs by dulcet-voiced singers began to climb the pop music charts. Perhaps Bing Crosby led the way with Red Foley's country tune "Chattanoogie Shoe Shine Boy" in 1950. Toney Bennett followed in 1951 with Hank Williams's "Cold, Cold Heart." The next year a pair of Williams's songs were popularized with Rosemary Clooney's cover of "Half as Much" and Jo Stafford's version of "Jambalaya (On the Bayou)."

The idea of pop singers performing country songs was remarkable in the early 1950s but not as much as the trend of white singers covering rhythm and blues. The rise of a black recording on the R&B chart often triggered a white rendition for the pop market. One of the most credible was country singer Hardrock Gunter's proto-rockabilly cover of the Dominoes' "Sixty Minute Man" (1951). In 1954, the year of Elvis's music industry debut, a spree of popular covers charted, including the McGuire Sisters' rendition of the Spaniels' "Goodnight, Sweetheart, Goodnight" and the Moonglows' "Sincerely," and the Crewcuts' version of the Penguins' "Earth Angel." Lost in translation was the steamy energy and enigmatic cool of the original recordings. Nonetheless a substantial market existed for bleached covers of rhythm and blues as many record buyers cautiously explored new options even as their more adventurous peers formed the growing white audience for contemporary black music.

Phillips had every reason to suspect that a large audience existed for a white singer who conveyed the essence of the black style. In the years preceding Elvis, several white singers who sounded black to contemporary ears became popular. Frankie Lane's "That Is My Desire" (1947) was a rhythm and blues hit before it crossed over to the pop charts. "Everybody thought I was colored," he explained. Similar confusion greeted Johnnie Ray, who enjoyed a number one pop hit with "Cry" (1951). "When my first record hit, a lot of people thought I was black," he said.[34]

The fusing of apparent opposites, of white and black, country and blues, was an idea that occurred only gradually to Phillips if his recorded output is any marker. In 1951 he launched a short-lived label with Dewey Phillips called Phillips Records. Although the two men were unrelated by blood, they belonged to the brotherhood of white Southern hipsters who sought out the blues. The label was aborted after the first recording by blues multi-instrumentalist Joe Hill Louis, also known as "the Be-Bop Boy." Only 300 copies were pressed and despite Dewey's influence as a popular DJ, they stirred little interest.[35]

Sam Phillips remained determined to break into the record business. In April 1952, Sun Records debuted with a bluesy vamp, Johnny London's "Drivin' Slow," an otherwise unremarkable number that displayed Phillips's love of echo, which would factor into his sessions with Elvis. Sun's bright yellow label boasted a cleverly stylized representation of a rooster crowing at the rising sun. Phillips later claimed calling his company Sun represented "A new day, a new opportunity,"[36] but to Memphis record buyers at the time, it probably signified the close ties his black artists maintained with their rural roots. There was nothing futuristic or even in the moment about Phillips's earliest recordings, which documented a blues tradition that was starting to fade.

The same month that Sun entered the marketplace, Bill Haley and his Comets streaked ahead of Phillips in achieving a country-blues fusion with their recording of a cover of Jimmy Preston's rhythm and blues hit "Rock This Joint" on Philadelphia's Essex Records. One year earlier Haley had already brought western swing to rhythm and blues with his cover of the Phillips-produced hit "Rocket 88." Given the uncertain distribution and radio play of independent record labels beyond their home region, it is possible that Phillips never listened to Haley until the latter scored his first hit on the pop chart, "Crazy Man, Crazy," in the spring of 1953.

Meanwhile Sun continued to release a steady trickle of blues recordings by African American performers. There was little hint of things to come in the rootsy blues of Joe Hill Louis's "We All Gotta Go Sometime" (released in January 1953). Jimmy & Walter's "Easy" (March 1953) was a thinly disguised version of Ivory Joe Hunter's hit "I Almost Lost My Mind." The novelty blues number by popular African American DJ Rufus Thomas, "Tiger Man" (March 1953), is unremarkable except that it resurfaced as part of Elvis's repertoire during his Christmas 1968 TV special and remained on his song list into the 1970s. All of these releases presumably received a measure of local attention. Dewey Phillips customarily received advance copies days before they went on sale.

Betting on a jackpot, Phillips conceived a tune called "Bear Cat" (March 1953) as Thomas's "answer record" to Big Mama Thornton's hit "Hound Dog," the same song that became Elvis's vehicle three years later. "Bear Cat" was among dozens of answer records to Big Mama Thornton but it was the one that raced onto the charts. Phillips had little time to enjoy his success. "Bear Cat" drew a copyright infringement lawsuit from "Hound Dog's" publisher, "Diamond" Don Robey, the most powerful African American mobster in the South and an important force on the business end of rhythm and blues and gospel music. Phillips lost the case.[37]

The local press devoted coverage to Sun's July 1953 release by the Prisonaires, "Just Walkin' in the Rain." The African American singing group was, in fact, imprisoned at Nashville's Tennessee State Penitentiary. Although Phillips was skeptical, his partner Jim Bulleit convinced him to record them. "Bulleit drove the five singing prisoners to Memphis, the [song's] composer having to stay in prison. An armed guard and a trusty came along, the record company paying the expenses."[38]

Perhaps the publicity surrounding "Just Walkin' in the Rain" encouraged Elvis to pay his first call on Sun Studio. The Prisonaires' record was neither blues nor rhythm and blues but a sweet group harmony effort harkening back to such popular black acts as the

Mills Brothers and the Ink Spots. The Prisonaires may have influenced Elvis's decision to sing an Ink Spots favorite for his recording debut. Their song would later be a hit in a cover version by Johnnie Ray.

Released later in July on Sun, "Feelin' Good" by Little Junior's Blue Flames became a national hit, reaching number five on the R&B chart. Although credited to bandleader Herman Parker, the song was a slightly rewritten version of John Lee Hooker's blues classic "Boogie Chillun" and was released over the writer's protests.[39] Parker wanted to be a contemporary black performer and was uninterested in Phillips's penchant for more rural sounding blues. The Blue Flames' next record for Sun, "Mystery Train" (November 1953), was more his style and would become one of Elvis's signature songs during his tenure at the label. The original version sounded nothing like "Feelin' Good" or Elvis's "Mystery Train" but was a suave, uptown rhythm and blues number.

If Phillips was already thinking about finding a white singer with a black sound, there was still no evidence of it in his recorded output by the time Elvis made a second vanity disc at his studio in January 1954. This time he recorded "I'll Never Stand in Your Way" by Italian American pop vocalist Joni James and "It Wouldn't Be the Same Without You" by country singer Jimmy Wakely. A better choice from James's repertoire might have been her gold record from 1952, "Why Don't You Believe in Me." By this time Elvis still had no reason to suppose he would ever get a hearing from Phillips but his shy persistence would soon pay off.

During the early months of 1954, Elvis attended the Assembly of God in South Memphis. The church was presided over by the Reverend James Hamill, a fiery preacher who condemned dancing and movies as sinful but encouraged speaking in tongues. Perhaps a touch of glossolalia rubbed off on Elvis's stuttering introduction to "Baby Let's Play House" for Sun, but the preacher's admonishments against movies had no apparent effect on the singer's actions or his Hollywood-colored dream world. Although Elvis would soon send millions of teenagers to the dance floor, the prohibition against dancing he had grown up with left a mark. He was never much of a dancer.

A large congregation with nearly two thousand members, the South Memphis Assembly of God probably did not provide Elvis with the close-knit sense of community he was used to. He may have joined because it numbered among its congregants the Blackwood Brothers, one of his favorite gospel quartets. Elvis's membership may have cemented his relationship with the singers. Churches have always served as centers for social and business networking as well as worship.

American Teenager

Elvis also met his girlfriend, Dixie Locke, at the South Memphis Assembly of God, where he stood out against the crew cut conformity of the other boys in the Bible study class. She was only 15, nearly three years Elvis's junior, but this was not considered unusual. In the South as in many traditional cultures, men tended to take younger women as their wives. Dixie found Elvis achingly shy yet always ready to call attention to himself. "I really think he was doing it to prove something to himself more than to the people around him," she recalled.[40]

It was a good pairing psychologically. Dixie has always been described as outgoing and uncomplicated. Although it may be purely coincidental, Dixie's appearance, dark shoulder-length hair with a short lock swept off the forehead, resembled Mary Marvel, Captain Marvel's twin sister. Perhaps his attraction was rooted in part in comic book fantasy.[41]

On date nights, Elvis picked Dixie up in the old Lincoln he borrowed from Vernon. She took his calls next door at her uncle's home. Dixie's parents were without a telephone. Despite the nearness of working class poverty, many of her memories are suffused with the "Happy Days" nostalgia of skating rinks, soda fountains with red leatherette booths, double dates with Elvis's cousin Gene and her sister Juanita, and nervous first encounters with parents. In the warm glow of her reflections, Dixie and Elvis were in some ways typical of 1950s teenage America. The few tense moments were easily overcome. Her folks found Elvis's hair and clothing off-putting but warmed under the pale glow of his unfailing courtesy. Dixie got along famously with Gladys but found Vernon to be "an outsider" in his own family. According to her, Gladys and Elvis "had such a strong love and respect for each other" that Vernon was relegated to a secondary role. Despite the Reverend Hamill's denunciation of movies, Elvis and Dixie took in shows at least twice a week.[42]

Sometimes Dixie met Elvis at one of his favorite haunts, Charlie's Record Shop, with its listening booths and huge inventory of rhythm and blues records. Although she never saw or heard Elvis's vanity recording of "My Happiness," Dixie remembers him saying that the disc was on the store's jukebox for a while. She also remembers him singing often, whether hymns or songs from the radio, and that he could pick up any melody easily on the piano. A guitar often accompanied them on dates. Like a misplaced romantic troubadour from a Hollywood movie, Elvis was always ready to serenade her and entertain passersby in the parking lot of Rocky's Lakeside refreshment stand. If Dixie's memory served her well, the outlines of Elvis's repertoire had already been drawn in that parking lot by the spring of 1954. "He sang songs that were popular and a lot of the old blues-type songs; he did some of the old spirituals, too." Sometimes he would goof around with familiar pop lyrics, rewriting their earnest words into little jests.[43]

Toward the end of April, Elvis began work at Crown Electric, a family-run electrical contractor around the corner from Humes Courts. The husband and wife owners, James and Gladys Tipler, kidded him about his "long hair" but found him to be a conscientious worker.[44] He drove a truck for Crown, delivering supplies to building sites, and was heading down the road to one possible future. Apparently, there were opportunities for Elvis at Crown. He was encouraged to go to night school and train as an apprentice electrician. It was a lucrative trade but one suspects that a career in electrical wiring would never have afforded the satisfaction craved by the dreamy young man.

"I was in doubt as to whether I would ever make it, because you had to keep your mind right on what you're doing, you can't be the least bit absentminded or you're liable to blow somebody's house up," Elvis recalled in 1956. His next sentence implies that he had no confidence in finding a better path. "I didn't think I was the type for it, but I was going to give it a try."[45]

One of his coworkers at Crown, Dorsey Burnette, played music with his brother Johnny in a band called the Rhythm Rangers in the upbeat Hank Williams style that presaged rockabilly.[46] Like Elvis, the brothers had grown up in Lauderdale Courts. Two years later as the Johnny Burnette Trio, they would release one of the greatest rockabilly records ever, the fuzztone guitar-powered version of Tiny Bradshaw's rhythm and blues number "The Train Kept A-Rollin'," which became a staple in the rock repertoire after recordings by the Yardbirds in the 1960s and Aerosmith in the 1970s.

During his tenure at Crown Electric, Elvis enjoyed less success in music than his coworkers. He cautiously tried his hand at performing in public, playing a couple of songs at the Hi-Hat club. He was not invited to return.[47] Elvis occasionally sang with other bands, with Johnny Burnette and a combo led by Jack Clement, who would go on to produce Johnny Cash, Carl Perkins, and Jerry Lee Lewis for Sun.

Photographs exist of Elvis hanging around the Eagles Nest, a rough honky tonk on Highway 78, the collar of his windbreaker turned up. Burnette remembers him going around with a guitar slung across his back. "Sometimes he used to go down to the fire station and sing to the boys there—they were the only ones around Memphis who seemed to have a lot of listening time," he recalled. "And every now and then, he'd go into one of the cafes and bars and slouch across a chair . . . Then some folks would say: 'Let's hear you sing, boy,' and old Elvis would stroll up to the most convenient spot, looking at the ground all the time. Then all of a sudden he'd slide that guitar round to his front and he'd near raise the roof with that real rocking sound of his."[48]

In the early months of 1954, Elvis and Dixie stood at the threshold of a conventional life together. They were "going steady," an arrangement that did not inevitably lead to the formality of engagement or the commitment of marriage, but often resulted in marriage from accidental pregnancy or genuine romantic feelings. "We were a big thing. I gave her my high school ring," Elvis recalled.[49]

Everything between them was happening fast in a teenage subculture that insisted upon dating but left the rules of the game unclear. The opportunities for acting on the raging sexual urges of youth were greater than ever, given the mobility afforded by cars and the proliferation of unchaperoned activities. However, social taboos about sexuality remained in place, enforced by religion and the greater fear of pregnancy in an era before birth control pills, when frank discussion about sexuality was scarce and knowledge among teenagers was often spotty despite the appearance of the Kinsey Reports on male and female sexuality on the bestseller lists in 1948 and 1953.

Dixie would join her parents on a two-week vacation in Florida during the early weeks of July, the period when Elvis's rockabilly sound coalesced in the Sun Studio. She worried about her absence, not because she feared that Elvis would cheat on her but because of his unreasonable jealousy. "He couldn't stand it if I was doing something that didn't involve him, he was kind of possessive in that respect," she said.[50]

As it turned out, Elvis would have other things on his mind. Although there is little to go on beyond Keisker's memories, it appears that Elvis continued to stop by Sun Studio from time to time, reminding her of his interest in joining a band. "Every time a song came up, I'd say to Sam, 'How about the kid with the sideburns?'" she said, adding that Phillips never seemed especially interested.[51] Elvis's persistence was finally rewarded when Phillips mulled over a demo recording of a song presented to him by a Nashville publisher, "Without You."

Phillips was intrigued by the yearning ballad and searched his memory for a singer who could cut a version for Sun. The story goes that Phillips, as usual, asked Keisker for advice. "Remember Elvis Presley?" she replied. "Yes, indeed. Give him a call," he said.[52]

Keisker rang him at noon on Saturday, June 26. For Elvis it was a dream come true. "She said, 'Can you be here by three?'" he recounted. "I was there by the time she hung up the phone."[53]

"Without You" was apparently beyond Elvis's range. For some reason, Phillips was not discouraged. He evidently recognized something in the voice that rang out from the painfully shy young man at the microphone in his cramped studio and asked him to keep singing. "I sang everything I knew—pop stuff, spirituals," Elvis said.[54]

Although the session for "Without You" was a failure, the effort to record the song was not time wasted. Elvis finally had Phillips's ear. By the end of June 1954, Elvis was already the product of a complex social and cultural layering. Ancient verities and pop culture coalesced within his imagination without contradiction. He was a white Southern Pentacostal and a white Southern hipster who worshipped Jesus while paying Marlon Brando his due. He was not simply a country boy in love with the blues, a *Grand Ole Opry* fan wandering down Beale Street in search of rhythm and blues. Elvis also loved the golden-throated singers of previous generations, from Bing Crosby to Mario Lanza. He was familiar with black gospel music but the white Southern quartets with their flashy yet essentially wholesome showmanship had the greatest influence on him.

The carnality of the blues and the spirituality of gospel, the fatalism of old-time country singers and the expansiveness of Frank Sinatra and Dean Martin, all made their marks on Elvis. Hollywood movies presented him with images of romance and heroism, duty and rebellion, and with notions of stardom that would have to be squared with the engrained sense of limitation he learned as the child of sharecroppers. Elvis was unfailingly courteous to authority figures but his deference was sometimes worn with a sullen shrug. He was a gentleman with women. His Southern chivalry was reinforced by a devotion to his mother that never eclipsed his respect for his father but left Vernon in the shade. Family, religion, and regional identity were the foundations on which Elvis added a superstructure of personality constructed from popular culture.

Elvis set himself apart from the working class Memphis of his teenage years for his adaptation of hip clothing and hair styles, but whether this rebellion against conformity was more than skin deep depends on the significance he accorded the choices he made. He sought distinction within his community of lower caste Southerners, not the severing of ties. He was no outlaw. On the other hand, Elvis was distinguished for his apparent lack of racial or religious bigotry. Elvis sensed an affinity with society's other outcasts that many working class Southerners of his time strenuously denied. He felt that he understood something about the Jews and African Americans he encountered. He also took the benign and universal implications of his religious faith to heart, without reservations based on complexion.

The comic books that Elvis devoured were also a factor in his makeup. His interest in the pulpy, loudly colored stories was not unusual. By many measurements the comic book had become the most popular form of entertainment in America, outpacing Hollywood movies with sales of more than 80 million copies a week at 5 or 10 cents a copy, mostly to younger readers.[55] Not unlike rhythm and blues and country music, comic books were largely drawn and disseminated by outsiders, in the comics' case Jews, Italians, and other urban ethnics from the East Coast.

Even before the end of World War II, comic books began drawing many of the same thunderbolts that would be hurled against rock and roll. The Roman Catholic Church condemned them for endangering "strict sex control," while the liberal *The Nation* claimed they had driven youth "several degrees toward illiteracy," and the *New York Times* was "deeply concerned over the moral and social effect of this flood of pulp paper."[56] A connection was drawn between pulpy picture stories and juvenile delinquency, as the spike in youthful crime and dissidence during World War II was labeled. Comic books were banned or restricted in New Orleans, Los Angeles, Cleveland, and other cities. In his bestseller *Seduction of the Innocent* (1954), respected psychiatrist Frederic Wertham blamed comic books for behavior disorders and personality difficulties in children that led to antisocial activities. He drew his findings on case studies of youthful criminals who avidly devoured comic books.

Concerns over juvenile delinquency grew during the war years as fathers and older brothers enlisted and mothers and older sisters went to work, leaving many children unsupervised and prone to crime. "These are symptoms of a condition which threatens to develop a new 'lost generation' more hopelessly lost than any that has gone before," J. Edgar Hoover warned in an editorial.[57]

Delinquency came to be a convenient label for young people involved in "an array of conscious deviations from the conventions of proper society: improper language, attitudes, modes of dress and personal grooming, tastes in music, and reading matter."[58] By this definition Elvis was a juvenile delinquent, albeit a dutiful son and a reliable worker without a single brush with the law.

From what is known of Elvis's reading habits, he favored superhero comics. He especially enjoyed Captain Marvel and his youthful sidekick, Captain Marvel Jr., whose own series of books debuted around the time of Elvis's birthday in January 1942.[59] Elvis was probably crestfallen to learn that the Captain and his cohort were driven from the news racks at drugstores in January 1954, when DC Comics, the publishers of Superman, won their case of plagiarism against Captain Marvel's creators.

Regardless of the color of their capes and the emblems they employed, superheroes inevitably supported the status quo. Captain Marvel may have been the most conventional of the masked crusaders. His visage modeled after popular everyman actor Fred MacMurray, the Captain was "an example of American naiveté, cheerfulness and undying optimism. He was Horatio Alger in superhero tights."[60] Superhero stories tapped into adolescent fantasies of rule breaking and destruction in the name of good. They were a projection of thwarted ambition, a daydream of supremacy in a world where mountains are hard to climb and obstacles may appear insurmountable, as well as an archetypal resurgence of ancient demigods.

Captain Marvel was the alter ego of Billy Batson, an unimposing young man of humble origins who began to channel great power after encountering a wizard called Shazam. In everyday life Billy remained, like Elvis, little noticed by coworkers and the public. Perhaps the young singer felt that in Sam Phillips he had discovered his Shazam.

Notes

1. The original acetate of "My Happiness" and "That's When the Heartaches Begin" emerged in 1988 "in the possession of a high school classmate." Booklet to *Elvis Presley The King of Rock'n'Roll: The Complete 50's Masters* (RCA, 1992).

2. Peter Guralnick, *Last Train to Memphis: The Rise of Elvis Presley* (Boston: Little Brown, 1994), p. 63.

3. Guralnick, *Last Train*, p. 63; Jerry Hopkins, *Elvis: A Biography* (New York: Simon & Schuster, 1971), p. 64,

4. Guralnick, *Last Train*, p. 497; Hopkins, *Elvis: A Biography*, p. 66.

5. John Storm Roberts, *The Latin Tinge: The Impact of Latin American Music on the United States* (New York: Oxford University Press, 1999, 2nd ed.; Ned Sublette, *The World That Made New Orleans: From Spanish Silver to Congo Square* (Chicago: Lawrence Hill, 2008).

6. Greil Marcus, *Mystery Train: Images of America in Rock'n'Roll Music* (New York: E. P. Dutton, 1975), p. 23.

7. Robert Palmer, "Rock Begins," in Rolling Stone *Illustrated History of Rock & Roll*, ed. Jim Miller (New York: Rolling Stone Press, 1976), p. 10.

8. "Statesboro Blues" is cited in Michael Gray, *Hand Me My Travelin' Shoes* (London: Bloomsbury, 2007), p. 205; "Blues" in Roy Carr, Brian Case, and Fred Dellar, *The Hip: Hipsters, Jazz and the Beat Generation* (London: Faber & Faber, 1986), p. 34; "Rocket 88," in *The Rolling Stone Encyclopedia of Rock & Roll*, ed. Jon Pareles and Patricia Romanowski (New York: Summit, 1983), p. 429; "Good Rockin' Tonight" in Palmer, *Rock & Roll: An Unruly History* (New York: Harmony, 1995), p. 27; "Sixty Minute Man" in Nick Tosches, *Unsung Heroes of Rock'n'Roll: The Birth of Rock in the Wild Years before Elvis* (New York: Da Capo, 1999, 3rd ed.), p. 106; "Crazy Man, Crazy" in Charlie Gillett, *The Sound of the City: The Rise of Rock and Roll* (New York: Da Capo, 1996, 3rd ed.), p. 3; "Sh-Boom," and "Gee" in Arnold Shaw, *The Rockin' '50s* (New York: Hawthorne, 1974), p. 77.

9. Tosches, pp. 6, 16; Bruce Pegg, *Brown Eyed Handsome Man, The Life and Hard Times of Chuck Berry* (New York: Routledge, 2002), p. 28.

10. Martin Jack Rosenblum and David Luhrssen, *Searching for Rock and Roll* (Mason, OH: Thomson, 2007), p. vii.

11. Shaw, *Rockin' '50s*, pp. 81–82.

12. Shaw, *Honkers and Shouters: The Golden Years of Rhythm and Blues* (New York: Macmillan, 1978), p. 64.

13. Crooning was seen as a bellwether of juvenile delinquency but not a challenge to racial and cultural segregation. The New York Singing Teachers Association declared, "Crooning corrupts the minds and ideals of the younger generation" and Boston's

Cardinal O'Connor called it "a degenerate form of singing." "These Pesky Crooners," *Air Time* (December 5, 1932).

14. Robert Johnson, "TV News and Views," *Memphis Press Scimitar*, May 4, 1956.

15. Charles Wolfe, "Presley and the Gospel Tradition," in *The Elvis Reader: Texts and Sources on the King of Rock'n'Roll*, ed. Kevin Quain (New York: St. Martin's, 1992), pp. 16–17; Nancy Anderson, "Elvis, by His Father Vernon Presley," *Good Housekeeping*, January 1978, p. 158.

16. Hopkins, p. 53.

17. Pareles and Romanowski, p. 429.

18. Tosches, p. 3.

19. Tosches, pp. 4–5; Gillett, p. 10.

20. Shaw, *Honkers and Shouters*, p. 182.

21. Johnny Cash with Patrick Carr, *Johnny: The Autobiography* (New York: Harper Paperbacks, 1997), p. 105.

22. Jeff Tamarkin, "Roy Orbison: An Interviewer's Dream," *Goldmine*, May 5, 1989.

23. Sam Phillips, "Sam Phillips Talks," jacket notes for *Sun Records Collection* (RCA/Rhino, 1994).

24. Pete Daniel, "Rhythm of the Land," *Agricultural History* 68, no. 4 (1994), p. 8.

25. Colin Escott with Martin Hawkins, *Good Rockin' Tonight: Sun Records and the Birth of Rock'n'Roll* (New York: St. Martin's, 1991), pp. 16–17; Guralnick, *Last Train*, pp. 61–62; Red West, Sonny West, and Dave Hebler as told to Steve Dunleavy, *Elvis: What Happened?* (New York: Ballantine, 1977), p. x.

26. Escott, pp. 14–15.

27. Mike Rowe, *Chicago Blues: The City and the Music* (New York: Da Capo, 1975), p. 126.

28. Escott, p. 13.

29. Palmer, *An Unruly History*, p. 24.

30. Guralnick, *Last Train*, p. 60.

31. Stephanie Capparell, *The Real Pepsi Challenge: The Inspirational Story of Breaking the Color Barrier in American Business* (New York: Wall Street Journal Press, 2007).

32. By the end of 1953, African Americans constituted only 5.7 percent of the record-buying public, Gillett, p. 14.

33. Hopkins, p. 66.

34. Shaw, *The Rockin' '50s*, pp. 49, 53.

35. Escott, pp. 19–20.

36. Escott, p. 35.

37. Escott, pp. 36, 40; For an account of Robey from the perspective of "Hound Dog's" authors, Jerry Lieber and Mike Stoller, see Josh Alan Friedman, *Tell the Truth until They Bleed: Coming Clean in the Dirty World of Blues and Rock'n'Roll* (New York: Backbeat, 2008), pp. 18–21.

38. Clark Porteous, "Prison Singers Find Fame with Record They Made in Memphis," *Memphis Press-Scimitar*, July 15, 1953.

39. Escott, p. 43.

40. Guralnick, *Last Train*, p. 68.

41. Elaine Dundy, *Elvis and Gladys* (New York: Macmillan, 1985), pp. 187–188.

42. Guralnick, *Last Train*, pp. 69–75.

43. Guralnick, *Last Train*, pp. 79–80.

44. Hopkins, pp. 61–62.

45. Guralnick, *Last Train*, p. 84.

46. Craig Morrison, *Go Cat Go! Rockabilly and its Makers* (Urbana: University of Illinois Press, 1996), p. 104.

47. Charles Raiteri, "Eddie Bond: A Reluctant Rockabilly Rocker Remembers," *Goldmine*, August 1, 1986.

48. Dundy, pp. 160–161, 185.

49. *New Musical Express*, September 11, 1959.

50. Hopkins, p. 68.

51. Guralnick, *Last Train*, p. 83.

52. Paul Lichter, *The Boy Who Dared to Rock: The Definitive Elvis* (Garden City, NY: Dolphin, 1978), p. 12.

53. Guralnick, *Last Train*, p. 84.

54. Robert Johnson, *Elvis Presley Speaks!* (New York: Rave Publications, 1956), p. 10.

55. David Hajdu, *The Ten-Cent Plague: The Great Comic Book Scare and How It Changed America* (New York: Farrar, Straus & Giroux, 2008), p. 5.

56. Robert E. Southard, "Parents Must Control the Comics," *St. Anthony Messenger*, May 1944; *The Nation*, March 19, 1949; "Comic Book Censorship," *New York Times*, February 25, 1949.

57. J. Edgar Hoover, "Youth Running Wild," *Los Angeles Times*, June 27, 1943.

58. Hajdu, *Ten-Cent Plague*, pp. 84–85.

59. Dundy, pp. 3–6.

60. Joe Brancatelli, "Captain Marvel," in *World Encyclopedia of Comics*, ed. by Maurice Horn (New York: Chelsea House, 1976), pp. 157–158.

4

How High the Moon

Sam Phillips was not entirely discouraged by his first recording session with Elvis Presley. In his version of the story, only a week passed before he fulfilled Elvis's dream by arranging an audition with one of Sun's recording acts, the Starlite Wranglers, a country combo. According to the popular and often repeated account, Phillips gave Elvis's phone number to the band's electric guitarist, Scotty Moore, and suggested casually, "Why don't you give him a call and get him to come over to your house and see what you think of him?" When he phoned, Elvis responded with characteristic diffidence. "He said he guessed so," Moore recalled years later when asked for Elvis's reaction to the invitation to try a few songs.[1]

Moore, 22 years old, was typical of the crossover that was occurring in country music. He was a U.S. Navy veteran like many of the young Southerners crucial in the formation of the emerging musical genre that soon would be called rockabilly. The word was apparently coined in 1956 by New York DJ Alan Freed to describe hillbillies who played rock and roll. Freed made several contributions to contemporary English. He was also first to apply the term *rock and roll* to the nascent musical revolution.[2] Moore was not alone in enjoying the songs of Hank Williams and the guitar playing of jazz instrumentalists Tal Farlow or Barney Kessel. The music he played with the Starlite Wranglers was already building bridges between apparently disparate genres. Their single "My Kind of Carrying On," released by Sun in June 1954, included the slapping upbeat rhythm that would become integral to Elvis's debut. The Wranglers' single was one of several Sun records from earlier in 1954 that edged toward the sound Phillips would achieve with Elvis.

If by the turn of 1954 Phillips was keeping his eyes open for that million-dollar white singer "with a Negro sound," he may have seen that none of the prototypes working at Sun had Elvis's sex appeal. The raw-boned Charlie Feathers, who recorded several rockabilly singles for Phillips in the aftermath of Elvis's success, maintained that he was already playing rockabilly in the Sun Studio long before Elvis. No recorded evidence survives to substantiate Feathers, but the financially strapped Phillips routinely taped over recordings that were not slated for release and may have erased his earliest efforts. Some authorities have given measured credence to Feathers, who often had the ring of a dejected lover recalling how he almost married Lady Luck, the woman of his dreams. Feathers was apparently an occasional engineer and arranger at the Sun Studio from 1950 and may have recorded a demo of Bill Monroe's "Blue Moon of Kentucky" that served as the template for Elvis's version.[3]

Feathers is not the only contender as Elvis's predecessor at Sun. In February 1954, a month after Elvis returned to Sun to record his second vanity disc, Phillips released "Boogie Blues" by Earl Peterson, "Michigan's Singing Cowboy." Peterson was an exponent of the hillbilly boogie sound that prefigured rockabilly, but the contrast in image between the "Singing Cowboy" and the "Hillbilly Cat" is probably the clearest measure of the distance between the forerunners of rockabilly and the new genre. In his cowboy clothes Peterson embodied nostalgia for country music's past while Presley's Beale Street fashion embraced the hipster world of the present moment. Phillips supposedly played "Boogie Blues" for Elvis as a model for the sound of "That's All Right."[4]

Two months before recording "That's All Right," Phillips issued "Fallen Angel" and "Gonna Dance All Night" by Hardrock Gunter. The singer had already pushed country music toward rockabilly with an original song for the indie Bama label, "Birmingham Bounce" (1950) and his Decca recording of the Dominoes' "Sixty Minute Man" (1951).[5] Elvis may have seen Gunter perform in Memphis and heard his recordings.

Harmonica Frank was another white man who claimed to have invented rock and roll "before I ever heard of Elvis Presley." With his folkloric hobo-at-the-campfire image, Frank cut a more romanticized profile than the stolid-looking, Stetson-wearing Gunter, and has received more attention from rock critics. In contrast to Charlie Feathers, Harmonica Frank left behind better documentation. Phillips produced several of Frank's songs and leased them to Chess Records in 1951 and 1952, evidence that owners Leonard and Phil Chess gambled they could market a white man to an audience of blues fans just up from the South. Their bid was not successful. Sun finally released a Harmonica Frank single simultaneously with Elvis's debut in July 1954. Frank's "The Great Medical Menagerist" harkens back to the singer's formative years traveling with carnivals in the 1920s. The flipside, "Rockin' Chair Daddy," is a free-spirited country blues number whose go-for-broke tempo may provide a foretaste of Elvis's Sun sound if one strains to hear a connection.[6] Where Elvis exuded youthful confidence on his early Sun discs, Frank sounded like what he was, a street corner showman given an opportunity to record. "The Great Medical Menagerist" showed the side of Phillips that was more concerned with preserving fading rural traditions than discovering a new sound. "He was really out of the old school—a one man band," Phillips recalled of the carnie performer who sang from one side of his mouth and played harmonica out of the other.[7]

The most widely circulated legends concerning Elvis's sessions at Sun make little or no mention of these forerunners. In the popular account, Elvis accepted Moore's invitation and drove to his house on Independence Day where he ran through songs with the guitarist and the Wranglers' bassist, Bill Black. Moore claimed that when asked, Elvis mumbled about not knowing what to play, but that the two Wranglers followed him through bits and pieces of ballads by the Ink Spots and Billy Eckstein, Eddy Arnold and Hank Snow. "He was green as a gourd," Moore said, describing a nervous and fidgeting singer, a young man too inarticulate or tongue-tied for conversation.[8]

What Moore and Black actually thought of Elvis at that point cannot be reconstructed with any certainty. The Wranglers had already gone through several singers and might have been looking for another. Then again, something in the quavering yearning of his voice may have struck a chord of promise.

In another version of the story, Elvis was no stranger to Moore and Black. They had already known each other for three years by then. Bill Black's widowed mother, Ruby, and his two younger brothers, Johnny and Kenny, lived at Lauderdale Courts during the Presleys' tenancy. The younger Blacks were around Elvis's age and attended Humes High. Bill's son Louis claims that Moore and his father knew Elvis since 1951 and casually sang and played with him in the Lauderdale courtyard. Louis claimed that when he first heard "That's All Right" on the radio in July 1954, he thought, "But that's just what they've been doing in the front yard."[9]

Another wrinkle in the story of Elvis's sudden invention as a rockabilly singer comes in the person of Johnny Burnette. Like Elvis, Johnny and his brother, Dorsey, worked at Crown Electric as delivery drivers and Johnny sang in the Starlite Wranglers before forming the Rock and Roll Trio with Dorsey and Paul Burlison in 1951. The net of musical association around Elvis seems too thickly woven for Elvis to have been "green as a gourd." Perhaps Elvis, in addition to his many other musical interests, was already a junior player in the developing rockabilly sound with other Memphis musicians well before that fateful July night in the Sun Studio.

Phillips arranged a session for Elvis, Moore, and Black at the studio for July 5. In what may be a revealing snippet of memory, Phillips supposedly told Moore that there was no need to bring along the rest of the Wranglers, whose lineup also included steel guitar and acoustic guitar. "Naw, just you and Bill come over, just something for a little rhythm. We'll put down a few things and we'll see what it sounds like. No use in making a big deal about it."[10]

The mood was apparently informal and without set expectations. In the conventional account, the trio regrouped at Sun and, as musicians will do when getting to know each other, searched for songs they had in common, looking for entire songs, not the snippets they played with the night before. Of course if they had been playing together even casually and infrequently for three years, they were already aware of songs they knew. The repertoire they shared that night crossed the boundaries set by the music industry and the *Billboard* charts. They recorded "Harbor Lights," a sentimental pop hit for Bing Crosby, and "I Love You Because," a lachrymose country favorite from Leon Payne and Ernest Tubb. Neither track was groundbreaking. Both were close in feel to Elvis's vanity recordings. With Phillips prodding them from behind the console, they ran through those songs over and over. During a break, the story goes, Elvis began goofing around with a song recorded in 1947 by bluesman Arthur "Big Boy" Crudup, "That's All Right."

White, Hot, and Spontaneous

According to Moore, "All of a sudden, Elvis just started singing this song, jumping around and acting the fool, and then Bill picked up his bass, and he started acting the fool, too, and I started playing with them." Within moments they gained Phillips's attention. He stuck his head out of the control booth and asked what they were doing. "And we said, 'we don't know.'" Moore remembered. "'Well, back up,' he said, 'try to find a place to start, and do it again,'" Phillips insisted.[11]

Like the broken amplifier of Jackie Brenston's "Rocket 88," the spontaneous performance that night was apparently random, a happy accident of fate embraced in the moment by Phillips. As usual when inspiration strikes, the luminous moment was followed by hours of hard work. The trio played and replayed the song, refining "That's All Right." By the time they went home," Elvis Presley's debut recording for Sun was completed.

As with any story concerning Elvis at Sun, there is an alternate take on the origins of "That's All Right." In this version the recording resulted less from an unanticipated descent of the spirit upon Elvis than at least a certain amount of planning. Elvis's recollection of the session involves a call from Phillips. "'You want to make some blues?' he suggested over the phone, knowing I'd always been a sucker for that kind of jive. He mentioned Big Boy Crudup's name and maybe others too." Elvis recounts having a detailed discussion with Phillips, apparently in the days before the famous "That's All Right" session. "We talked about the Crudup records I knew—'Cool Disposition,' 'Rock Me Baby,' 'Everything's All Right,' and others, but settled for 'That's All Right,' one of my top favorites."[12]

Regardless of how they got there, Elvis and the band brought a new spirit to the old song. Crudup's original version is a characteristic example of early Chicago blues, with the music's Mississippi roots branching out into the big city and the guitar plugged in for some stinging electric leads. Unlike the heavy rhythm of many Crudup recordings, "That's All Right" moved at a frisky, jumpy pace. He sang it like a man who had already lived through the lyrics' optimistic forecast of freedom after the end of an affair. He had seen it before. Elvis's version was lighter and freer from experience and eager to taste the unknown experiences of adult life. He sang it with a confidence that sounded spontaneous and unselfconscious, even if the recorded performance may have been refined from a raw moment of inspiration through the alchemy of Phillips's recording process, the new magic of the studio. Elvis would always honor "That's All Right" as the genesis of his stardom. It remained in his concert repertoire through the end of his days.

Dewey Phillips was a regular visitor to the Sun Studio. A few days after the recording of "That's All Right," he dropped by, popped open a beer, and listened as Sam played a tape of "That's All Right." As Sam tells it, Dewey called the next morning to say, "I didn't sleep well last night, man, because [I] kept thinking about that record." Dewey asked for two acetate copies of the song to spin that night on *Red, Hot and Blue*. Sam was happy to oblige.[13]

The radio audience responded avidly. Dewey played the record over and over again as he often did when he liked what he heard. Calls poured into the studio. In the white-hot spontaneity of *Red, Hot and Blue*, Daddy-O-Dewey decided to interview Elvis on the air.

Sam informed Elvis that the acetate would likely be aired on Daddy-O-Dewey's show that night. Before leaving for the movies with Dixie, Elvis "fixed the radio and told us to leave it on that station," Gladys said. "I guess he was just too nervous to listen." The mention of her son's name as much as the sound of his voice on the radio left her flabbergasted. After being called by Dewey about interviewing Elvis that night on the air, the Presleys went to the cinema in search of their son.[14] "I was scared to death. I was shaking all over," Elvis recalled. "I just couldn't believe it, but Dewey kept telling me to cool it."[15]

Dewey later said that he drew out the nervous young singer with a ruse after he arrived in the studio. "He sat down, and I said I'd let him know when we were ready to start. I had a couple of records cued up, and while they played we talked. I asked him where he went to high school, and he said, 'Humes.' . . . Finally I said, 'All right, Elvis, thank you very much.' 'Aren't you gone interview me?' he asked. 'I already have,' I said. 'The mike's been on the whole time.' He broke out in a cold sweat."[16] In a city whose schools were strictly segregated, the Humes reference was a sly way to identify Elvis racially. Daddy-O-Dewey was introducing Elvis as a white hipster to a mixed audience of black and white listeners that had grown used to his integrated roster of guests. *Red, Hot and Blue* had featured live interviews with Fats Domino, Ivory Joe Hunter, and Lionel Hampton as well as Patti Page, Hank Williams, and Les Paul.[17] By asking about Elvis's high school, Dewey was implying that the sound of "That's All Right" was not readily categorized as black or white to contemporary audiences.

The impact of Elvis's broadcast on *Red, Hot and Blue* was felt not only widely but also deeply among listeners. Radio was an intimate medium that seemed to speak more directly to its audience members than television, especially through the voices of distinctive personality DJs such as Phillips. It was able to stir the imagination more profoundly. In an age before music video, listeners were able to visualize the stories told by the songs unfiltered through anyone else's vision. Sung with unforced mastery, Elvis's rendition of "That's All Right" painted a picture of freedom through cutting old ties.

With the exposure he received on *Red, Hot and Blue*, Elvis found himself with an avid audience for a product that did not exist. Phillips rushed Elvis back into the studio to record the flipside of "That's All Right" while the excitement was still electric. The weak renditions of "Harbor Lights" and "I Love You Because" would never do.[18] The flipside for "That's All Right," "Blue Moon of Kentucky," became at least as important for building an audience in the South as side A. By the time "That's All Right"/"Blue Moon of Kentucky" was rushed into the stores on July 19, six thousand advance orders had been taken, the demand stoked by Memphis radio. A hit on the hillbilly charts from 1947, "Blue Moon of Kentucky" was the signature song for the Father of Bluegrass, Bill Monroe. Elvis recorded it in a rockabilly rhythm similar to "That's All Right" with Black keeping up a lively tempo on string bass and Moore pushing the song into overdrive.

Engineering the Sound

As the fourth participant in the recording session, Phillips was just as integral to the finished artifact as the musicians. It was not the first time Phillips employed "slapback echo" generated by running the signal through a second Ampex tape recorder to add a sonic shadow. Phillips was neither the inventor of slapback echo nor the first recording engineer to cross the new frontier opened by magnetic recording tape. An early use of slapback echo was heard on Little Walter's "Juke" (1952), a number one hit on the R&B chart for Chess and recorded at the label's Chicago studio.[19] Although not the first to use an echo, Phillips was an important contributor to the evolution of sound recording from its initial purpose of documenting "real events" or recreating them in a controlled setting. He was aware of all developments and willing to break the bounds of conventional audio engineering to achieve an emotional resonance in listeners.

As with many other developments in 20th-century vernacular music, the evolution of sound recording can be foreseen in the 1936–1937 recordings of Robert Johnson, where his hushed whisper suggests he was consciously creating an artifact to be heard by the intimacy of the gramophone, not recreating a performance from a noisy juke joint or rent party.

The postwar adaptation of recording tape increased the possibilities for musical recordings to transcend their origins as live performances in real time. Although recording engineers had worked with reverb as early as the 1930s, the resonance was intended to make performances sound more real and less wooden. After the war, sound recording began to move from naturalism to expressionism. Jerry Murad and the Harmonicats' million-selling "Peg o' My Heart" (1947) popularized the echo chamber in pop music as it conjured an aural landscape of loneliness. The distinction of Vaughn Monroe's hit "Riders in the Sky" (1949) resulted from the use of echo to underscore the ghostly vision of the cowboy narrator.

The next steps in the story of sound recording can be credited to Les Paul. The guitarist and engineer had already developed a laborious method for multitrack recording without tape. When he finally got his hands on tape machines, he employed them to startling effect on "How High the Moon" (1950). A familiar jazz standard, "How High the Moon" was transformed into a demonstration disc for emerging technology in aural engineering. The vocal by Paul's wife, Mary Ford, was tripled by multitracking to simulate a vocal trio such as the Andrews or Boswell sisters. The echo added drive and urgency to the guitar parts. It sold a million and a half copies.[20]

For the public, "How High the Moon" was a revelation. Recordings were no longer merely the recorded evidence of an event, as the word record suggests, but could be events in themselves constructed by engineers and producing effects impossible in real time. The sonic evolution begun in postwar America continued through the early rock and roll period and accelerated into a revolution by the time the Beatles turned their backs on live performance and crafted *Sgt. Pepper's Lonely Hearts Club Band* (1967), an album whose music could only have been achieved within the walls of a recording studio.

For all of his technical dazzle, Les Paul's recordings drew from the limited emotional palette of relentless cheer. It was left to less proficient engineers working with more dramatic or emotive material to explore the potential of echo and the recording studio to increase the range of expression in contemporary music.

The first fruits to ripen from these seeds came from the Chess Records studio. Co-owner Phil Chess claimed he was looking for "gimmicks" or "something new" to catch the ears of the blues audience. "So we developed a sensibility to look for that and help develop it on our own, with echo, with our studio," he said.[21]

Beginning in 1947, the recordings Muddy Waters made for the Chess brothers painted moods "with effects created through judicious manipulation of room acoustics and recording technology." Among them was the use of the studio's tile bathroom as a resonating chamber for Waters's electric guitar and recording his voice and guitar close to the distortion line on the VU meter.[22]

Given the subject of some blues lyrics, with their references to voodoo, hints of shamanism and unholy pacts, and suggestion of dark forces at work in the world, the fascination with sonic distortion may have had roots in Hollywood. In popular horror films such as *Cat People* (1942) and *I Walked with the Zombie* (1943), reverb was used to summon the uncanny or compound the eeriness. Phillips may have been consciously aware of this when he recorded Elvis's version of "Mystery Train."

Having leased a number of recordings to Chess before founding Sun Records, Phillips was well aware of developments at the Chicago label. His recording for Chess of Howlin' Wolf's "Moaning at Midnight" (1950) opens as wordless humming overloads the microphones. The deeply reverberant electric guitar on Joe Hill Louis's Sun recording of "When I'm Gone" (1952) summons vistas of "graveyards at midnight, of lonely dark spaces."[23] Despite or because of his training in broadcasting, where perfect modulation was the ideal, Phillips was willing to break any perceived rule or norm in recording engineering to achieve a certain effect, even or especially when the effect was unanticipated. Sun recording artist Carl Perkins recalled saying of a flubbed moment in the studio, "'Mr. Phillips, that's terrible.' He said, 'That's original.'"[24]

"Blue Moon of Kentucky" became an important step on Elvis's journey from obscurity to fame. Memphis country DJs began playing acetates of the song in preference to the ostensible A-side, "That's All Right." Among those to embrace the new version of the Bill Monroe classic was WHHM's Sleepy Eyed John, who booked the Eagle's Nest, and Bob Neal, host of WMPS's popular *High Noon Round-Up*. The former may have already heard of Elvis through the honky-tonk grapevine and the latter may have already met the young singer, who is said to have watched *High Noon Round-Up* through the glass studio window during his lunch break from Crown Electric.[25] With all of the sudden attention, a manager was needed to mind Elvis's affairs. Scotty Moore filled the job but not for long. Bob Neal would play the role before being edged out by Colonel Tom Parker.

Rural Rhythm

By 1954 the musical miscegenation of white and black was not the unprecedented phenomenon described by Elvis's more careless chroniclers. "Rural rhythm," as Elvis's blend of country and blues was called at first, was already an established field within country music.[26] The gap between Elvis and his predecessors continued to be more a matter of style than substance. However, style was not without substance and the greater appearance of identification with African Americans would eventually provoke a backlash from racists under pressure to desegregate public facilities. Where Hardrock Gunter sang rhythm and blues wearing a Western suit and a cowboy hat, Elvis's "cat clothes" represented an aggressive embrace of black hipster attitude. The words being used for nearly all but the most traditional Appalachian folk-based music of white Southerners tells the story. Rural rhythm, hillbilly boogie, and western swing were genres or descriptions for prototypes of rockabilly, and each contained an obvious allusion to the music's biracial, white-black roots. Any discomfort about this was entirely muffled through the early 1950s. The mixing of music did not necessarily imply social desegregation or civil rights for the black minority. Within a few short years the battle lines over racial equality would be set and rock and roll music would be drawn into the fray.

The release of "That's All Right"/"Blue Moon of Kentucky" coincided with the advent of legal desegregation and the civil rights movement. Only two months earlier, on May 17, 1954, the U.S. Supreme Court handed down its landmark school desegregation ruling in *Brown v. Board of Education*. However, the mood in the South during the summer of 1954 was not one of rising tension but of vague uncertainty. No one knew how the court's ruling would be enforced or what the pace of implementation would be. The president, Dwight D. Eisenhower, made no public comment. The prominence of Elvis and rock and roll in general as a lightning rod for racists would grow by stages along with the rise of "massive resistance" in the South to desegregation.[27] There was no panic among the white populace until after the Supreme Court's implementation decree of May 31, 1955, calling for "all deliberate speed" in school desegregation, and the December 1955 Montgomery Bus Boycott led by Reverend Martin Luther King Jr.[28]

The reaction among Elvis's earliest listeners in Memphis mingled curiosity and excitement over a local white boy who sang the blues with such panache. Much of the excitement in July 1954 had less to do with a white singer performing a song of black origin than with the startling transformation of Bill Monroe's stately waltz into the hipster idiom of rural rhythm. It was a familiar song handled in an unfamiliar way, both from the performance by Elvis and the boys and from Phillips's liberal application of slapback echo. As Carl Perkins pointed out, "There's a lot of kinship between bluegrass and early rockabilly—I mean a lot."[29] Realizing he had a hot number on his hands with Elvis's single, Phillips began to lay his plans. He may have arranged for Elvis, Moore, and Black to perform at the Bon Air Club, but his assertion that "this was Elvis's first appearance, period, and he was absolutely mortified," is typical of an irrepressible tendency to add to his own importance.[30] What's not in question is Phillips's hard work on behalf of Elvis's single, which he pitched with the fervor of a traveling salesman living on his commission. Packing cartons of 45s and 78s into his trunk, Phillips drove across Tennessee, Mississippi, and Arkansas, and perhaps as far as Texas and Florida, wholesaling "That's All Right"/"Blue Moon of Kentucky" to jukebox operators as well as music stores and shoeshine stands, any place where records were sold. His efforts would be justly rewarded.

Elvis remained tongue tied with strangers and authority figures. Marion Keisker, who brought him to the office of the *Memphis Press Scimitar* for his first newspaper interview, was forced to provide the journalist with virtually every quote. "The odd thing about it is that both sides seem to be equally popular on popular, folk and race record programs," she told the reporter, referring to "That's All Right"/"Blue Moon of Kentucky." "The boy has something that seems to appeal to everybody," she added prophetically.[31]

Hustling with great speed, Phillips helped arrange Elvis's first concert appearance before a large audience. It was a July 30 "hillbilly hoedown" at the Overton Park Shell promoted by Bob Neal. Slim Whitman, a popular singer on the *Louisiana Hayride* radio program where Elvis would soon become a regular, headlined the lineup on that muggy afternoon and evening. A last-minute addition to a roster with at least five other performers, the young singer was misidentified in one newspaper ad as "Ellis Presley" and ignored entirely in others.[32]

"I was scared stiff," Elvis recalled. "I came out and I was doing a fast type tune, one of my first records, and everybody was hollering and I didn't know what they were hollering at. Then I came off stage and my manager told me that everyone was hollering because I was wiggling. So I did a little more and the more I did, the more I got."[33]

The crowd at Overton Park may have been the first to witness the gyrating that would soon make Elvis famous the world over. By some accounts, Elvis was all shook up from stage fright and may have transmuted his nerves into sexually provocative body language. The showmanship of gospel quartets and the Pentecostal possession of the Holy Spirit are also plausible references. Regardless of the source,

Elvis's performance was greeted by screaming girls in the audience. "We hadn't gone out and arranged for anybody to squeal and scream. For Elvis they just did it automatically," said Bob Neal.[34]

Soon afterward, *Billboard* reviewed Elvis's first single, calling him "a strong new talent" and insisting that he "can sock over a tune for either the country or the R&B markets."[35] In the early months of his rise, however, it was primarily the country market that took interest. RCA's field agent for the upper Southern states, Brad McCuen, recalled witnessing a 50-year-old white Tennessee man purchasing "That's All Right" in a record store and realizing that a record he had pegged as rhythm and blues was selling to a country audience.[36]

Elvis and his combo, calling themselves the Blue Moon Boys to capitalize on their hit, spent many nights on the road, even as the singer continued to drive for Crown Electric. The cash-strapped Phillips was unable to pay an advance on royalties.[37] In the perception of many latter-day fans, Elvis seemed to leap from obscurity onto television, and from there into the movies, and, finally, to Las Vegas. Largely overlooked is the period spent by Elvis and the Blue Moon Boys traveling lost Southern highways in Moore's Chevrolet Bel Air, playing the Eagle's Nest and other Memphis venues while venturing as far as Arkansas, Mississippi, and Texas. Some of the acts he was booked with seem curious when seen through the distorting lens of the rock critics who composed the earliest serious chronicles of his life. Elvis appeared several times with the Louvin Brothers, an influential harmony duo whose songs of heartbreak, devotion to family, and faith in an uncompromising God were in the Appalachian tradition of the Carter Family, not the honky-tonk lineage of rockabilly.[38]

A Night at the *Opry*

Elvis was rebuffed when he auditioned for the *Grand Ole Opry* on August 9, 1954.[39] Phillips arranged the session with *Opry* talent scout Jim Denny, the man who famously told Elvis that he should stick to driving a truck.[40] Usually portrayed as belligerently myopic, Denny had been a man of some foresight, booking rising talent such as Hank Williams, Faron Young, and Ray Price. It escapes most commentators that Elvis, still unknown outside of Memphis, should receive any attention from the *Opry* so early in his career. An audition and soon thereafter an appearance on country music's most important radio program, a show with national reach, were remarkable accomplishments, a testimony to Phillips's persistence and network of connections. Even Keisker was amazed Elvis traveled so far so soon. "For all of us the *Grand Ole Opry* was the summit, the peak, the show you hoped you'd get eventually—not when you had just one record out," she said.[41]

Elvis's lukewarm response at the *Opry* is usually interpreted as a watershed signifying a rupture between him and country music. This was not the case. By August 28, "Blue Moon of Kentucky" appeared on *Billboard*'s "Country and Western Territorial Best Seller" chart, measuring regional popularity by record sales and jukebox plays at a time when record sales in one city often differed greatly from the town down the road. Likewise, jukebox operators programmed selections to match the clientele of each tavern or other coin-machine venue. At the end of 1954, Elvis was named by *Billboard* as number eight on its list of most promising country acts. The press referred to him as a "young hillbilly singing star."[42]

That Elvis was given a second chance on the *Opry* was not inevitable, despite his growing regional popularity. On October 2, 1954, Elvis and the boys returned to Nashville's Ryman Auditorium, whose cramped stage and run-down interior was a surprisingly drab setting for country's grandest show, for his only performance in that venue. One *Opry* musician remembered Elvis worrying, "They're going to hate me," but his worst fears were not realized. The audience response was polite if not overly enthusiastic. *Opry* regular Bill Monroe, known as a solemn and stoic figure, surprised everyone by complimenting the Sun rendition of "Blue Moon of Kentucky" and remarking that he had recorded a new rendition influenced by Elvis's interpretation.

A Hit on the *Hayride*

Elvis never returned to the *Grand Ole Opry* but solidified his regional popularity as a regular on country music's second most important radio show, the *Louisiana Hayride*. Broadcast on KWKH in Shreveport, Louisiana, one of a handful of American radio stations with a 50,000-watt signal, the *Hayride* was heard over much of the United States. With roots going back to the 1930s, the program was heard live each Saturday night from the Shreveport Municipal Auditorium, a 3,800-seat facility slightly larger than the *Opry*'s Ryman. The *Hayride* enjoyed a maverick reputation. It was where Hank Williams climbed from local to national acclaim and it re-embraced him after the country star was fired from the *Opry* for drinking and missing shows.

The *Louisiana Hayride* had a deserved reputation for being more open to new artists than the *Opry*. Among the regulars on the show at the time of Elvis's rise were the Maddox Brothers and Rose, whose recordings bristled with yelps and howls, slapping bass, and driving electric guitar. They were yet another precursor to rockabilly. The Maddox Brothers sometimes wore pink costumes, which Elvis admired. "One of these days, I'm going to have me a suit like this," he supposedly told Rose Maddox.[43]

On August 19, 1954, Elvis and the boys drove the four hundred miles from Memphis to Shreveport to audition for the *Hayride* with the show's producer, Horace Logan. Logan cut a deal, offering Elvis a chance on the show if he performed successfully at several clubs affiliated with the *Hayride*. The response from club owners and audiences was enthusiastic. On October 16, scarcely two weeks after the *Opry*, Elvis, Moore, and Black debuted at the Shreveport Auditorium. The *Hayride*'s announcer, Frank Page, introduced Elvis as "a singer who's forging a new style." With the show of modesty customary to country singers, Elvis began with, "I'd like to say how happy we are to appear on the 'Louisiana Hayride.' We're gonna do a song for you we got on Sun Records that goes like this." It was "That's All Right," which the multigenerational audience greeted with cheers.[44]

Elvis also performed "Blue Moon of Kentucky," which was still climbing on *Billboard*'s country-and-western territorial charts by the time of his second *Hayride* performance later in October. "Blue Moon of Kentucky" reached number six in New Orleans and number three in Nashville. Sales for the single were picking up in many Southern cities.[45] Within weeks of his Shreveport debut, the singer and his parents cosigned a contract making him a regular on *Louisiana Hayride* at the standard union rate of $18 per appearance for the bandleader, Elvis, and $12 apiece for Moore and Black. Elvis needed his parents' consent. He was only 19 and still a minor under the law. He was praised for the accomplishment in his hometown newspaper, which noted, "The 'Hayride' specializes in picking promising young rural rhythm talent, and it took just one guest appearance [for Elvis] to become a regular."[46]

The contract was beneficial to both the performer and the radio station. "As word got around that he'd be on our show all the time, young people from a half-dozen states started flocking to the Municipal Auditorium on Saturday nights," Logan recalled. Elvis was rapidly elevated to the *Hayride*'s headline act. The women in the audience "screamed themselves into hysteria until the noise level became deafening," Logan said.[47]

Logan was impressed by Elvis's scope as a performer, a range that would never be apparent in the recordings he made for Sun. "He had a rare gift for being able to sing just about any kind of song," he said. Logan also recalled that when Elvis expressed his love for Hank Williams and Hank Snow, he added, "but Dean Martin's one of my favorite singers, too."[48]

The *Hayride* producer noticed that in performance, Elvis was transformed into something other than the young, unassuming Southern boy he continued to be when offstage. The microphone became the talisman that turned Elvis into the superhero of his imagination. "When he sang, his shy innocence melted away, and there was something fierce, almost cocky about him," Logan said. "Offstage, though, he was still as polite and reserved as ever, and he was unfailingly respectful toward everybody."[49]

Whether or not an occasional honky-tonk angel offered herself to Elvis on the earliest road trips with the Blue Moon Boys, it was in Shreveport where Elvis's rising stardom and sexual allure unlocked the gates of almost unlimited gratification. The term *groupie* would not be coined until at least 10 years later, but Elvis for the first time became the object of sexually adventurous women attracted by the bright light of his fame.

The setting was not the grand hotel, high glamour of the Rolling Stones at their peak, but cheap rooms at the Al-Ida Motel on the busy commercial strip in nearby Bossier City. Long lines of teenage girls formed outside his room Saturday nights after the *Hayride* for "a chance to see Elvis up close or say something to him. Others had more intimate encounters in mind," Logan said. "It was a brand new experience for him . . . They kept his adrenalin pumping, and he never seemed to get tired of having them around." Logan added that Elvis never touched alcohol or took "so much as a puff from a regular cigarette, much less a marijuana cigarette. But he had an insatiable addiction to girls."[50]

The *Hayride* producer also remembered that during his first weeks on the show, Elvis returned to Memphis fairly often to visit Dixie Locke. "But before long, girls were swarming around him by the hundreds, making him forget about his homesickness for Dixie."[51] Celebrity mania was not entirely novel to the 20th century but was intensified by new technology that exposed audiences across continents to the same sounds and images. Projected onto big screens or heard simultaneously across vast distances on gramophones or radio, their faces splashed across periodicals, the stars of popular culture became, as cultural critic Max Lerner complained in 1957, "the legislators of American mores."[52]

Psychologically, the stars fulfilled a need for contemporary figures that embodied meaning in the increasingly commercialized, mechanical, and impersonal world of modernity. In a society whose organizing principle was the routine order of the assembly line, where conformity was equated with reliability, the star was an individual who lived more largely and stood apart. Stars were the screens on which everyday people could project their desires and aspirations, especially those desires that could never be realized. To copy a star's haircut, clothing, or other elements of style was an act of identification and an attempt to capture a spark of their charisma. The mirage produced by the entertainment industry was not simply an avenue of escapism. It also engendered "ambition-and-attainment dreams" in audiences responding to rapid social change. "It is impossible that a people should reach for new living standards without at the same time reaching for new emotional experiences," Lerner said.[53]

The fan mania that would follow Elvis and eventually lead to his retreat into isolation was one such experience. The prototype for the phenomenon of screaming female fans in hot pursuit that Elvis began to experience in Shreveport was established by one of the great movie stars of the silent era, Rudolph Valentino.

In the years before Valentino succumbed in 1926 at age 31 from a perforated ulcer, aggravated by the adulation and hostility he aroused, Valentino broke with expectations by broadening accepted ideas of masculinity. He was not the square-jawed all-American but an exotic with sideburns, longish hair in the era of weekly visits to the barber, and dark hooded eyes. In some photographs taken of Elvis in 1954 and 1955, the aspiring star bares some resemblance to his silent predecessor. On occasion Elvis even wore bolero costumes that suggested several of Valentino's screen characters, although the influence could have derived from Hollywood "Latin lovers" of more recent vintage.

To women in the 1920s, Valentino seemed a wildly romantic and erotic figure, the symbol of all that was unmet in the drab, confined bedrooms of the middle class. Like Elvis, the Italian-born actor was a slightly androgynous dandy who emerged from society's lower tiers. He had been homeless on the streets of New York. After he became a matinee idol, Valentino toured theaters as a dancer and attracted more than full houses. In New York he was "stampeded by two or three hundred feminine worshippers" in the words of a reporter. A probably hyperbolic Boston headline claimed "10,000 Girls Mob World's

Greatest Kisser." Not unlike the Beatles in *A Hard Day's Night*, he was forced to make his escape by dashing across rooftops.[54]

At the same time, Valentino was regarded as an ethnically alien intruder in American culture. A *Chicago Tribune* editorial condemned him for causing the "degeneration into effeminancy" of the American male, linked him to Communism by wondering about the relationship between effeminate "pink parlors and parlor pinks" and implied that he inspired "a disregard for the law and an aptitude for crime."[55]

The eruption of pent-up desire caused by Valentino crossed generational boundaries, affecting women of all ages. Frank Sinatra may have been the first public figure to become the specific focus of teenage girls. He was also emblematic for the barely articulated yearnings of a youth subculture emerging among predecessors of the baby boomers, teenagers whose formative years were stamped by the Great Depression but suddenly found themselves in a wartime society of greater mobility and laxer supervision. Fathers and older brothers were in the service. Mothers and older sisters went to work at the defense plants. *The New Republic* described Sinatra's seemingly unprecedented appeal as "a hunger still unfulfilled, a hunger for heroes, for ideal things."[56]

The ecstatic reaction to Sinatra by teenage girls, "bobbysoxers" as the media dubbed them, became apparent at his December 30, 1942, concert at New York's Paramount Theater. "The sound that greeted me was absolutely deafening. It was a tremendous roar . . . I was scared stiff," Sinatra said in language similar to Elvis's description of the crowd at Overton Park.[57] Similarities between Sinatra and Elvis are numerous. Both became "self-made men" in the Horatio Alger mode, rising from obscure circumstances through hard times and onto the highest rung of success. Across the cultural differences between the Italian American neighborhood of Hoboken and the sharecropper shantytown of East Tupelo, the parents of both singers shared the aspiration for respectability in a society that did not respect them. Both singers communicated desire and empathy to the ears of young women. Both appeared tough yet sensitive.

The mania Sinatra stirred would not be the last such phenomenon before the coming of Elvis. After he became a country star on the strength of his appearances on *Louisiana Hayride*, Hank Williams was pursued by gaggles of teenage girls in the South. The most adventurous were keen to cut off pieces of his clothing as souvenirs and let the air out of his tires to slow his escape.[58]

Like Williams before him, the exposure Elvis received on the *Hayride* triggered airplay on other Southern stations. The *Hayride* also booked Elvis on package tours through Louisiana, Texas, and Arkansas during November and December of 1954. The Blue Moon Boys were almost always garbed in western fashion; sometimes for *Hayride* shows, even Elvis sported a western shirt and cowboy belt.[59]

While the *Hayride* tours helped Elvis solidify his hold on Southern country music audiences, the milieu of Shreveport would exert an enduring influence on him. As with Memphis, Shreveport had long enjoyed flourishing opportunities for African American musicians. Leadbelly had once been a regular entertainer in the brothels of Fannin Street, Shreveport's answer to Beale. By the late 1940s, local white musicians of Elvis's generation already had one foot in country and the other in rhythm and blues. *Louisiana Hayride* drummer D. J. Fontana, soon to become a member of Elvis's band, recalled the jam sessions in Shreveport clubs and the Bossier City strip near the motel where Elvis would later entertain his female fans. "Amongst musicians we had no problems," he said of the racial divide and the easy atmosphere of the city's clubs. "We'd go to a black club and maybe play and they wouldn't bother us cause we were with that band."[60]

Shreveport already had its own radio program featuring a white hipster spinning black recordings. *Hayride* announcer Ray Bartlett, calling himself Groovie Boy, hosted a nightly show on KWKH called *In the Groove* or *Groovie's Boogie*. Fontana as well as *Hayride* guitarist James Burton, who would also become a regular in Elvis's band after the singer went on to greater stardom, spent many hours learning about rhythm and blues while listening to Groovie Boy.[61]

Although the *Hayride* broadcasts and Southern tours occupied much of his time, Elvis continued to return to Memphis to record for Sun with Moore and Black. Their second single continued Phillips's black-white strategy. The A side, "Good Rockin' Tonight," was a cover of a rhythm and blues song that had been a hit for its author, bluesman Roy Brown, as well as uptown rhythm and blues singer Wyonie Harris in 1948 and 1949, but Elvis's version stands alone for its marvelous understanding and understatement. He sings the lyrics slyly as his combo plays in a relaxed groove. Even Moore's solo is steady as it goes. In context the song's climactic call-out, "Let's rock, come on let's rock, we're gonna rock all our blues away," is obviously sexual, but could have later gathered an additional allusion to rock and roll music as a departure from the old world into the new.

The B side, "I Don't Care if the Sun Don't Shine," originated in Walt Disney's 1949 animated feature *Cinderella* and had been covered for the pop market by Patti Page and Elvis's favorite singer, Dean Martin.

Its inclusion in the Sun catalog may have been Phillips's concession to Elvis's taste for pop crooners. Upon its release on November 3, 1954, "Good Rockin' Tonight" leaped onto the Memphis country chart but sold less briskly elsewhere than its predecessor. Given the relatively light tone of the B side, perhaps the release lacked the double-barreled impact of "That's All Right"/"Blue Moon of Kentucky."

A late December session resulted in a third single, "Milkcow Blues Boogie"/"You're a Heartbreaker," released on January 8 1955, Elvis's 20th birthday. The A side begins with a false start as Elvis pretends to sing the song as a ruminative blues. Suddenly he announces in a hipster voice, "Hold it fellas! That don't move me! Let's get real gone for a change!" Elvis pushes into a falsetto over the combo's rumbling-on-the-rails rhythm, with Moore occasionally tearing up the tracks on guitar.

"Milkcow Blues Boogie" has a complicated provenance. It was originally written and recorded by bluesman Kokomo Arnold in 1934. As early as 1937 it was covered by a country singer, Cliff Bruner, and found its way into the record catalogs of western swing bandleader Johnnie Lee Wills (1941) and hillbilly boogie singer Moon Mullican (1946). Elvis's role model in Tupelo, Mississippi Slim, played the song on his radio show. It was familiar to Elvis and like an itinerant bluesman, he plucked verses from here and yon, reassembling the song out of a stock of commonly held verses, lyric lines, and rhythms until it became a montage of conflicting emotions around the milk cow as a rural metaphor for a straying woman. Elvis combined parts of Arnold's song with a 1946 number by western swing star Bob Wills, "Brain Cloudy Blues."[62]

"You're a Heartbreaker" originated in Phillips's frustration over lost opportunities. He did not own publisher's rights for any of Elvis's previous recordings and, like many indie label owners, wanted a piece of the publishing revenue. Why Elvis was not encouraged to write his own songs, which Phillips could then publish, is unknown. Instead, Phillips commissioned "You're a Heartbreaker" from Jack Sallee, a Tennessee theater owner. "Heartbreaker" was a conventional country song where a swift backbeat overcame a broken heart. The narrator addressed a high-stepping, unfaithful ex-girlfriend with the news that he has found a better woman. It was Sallee's first and last published song. "Milkcow Blues Boogie"/"You're a Heartbreaker" was also Elvis's worst selling single at Sun.[63]

Slumping sales could have resulted from problems that often dogged independent labels. Once they had a hit on their hands, as Sun did with "Blue Moon of Kentucky," indies were often hard put to find ready cash to support a follow-up. Receipts from sales routinely tied up in the accounts of slow-to-pay distributors and retailers. It may also be true that the third Elvis single was not as compelling to a contemporary audience. "Milkcow Blues Boogie" represented Phillips's interest in older forms of black music that younger black listeners were rejecting and the white pop market was not buying. As for "You're a Heartbreaker," it was not a standout.

Elvis was named eighth among 1954's "Most Promising Country and Western Vocalists."[64] His career progressed almost exclusively in country music circles. He opened the New Year with a January 1, 1955, live broadcast on KNUZ Houston's Grand Prize Saturday Night Jamboree. The bill, which also included George Jones and *Hayride* regular Tommy Sands, took place at Eagle's Hall, a country venue. Introduced by the MC as "the bopping hillbilly," Elvis performed "Good Rockin' Tonight," "Blue Moon of Kentucky," and a pair of rhythm and blues songs he would eventually record, Ray Charles's "I Got a Woman" and Arthur Gunter's "Baby, Let's Play House," to a wildly cheering crowd. The audience was described as a "sea of cowboy hats, flannel shirts and frilly women's dresses."[65]

During the early months of 1955, the Blue Moon Boys, now augmented by Fontana on drums, toured with respected country acts such as Faron Young, Hank Snow, Ferlin Husky, and Mother Maybelle Carter from the seminal Carter Family country singing group. On May 25, 1955, Elvis performed at the annual Jimmie Rodgers Memorial Celebration in Meridian, Mississippi, as part of a caravan of *Louisiana Hayride* artists honoring another legend from country music's early days. During 1955, features on Elvis were published in nationally circulated magazines such as *Cowboy Songs, Country Song Round-Up* and *Country and Western Jamboree*.[66]

As January began, Elvis and his parents cosigned a contract granting "exclusive personal management" to Bob Neal. The Memphis DJ also owned a record store and the Memphis Promotions booking agency, and was well situated to oversee the rising regional career of the young singer he called "the king of western bop," a genre description later claimed by Buddy Holly.[67]

One of the connections Neal made for Elvis was a spot on Hank Snow's *All Star Jamboree*, a cavalcade of country stars on tour through the South. Snow's manager, a balding, pear-shaped, and middle-aged man calling himself Colonel Tom Parker, promoted the tour vigorously through advertising in print, radio, and television, along with the more traditional handbills pasted on barns and fence posts. According to the colorful legend that he wove around himself, Parker once trapped sparrows, painted them yellow and sold them as canaries.[68] He was proud of his reputation as a W. C. Fields–style hustler of the "never give a sucker an even break" school. The colonel's underlings remembered him as a genius but the millions of Elvis fans came to view him warily. In comic book terms, the Colonel was a dark lord masquerading as a white knight. As Elvis reached the crossroads of his career, with one road leading to national acclaim and the other path to an endless blur of country roadhouses, Elvis signed away part of his soul to the mastermind who offered him stardom of unprecedented magnitude.

Notes

1. Peter Guralnick, *Last Train to Memphis: The Rise of Elvis Presley* (Boston: Little Brown, 1994), p. 91; Jerry Hopkins interview, Mississippi Valley Collection, Memphis State University.

2. According to Paul Burlison of Johnny Burnette's Rock'n'Roll Trio, Freed referred to his band as "all you rockabilly guys" in 1956. "Ever since we started calling it rockabilly," Burlison explained. Later that year the Rock'n'Roll Trio released a song called "Rockbilly Boogie" that included the word *rockabilly* despite a slightly different song title. Craig Morrison, *Go Cat Go! Rockabilly Music and Its Makers* (Urbana: University of Illinois Press, 1996), p. 5. The first appearance of rockabilly in print may have occurred in a June 1956 record review in *Billboard*.

3. Morrison, *Go Cat Go!*, p. 208. For an account of Feathers's views, see Guralnick, *Lost Highways: Journeys and Arrivals of American Musicians* (Boston: David R. Godine, 1979), pp. 106–115.

4. Howard A. DeWitt, *Elvis: The Sun Years, The Story of Elvis Presley in the Fifties* (Ann Arbor, MI: Popular Culture Ink, 1993), p. 139.

5. "Birmingham Bounce" has been pronounced by some latter-day fans as the first rock and roll record.

6. Greil Marcus, *Mystery Train: Images of America in Rock'n'Roll Music* (New York: Dutton, 1975), pp. 11–20.

7. Colin Escott with Martin Hawkins, *Good Rockin' Tonight: Sun Records and the Birth of Rock'n'Roll* (New York: St. Martin's Press, 1991), p. 113.

8. Guralnick, *Last Train*, pp. 91–92.

9. Elaine Dundy, *Elvis and Gladys* (New York: Macmillan, 1985), pp. 157–159.

10. Guralnick, *Last Train*, p. 93. In an earlier interview, Moore remembered Phillips's words this way: "Just you and Bill come over, just something for a little rhythm. We'll put down a few things and we'll see what it sounds like coming back off the tape recorder." Jerry Hopkins, *Elvis: A Biography* (New York: Simon & Schuster, 1971), p. 71.

11. Guralnick, *Last Train*, p. 95.

12. *Hit Parade*, January 1957.

13. Guralnick, *Last Train*, p. 99.

14. Editors of *TV Radio Mirror, Elvis Presley* (1956), p. 21.

15. *Memphis Commercial Appeal*, September 29, 1968.

16. Stanley Booth, "A Hound Dog to the Manor Born," *Esquire*, February 1968.

17. Louis Cantor, *Dewey and Elvis: The Life and Times of a Rock 'n' Roll Deejay* (Urbana: University of Illinois, 2005), p. 11.

18. Phillips never released either track. "Harbor Lights" and "I Love You Because" first surfaced in the early 1970s on a pair of LPs released by RCA, *Elvis: A Legendary Performer*, vols. 1 and 2.

19. Peter Doyle, *Echo and Reverb: Fabricating Space in Popular Recording, 1900–1960* (Middletown, CT: Wesleyan University Press, 2005), pp. 179–180.

20. For an overview of the impact of magnetic recording tape in the years before the rock era, see Doyle, pp. 143–162.

21. Phil and Marshall Chess interview on National Public Radio, n.d., transcript at http://www.wgbh.org.

22. Robert Palmer, *Deep Blues* (London: Macmillan, 1981), pp. 334–335.

23. Doyle, p. 169.

24. Guralnick, *Lost Highways*, pp. 334–335.

25. Charles Wolfe, "Presley and the Gospel Tradition" in Kevin Quinn, ed., *The Elvis Reader: Texts and Sources on the King of Rock 'n' Roll* (New York: St. Martin's Press, 1992), p. 16.

26. *Memphis Commercial Appeal*, October 14, 1954.

27. Perhaps the first white backlash against Elvis occurred in Greenwich, Mississippi, in September 1954, when the American Legion post banned Elvis from performing in their hall because of his "Negro sound." DeWitt, p. 151. It should be no surprise that the first such incident occurred in Mississippi, where white resistance to desegregation was most intractable.

28. For an analysis of the diversity of Southern response to *Brown vs. Board of Education*, see George Lewis, *Massive Resistance: The White Response to the Civil Rights Movement* (New York: Oxford University Press, 2006).

29. David McGee, "Carl Perkins," in *Rolling Stone: The Decades of Rock & Roll* (San Francisco: Chronicle Books, 2001), p. 49.

30. Guralnick, *Last Train*, p. 105. DeWitt, p. 293 lists no less than 31 previous public performances by Elvis at amateur nights and other occasions, not including any informal encounters on the lawn of Lauderdale Court.

31. Edwin Howard, "In a Spin," *Memphis Press Scimitar*, July 28, 1954.

32. Ger Rijff, ed., *Long Lonely Highway: A 1950's Elvis Scrapbook* (Ann Arbor, MI: Pierian Press, 1987), pp. 11–15.

33. *New Musical Express*, September 11, 1959.

34. DeWitt, p. 154.

35. "Review Spotlight: Talent," *Billboard*, August 7, 1954.

36. Guralnick, *Last Train*, pp. 122–123.

37. The end date for Elvis's employment at Crown is, like many facts in his chronology, in dispute. Dave Marsh claimed he kept his day job until January 1955, *Elvis* (New York: Rolling Stone Press, 1982), p. 48, but given the amount of time and travel spent with the Blue Moon Boys, that seems unlikely unless Elvis became a part-time or occasional worker. Horace Logan, producer for the *Louisiana Hayride*, claims that Elvis was able to quit driving a truck once he became a regular on the radio program by the start of November 1954. Horace Logan with Bill Sloan, *Elvis, Hank, and Me: Musical History on the* Louisiana Hayride (New York: St. Martin's Press, 1998), p. 141.

38. For a roster of Elvis's performances from August through December 1954, see DeWitt, pp. 293–95.

39. DeWitt, p. x.

40. Hopkins, p. 78.

41. Hopkins, p. 77.

42. Rijff, p. 28.

43. Tracey E. W. Laird, Louisiana Hayride: *Radio and Roots Music along the Red River* (New York: Oxford University Press, 2005), p. 126.

44. DeWitt, p. 167.

45. *Billboard*, October 23, 1954.

46. *Memphis Press Scimitar*, October 30, 1954.

47. Logan, pp. 137–138, 142.

48. Logan, p. 139.

49. Logan, p. 140.

50. Logan, p. 143.

51. Logan, pp. 142–143.

52. Max Lerner, *America as a Civilization: Life and Thought in the United States Today* (New York: Simon & Schuster, 1957), p. 780.

53. Lerner, p. 820.

54. Emily W. Leider, *Dark Lover: The Life and Death of Rudolph Valentino* (New York: Farrar, Straus & Giroux, 2003), p. 247.

55. *Chicago Tribune*, July 18, 1926.

56. Bruce Bliven, "The Voice and the Kids," *New Republic*, November 6, 1944.

57. Arnold Shaw, "Sinatrauma: The Proclamation of a New Era," in *The Frank Sinatra Reader*, ed. Steven Petkov and Leonard Mustazza (New York: Oxford University Press, 1995), p. 19.

58. Paul Hemphill, *Lovesick Blues: The Life of Hank Williams* (New York: Viking, 2005), p. 78.

59. Logan, p. 146; For a photograph of Elvis in Western attire at a *Louisiana Hayride* concert, see DeWitt, p. 180.

60. Laird, p. 136.

61. Laird, p. 128.

62. For an interesting exegesis of "Milkcow Blues Boogie," see Marcus, *Mystery Train*, p. 172.

63. Escott, Hawkins, *Good Rockin' Tonight*, p. 72.

64. *Billboard*, November 13, 1954.

65. DeWitt p. 174.

66. Susan Doll, *Understanding Elvis: Southern Roots vs. Star Image* (New York: Garland, 1998), pp. 54–55.

67. DeWitt believes that Elvis took an active role in his business affairs early on, forcing Neal to "audition" for the right to manage him and encouraging the promoter to set up an office across from the Peabody Hotel, a prestigious Memphis address, p. 164.

68. Hopkins, *Elvis*, p. 92.

5

His Master's Voice

During his career in show business, Colonel Tom Parker passed himself off as a good old boy from Huntington, West Virginia. He gleefully spoke of his life in the traveling circuses that crisscrossed North America in the 1930s, entertaining the masses while relieving "suckers" and "rubes" of their money through bait and switch and sleight of hand. He reveled in his role as a trickster, but only began to admit, under duress of legal proceedings following Elvis's death, that his greatest trick was passing himself off as a Southerner named Tom Parker. He was actually Andreas Cornelius van Kujik.[1] He was Dutch by birth and was never naturalized in the United States. For reasons that might never be sorted out, the inscrutable Parker spent his entire life in America as an illegal alien.

With the obsession for detail that has characterized European aficionados of American music as far back as the jazz clubs of 1930s Paris, Dutch Elvis fans began circulating rumors in their own obscure publications that Parker was a countryman as far back as 1969. Little note was taken of these assertions until Albert Goldman picked them up in his infamously negative biography, *Elvis* (1981). Goldman's chief contribution was not a greater understanding of Elvis Presley but his exposition of the origins of Elvis's manager.[2]

Some facts about Parker's early life have been established with certainty. He was born on June 26, 1909, in Breda to a lower-middle class, Roman Catholic family. Sometime around 1926, he left Holland and by 1931 or 1932 he was riding the rails six months of the year with Royal American, a traveling show second only to Barnum and Bailey in popularity. By 1938 he had left the circus and begun work as a show business promoter.

The details linking these few facts are obscured by a confusion of vague and conflicting recollections swirling around the Colonel and the people who thought they knew him. It is likely, however, that no one ever knew much about Tom Parker. His stepson and employee, Bobby Ross, died a year after Elvis, unaware that the man who headed his household from his tenth year was not what he claimed.

The paper trail on Parker is sketchy at best. No records show how or when he entered the United States; the evidence of his reported service in the U.S. Army during the 1930s is murky, and even the documentation for his years with Royal American has been destroyed. There is no certificate showing that he was legally married to the woman he called his wife, Marie Mott, whom he met in Royal American.[3]

The show of amiable gregariousness staged by Parker in his business and social dealings may have been a ruse concealing a profoundly secretive nature. There have even been accusations that he killed someone in Holland, either knifing a man on the fairgrounds where his life in the carnivals began or accidentally murdering a woman during a botched burglary.[4] Parker's secrecy may have been rooted in his socialization rather than in acts of crime. His habit of concealment probably began in childhood as a way of asserting himself against his strict father, a former soldier who continued to live according to an almost military regimen. Young Andreas took after his maternal grandparents, peddlers along the Dutch waterways. The carnival life suited him, and as an American carny, he disappeared into a clannish subculture that distrusted outsiders and developed elaborate patterns of deception and avoidance of authority figures.

Parker was by all accounts tin eared and cared little for music, but possessed an appreciation for making a buck. His skills as a hustler were well honed by the time he struck out on his own. In 1938 he was an agent for the faded crooner Gene Austin, a star eclipsed by the rise of Bing Crosby in the 1930s and reduced to headlining a traveling tent show touring the South. Parker secured bookings and sponsorships for the singer, drumming up business like a carnival spieler.[5] Years later Austin claimed it was only Parker's "knack of handling people" that saw him through those difficult times.[6]

Guided by his experience on the circus circuit, Parker seized on every angle when promoting concerts for his next client. Working for *Grand Ole Opry* star Roy Acuff, the "King of the Hillbillies," Parker arranged for grocery stores to sell discount tickets as part of a newspaper coupon deal paid for by store owners. Acuff suggested that Parker keep an eye on a rising country singer called Eddy Arnold. In 1944

Parker promoted an *Opry* tour featuring Arnold, who was about to debut as a recording artist for RCA Victor, the major label where Elvis would spend most of his career. Soon enough the "Tennessee Plowboy" took him on as manager. Arnold later recalled how Parker's disarming country manner left everyone off guard during business negotiations. "He's sharp with horse sense; he fools 'em. They think, because his English might be faulty (he might say a word wrong here and there), 'Oh, I'll handle him.' They walk right into his web!"[7]

During the years spent with Arnold, Parker drew the blueprint for the strategy he would apply on a larger scale to Elvis. He was often the one shrewd operator in a field of rubes. Many country performers were innocent of bank accounts and carried all their money with them. They could easily be bamboozled and won over by Parker's greasy charm over long games of cards and dice. At least one country singer who employed him as a booking agent, Ernest Tubb, refused to commit himself to the Colonel because "he'd constantly try to put one over on you—that was the life he led as a carny."[8] Many of the early *Opry* tours were tent shows, just like a small circus, with Parker pitching the big top at strategic points near small towns. He pretended to befriend the musicians he worked with. "He was the nicest guy in the world when he needed you," said Gabe Tucker, a musician and talent agent who worked with Parker.[9]

The shows Parker booked often included a comedian and he would continue hiring comics to back Elvis long after such pairings seemed anachronistic. He was determined to move Arnold into bigger venues and out of the rodeos, roadhouses, and barns, where cows and cow droppings had to be cleared out before the crowd could enter. Parker's objective was not only to boost ticket sales but to separate his star from the public, enhancing Arnold's luster in the eyes of his fans.

The handshake agreement Parker finally concluded with Arnold in 1945 was essentially the same contract Elvis would later sign, giving the Colonel 25 percent of all income plus expenses. It was a high percentage in an industry where a 15 percent commission was considered normal. As Arnold said years later when recalling his former manager, "He was a ball of fire, he worked hard, he got up early, and he was a nondrinker . . . He was absolutely dedicated to the personality that he represented."[10] Parker's devotion was almost obsessive. "I said to him once when he was managing me, 'Tom, why don't you get a hobby—play golf, go boating, or something?' He looked me straight in the eye and said, 'You're my hobby.'"[11]

Parker was always ready to play hardball for money; when dealing with unreliable promoters and theater owners, Parker refused to let Arnold sing until he had every promised penny in hand. In print advertising the inscription "UNDER EXCLUSIVE MANAGEMENT OF THOMAS A. PARKER" ran in type almost as large as Arnold's name. In 1948 he added an impressive prefix to his name when Louisiana Governor Jimmie Davis, himself a country singer, granted him the title of colonel. From then on he insisted on being addressed as Colonel Parker.

Parker's strategy appeared successful. Arnold often reached number one on the country charts, was a guest on Milton Berle's TV variety show, hosted his own program on the short-lived Mutual network, performed in Las Vegas, and starred in a pair of forgettable Hollywood westerns. Although Parker viewed himself as indispensable, Arnold fired him in 1953 for violating his understanding of exclusivity by working with country singer Hank Snow. Parker would not make the same mistake with Elvis and focused entirely on his career.

That no one knows how and when Parker became aware of Elvis has not prevented many bystanders from offering themselves as the man who brought the young singer to the Colonel's attention.[12] Parker claimed only that he first saw Elvis perform in Texarkana, probably in the waning months of 1954.[13] Elvis's drummer, D. J. Fontana, who played at the Texarkana shows, supports the assertion. "We would see him walkin' around, hanging back in the shadows, but he never would say nothin'. A lot of people just didn't want to deal with him."[14]

Parker was a hungry man by the fall of 1954, looking for a major new talent to represent after the ignominious end of his relationship with Arnold. His business relationship with Tommy Sands, a handsome young *Louisiana Hayride* singer pushing toward rockabilly, indicates that Parker was searching for a country performer with sex appeal for the younger generation. Meanwhile, Bob Neal was searching for a helping hand. Days after assuming management of Elvis at the start of 1955, Neal was already eager to gamble on the Colonel, whom he later called a "razzle-dazzle character, but honest and very sharp." Neal's aim was to extend Elvis's range as a touring performer.[15]

By this time Parker was a business partner with RCA recording artist Hank Snow. In effect, Snow paid the bills for Hank Snow Jamboree Attractions while Parker did the legwork. Their arrangement stipulated that Parker retained the right to enter into other managerial deals, a loop hole that allowed Parker to leverage his ties to RCA through Snow on behalf of Elvis while shutting Snow out of the deal.[16]

The traveling Hank Snow Jamboree was an ongoing tour teaming its star attraction with a revolving cast of big names in country music, including Mother Maybelle Carter, Slim Whitman, and Minnie Pearl. After Elvis was added to the roster, Parker and Davis met with Phillips, Neal, Moore, and Elvis in a coffee shop across the street from Memphis's Ellis Auditorium. Elvis was playing at the Ellis on a bill with country singers Faron Young and Ferlin Huskey and white gospel singer Martha Carson, whose ecstatic body language and repertoire of "colored spirituals" was another example of the musical miscegenation occurring all around Elvis.

Exclusive Contract

At the meeting, the cigar-smoking Parker was on the offense, needling Phillips about Sun Records' limited reach in an industry dominated by giants. Perhaps Elvis already understood that the dreams he nurtured in the darkened cinema of his imagination of being a contender with Bing Crosby, Frank Sinatra, and Dean Martin could never be reached on the closed circuit of country music radio and road shows. The Colonel was steeped in country but had connections with RCA and maybe even Hollywood.[17] Even before this meeting, Parker tempted Neal with the promise that one day he might book Elvis in "one of the big resort hotels in Nevada."[18] It was a pledge the Colonel intended to keep.

Elvis's reputation as a naïve rube in the clutches of the scheming Parker might not reflect the whole truth. Some recalled him as an avid reader of *Billboard* and other trade papers who managed to conceal his interest in the business side of show business. "I remember how dedicated Elvis was to his craft. He was always concerned about management and business tactics," said Tommy Sands.[19] Elvis likely took notice of a man with the title of colonel, which in the South in those years was a mark of association with power and authority.

If Sands was correct, Elvis was aware that the wily Colonel had made inroads into the entertainment industry that were well beyond the realm of his musical benefactor, Sam Phillips, or of Neal, the congenial man who soldiered on his behalf. Elvis was working continually as a performer in the early months of 1955, although his income was not dramatically rising owing to low guarantees offered by many local promoters. Progress came in slow, steady steps. "Milkcow Blues Boogie," the first of his singles to be placed in jukeboxes outside the South, was praised in *Billboard* for its "slick country-style reading" but never rose beyond number 80 on the charts.[20] Elvis balked at the prospect of being just another honky-tonk singer trapped on an endless, looping road trip through Dixie. The future he desired was larger than roadhouses and indie labels. The pact he signed with Parker may have been a Faustian bargain, but like Faust, Elvis was not entirely unaware of the consequences.

One report has Elvis seeking out a second meeting with Parker in April 1955, ostensibly to thank him for the opportunity of touring with Hank Snow. "I've heard a lot about you, Colonel, and I want you to know that it's very nice of you to have me on this show," he said. "Me and my band appreciate the work. You just tell me what you want us to do, and we'll sure do it."[21]

Because Elvis was still only 20 years old and legally a minor, the contract between him and Parker needed the signature of his parents. Given the close relationship inside the Presley family, Elvis would have sought the approval of Gladys and Vernon even if the law had not demanded it. The Colonel began courting Elvis's parents as early as May, finding Vernon to be an easy mark for his not implausible assertion that Elvis could make a million dollars as a singer. Gladys was more difficult to move. She instinctively distrusted the man. Gladys was finally persuaded to overlook her doubts by the friendly ministrations of Hank Snow, who had no idea he was handing his partner the key to a fortune he would never share, and Bob Neal, who imagined that he might remain a junior partner in Elvis's rising career.[22]

The agreement signed by the Presleys with Parker on August 15, 1955, was the first in a complicated string of deals that would link Elvis to the Colonel in perpetuity. The pact named Parker as "special adviser to Elvis Presley and Bob Neal for the period of one year" in exchange for a payment of $2,500 plus expenses "as approved by Elvis Presley and his manager" and imposed a set of expectations for Elvis's "personal appearances" in a variety of cities. Elvis expected to profit from Parker's promise of bookings across the United States, and Neal would profit by retaining his commission. The far-ranging implications of the agreement's final clause, "Col. Parker is to negotiate all renewals on existing contracts," seems to have escaped all parties except the author of the contract.[23]

The Colonel was always proud of his handiwork. "I'm not snowin' you. I prepared the contract myself, every single clause of it," he told New York music executive Arnold Shaw. "See, here's where you city slickers can learn a little somethin' from us country boys."[24]

Parker paid closer attention to Elvis's audience than to the singer himself, but may have coached him on his increasingly exaggerated stage moves, drawing on examples of bump and grind from the burlesque tents of the carnival. If so, his advice was paying off.

At a May 10 show in Ocala, Florida, before an audience of three thousand, the girls in the seats screamed like Sinatra fans of 10 years earlier at the sight of Elvis's insinuating body language. Hank Snow and the other country singers on the bill were received politely. Three days later Elvis played a baseball field in nearby Jacksonville before a cheering crowd of fourteen thousand. The Colonel's training in the sawdust world of the big top helped him maximize profits; he sold large quantities of cheap Elvis trinkets, including hats and pillows, but it should be added that there was nothing new about merchandizing in popular culture. As far back as the 1830s, entrepreneurs turned the characters from Charles Dickens's *The Pickwick Papers* into chintz upholstery, Toby jugs, and even pastries.

Parker assiduously worked the local press in advance. Playing with the sensation-seeking credulity of the journalists, he led them to report that the Jacksonville show had turned into a riot. He considered it good publicity.

Pink Cadillac

The reaction of the exuberant crowd was greatly exaggerated. Screaming teenage girls did follow Elvis to his motel where, rather like a coquettish burlesque dancer, he did a sort of strip tease for them by removing his shirt in the window of his room. Girls leaving their phone numbers and other messages in lipstick and nail polish defaced one of the first things Elvis purchased with the proceeds of his growing fame, a pink Cadillac. The singer was upset that this hard-earned token of his rising status was scratched during an upheaval of childish enthusiasm. According to legend, the Colonel laughed. With crowds like this, Parker told Elvis, he could soon afford to buy as many Cadillacs as he desired.[25]

As early as 1905, popular songs such as "My Merry Oldsmobile" forged a link in the imagination between cars and good times. The automobile became the key to the highway that ran through the emerging American Dream of liberty and consumption for all. Henry Ford's Model T (introduced in 1908) began to bring car ownership within reach of many middle class Americans. The Great Depression slowed the industry's growth, depressing sales of new cars, but many teenagers scraped together money from part-time jobs to purchase a used jalopy that insured greater autonomy from parents, schools, and authority figures.

After World War II, the pent-up hunger for consumer goods resulted in an appetite for new models. Cheap gasoline encouraged the spread of bedroom suburbs on the outskirts of cities, where another facet of the American Dream, a home on the range, found expression in subdivisions of ranch houses. The new class of suburbanites drove to work and the supermarket in the gleaming, chrome-trimmed products rolling off the Detroit assembly lines. Advertising increased the hunger for cars even among those who could least afford them, the African American teenagers of New York City who formed hundreds of rhythm and blues singing groups on the street corners of their city. Many of these "doo-wop" groups took the names of cars, including the Fleetwoods, the Impalas, the Imperials, the El Dorados, and the Cadillacs.

The Cadillac had long been associated with power and wealth. It was the car of presidents and bankers, and driving a Cadillac was a status symbol. As an outsider from a family that had never owned a new car, Elvis embraced the status symbol but gave it a funky twist. Dwight D. Eisenhower would never be chauffeured to events of state in a pink Cadillac. It was a daring juxtaposition of styles, an act of rebellion as well as conformity to the status quo. Elvis craved acceptance but wanted to dictate the terms.

The pink Cadillac turned up in the lyric to one of Elvis's most remarkable recordings, "Baby Let's Play House," issued by Sun in April 1955 as B side to the rhythmic country lament, "I'm Left, You're Right, She's Gone." Written by blues singer Arthur Gunter, the original 1954 recording of "Baby Let's Play House" reached number 12 on the R&B chart.

Gunter's version was a playful shuffling country blues, rooted in the juke joints of the Mississippi Delta. The music's light tone belied the threat at the climax of the lyrics: "I'd rather see you dead little girl than to be with another man." Gunter's theme of "playing house," a widely understood term for a couple living together outside of marriage, was acceptable to blues and country audiences of the 1950s, even if the subject was out of bounds for the pop market. In yet another case for the cross-pollination of white and black music in segregated America, Gunter derived his song from Eddy Arnold's 1951 country hit, "I Wanna Play House with You."

Elvis radically transformed "Baby Let's Play House," remaking the easy blues rhythm into a runaway rockabilly train pulled by

Scotty Moore's searing guitar solos and Bill Black's thumping bass. Elvis opened and closed the number with a furious stutter ("ba-ba-ba-ba-ba-ba-ba-baby, baby, baby") reminiscent of speaking in tongues, and tore into the lyrics with the confident swagger of a sociopath who would flinch at nothing, not even murder, to keep his woman from falling into the hands of a rival.

Elvis changed nothing in Gunter's lyric but one line. "You may get religion but don't you be nobody's fool," with its implied criticism of evangelical Protestantism, became "You may drive a pink Cadillac but don't you be nobody's fool." The shift would be echoed many years later in Aretha Franklin's interpretation of the Beatles' "Eleanor Rigby," where "No one was saved" was abbreviated to the silence of an ellipsis followed by "Saved." Like Elvis, her singing voice was first heard in church, and she was loath to cast a stone against the crucible of her spirituality. As for why Elvis substituted a pink Cadillac for religion, it may have been the flashiest image that came to mind, a symbol of earthly success that could go to the head of a woman who became too uppity to keep her relationship with a poor country boy.

An advertising flyer issued by Neal to promote the single showed that Elvis was still being marketed as a country act, regardless of his dark rhythm and blues roots. The pictorial circular declared the singer "The Freshest, Newest Voice in Country Music" and offered a few words ascribed to Elvis for the hillbilly fan base: "Howdy to all my friends at the Jimmie Rodgers Memorial."[26]

Elvis released only one more single for Sun, "Mystery Train"/"I Forgot to Remember to Forget," in August. "Mystery Train" was a rhythm and blues number whose lyrics derived from the Carter Family's enigmatic hillbilly classic, "Worried Man Blues." The lyrics and mood continue to haunt the imagination of rock fans, and books and movies have borrowed the title, but at the time, "I Forgot" was the show business milestone—Elvis's first national hit, reaching number one on the country charts. The momentum surrounding his career continued to gather speed, especially after signing with Parker, and his direction inexorably led away from Phillips.

The Major League

Even before he began his campaign to win over Gladys and Vernon, Parker devised a strategy for Elvis, which involved drawing him away from Sun Records and signing him with RCA. The first part of the plan proved relatively easy. Elvis sought a level of success beyond the reach of any indie label while Sun was mired in the frustrations that usually dogged the indies. Phillips was selling records but unable to collect his share of the proceeds quickly enough from storekeepers and distributors, making it financially difficult to maintain momentum. He was unable to pay Elvis the royalties owed on his Sun recordings, a problem Parker may have used to pressure the label owner with the threat of a lawsuit. Phillips's decision to sell Elvis's contract to a major company, and use the money to build up the stable of players that gathered at Sun in the wake of Elvis's success, coincided with Parker's scheme. Phillips saw the Colonel as a huckster and wanted to cut him out of the deal, if possible. "Sam had a great deal of contempt for him," Marion Keisker said, adding that Phillips rued turning Elvis's destiny over to Parker but felt it became "inevitable."[27]

Shrewdly, Parker spread the rumor that Phillips had put Elvis's contract up for sale, which at that point may not have been a move Sun's owner had firmly decided upon. According to Phillips, he made the Colonel an offer he expected would be refused. In those years, $35,000 for a regionally popular country singer was a princely sum. "I absolutely did not think Tom Parker could raise the $35,000 and that would have been fine," Phillips said. "But he raised the money, and damn, I couldn't back out then."[28]

The only record label of consequence Parker had worked with was RCA Victor, and he invested a great deal of effort to convince RCA executives that Elvis was worth such a large sum. Realizing that many trunk roads led to the seat of power in the industry, Parker worked any connection he could make. When Arnold Shaw came to Nashville in 1955, looking to purchase new songs in his capacity as general manager for New York's Albert B. Marks Music Corporation, he received a solicitous phone call from Parker. It was no coincidence that the music publisher's offices were located in the RCA building. Shaw not only brushed against RCA executives in the elevator but also enjoyed a convivial relationship with them in the era of two-martini lunches and three-martini happy hours. As a guest in Parker's home, Shaw was exposed for the first time to Elvis's Sun recordings and to glossy promotional photographs of "a tough-looking white youngster," as Shaw recalled him, his lips "curled in a wise-guy sneer."

The Colonel continued his sales pitch, appealing to Shaw's vanity by giving him a challenge. "In Georgia and Florida the girls are tearing off his clothes," Parker said. "He's unknown north of the Mason and

Dixon line. You're a big man up north. Let me see if you can get his records played in the Big City."[29]

Shaw returned to New York with copies of Elvis's singles. Executives over the age of 40 rolled their eyes at those "unmusical" recordings, but he got "the feeling in watching some of the under-twenty [office] girls . . . that they were reacting to something visceral and vibrant in the grooves."[30]

Parker's hunch that Shaw represented one road to his destination paid off when the song publisher presented copies of Elvis records to Bill Randle, a prominent DJ on Cleveland's station WERE, who also hosted a weekly show in New York on CBS. An erudite man of scholarly interests, Randle was known for his power to "break" records, picking winners and promoting them until they reached the top of the charts. Within days, Randle phoned Shaw, telling him that WERE's switchboard "lit up like Glitter Gulch in Las Vegas" when he played Elvis.[31]

Randle, who may have entertained the dream of pushing aside Parker and Neal and becoming Elvis's manager, began making contacts on the singer's behalf, especially to a prominent country music publisher, Hill and Range Songs, a firm that would figure in Elvis's move to RCA. Randle also arranged to produce a short music film for United International Pictures featuring performances in a Cleveland high school auditorium by Bill Haley, the Four Lads, Pat Boone, and Elvis. The project foundered; the movie's director, Arthur Cohen, refused to film Elvis, calling him "pitiful."[32]

Not unlike Dewey Phillips in Memphis, Randle spun Elvis's records several times an hour but his enthusiasm had greater impact on the national music industry. Randle's word was taken seriously. The Cleveland DJ piqued interest in Elvis at Mercury and Columbia, yet skepticism remained over how much the singer was worth. Shaw recalled rumors that Columbia's powerful director of artists and repertoire, Mitch Miller, dismissed Sam Phillips's asking price of $15,000 as "ridiculous."[33] Miller, who in the aftermath of Elvis's national success mounted a futile campaign against rock and roll, would have gone apoplectic if Parker had approached him for $35,000.

According to other reports, Phillips tried to offer Elvis at a variety of prices, including $5,000 to Decca and $7,500 to Dot Records in an effort to bypass Parker. He may even have hoped to launch a bidding war on his own terms but was unable to close the deal.[34] Atlantic Records, the giant among rhythm and blues indies, offered $25,000. "That was everything we had, including my desk," said Atlantic's chief

Ahmet Ertegun, adding, "the Colonel said he had to have forty-five thousand, which at that time was not only outrageous but silly."[35] Shaw remembered that even Neal made a faltering effort to sell Elvis.[36] Parker used the bidding or the rumors of bidding to his advantage, leveraging the interest shown by other labels with his contacts at RCA, especially the label's president Frank Folsom and the head of RCA's country and western division, Steve Sholes.

Meanwhile, Parker worked tirelessly to promote Elvis outside the South, where the migration of white rural folk to the factory towns of the North and the West helped spread country music, transforming it from a regional into an American music. In September 1955, the national magazine *Country Song Roundup* lauded Elvis as a wholesome yet exciting performer.[37] A month later Elvis was the opening act at a country show up North, in Cleveland, featuring Kitty Wells and Roy Acuff. "Mystery Train" appeared on playlists beyond Elvis's home territory in Seattle, San Francisco, Philadelphia, Cleveland, Boston, Detroit, and Chicago.

The deal Parker finally engineered netted $40,000, including the $35,000 he promised to Phillips plus $5,000 for Elvis, covering outstanding royalties on his Sun recordings. In addition to Elvis's contract, RCA purchased all recordings, released or unreleased, that Elvis had made for Sun.[38]

The $40,000 was not paid by RCA alone. A share of $15,000 came from Hill and Range Songs. The New York firm was owned by brothers Jean and Julian Aberbach, Viennese refugees from Hitler's Europe. The Aberbachs' stake in the arrangement was the acquisition of Sam Phillips's tiny publishing company, Hi Lo Music, which owned rights to most of the songs Elvis recorded for Sun.[39] Hill and Range agreed to establish a pair of subsidiaries, Elvis Presley Music and Gladys Music, as publishers of the songs Elvis would record for RCA. Elvis received half ownership of those corporations.[40] It was the way the Aberbachs had done business over the years, drawing big name country acts such as Hank Snow, Bill Monroe, Bob Wills, and Earnest Tubb into their fold by offering them a generous share of the profit from the songs they wrote or sang. The Hill and Range deal netted Elvis a fortune in royalties over the years as small-time publishers and songwriters were forced to sell all or most of their rights to Elvis Presley or Gladys Music in exchange for a chance to be recorded by the King of Rock and Roll.

The contract was signed on November 21, 1955. From now on, the label on Elvis's recordings would no longer display a rooster greeting the new day but RCA's famous logo, a dog listening to his master's voice on a gramophone. With RCA's links to television and movies and its national distribution, it seemed like a promised land for a young man of Elvis's ambitions.

Elvis had every reason to be impressed by the Colonel's wizardry because the deal entered into by RCA and Hill and Range had little precedent. The two well-established firms were gambling a large sum of money on a regional country star who was only beginning to make waves outside his home waters. With the $5,000 he received, Elvis could have purchased a pair of Cadillacs.

For RCA and Hill and Range it was risky but not entirely foolhardy business. In the South, Elvis had demonstrated crossover appeal to black and older audiences as well as the growing teenage market.[41] Moreover, sounds and songs from outside the mainstream of popular music were penetrating the hit parade, if often in watered-down recordings by Pat Boone and other white singers. Phillips was not the only music executive wondering whether a white man who sang black, or at least sounded that way to white ears, might become a bright comet across the show business horizon. The investment in Elvis can be understood as a chance to be taken at a time of uncertainty in the music industry. The pop charts of 1955 were a sonic jumble, including Dean Martin crooning on "Memories Are Made of This" and the Cuban mambo of Perez Prado's "Cherry Pink and Apple Blossom White," the ersatz folk of Mitch Miller's "The Yellow Rose of Texas," as well as the more genuine article in Tennessee Ernie Ford's "Sixteen Tons." During that summer, Bill Haley's "Rock Around the Clock" hit number one.

Rock critic Dave Marsh may have been correct when he wrote that Phillips was, in the end, happy to be rid of a protégé who wanted to become a star of stage and screen and was not content to explore the seam between black and white Southern traditions. In any event, Phillips "had newer, more congenial musicians to work with," especially Carl Perkins, Johnny Cash, and Jerry Lee Lewis, who flocked to Sun in the aftermath of Elvis's success in the South. The $35,000 was a godsend for his own label and the foundation for a comfortable future. Phillips invested a portion of the money in a fledgling hotel chain named after a popular Bing Crosby movie of a decade earlier, Holiday Inn.[42]

For the time being, Elvis's career continued to ascend on the gravel road of country music, often literally. Presley and his band, which by then included drummer D. J. Fontana, sometimes covered hundreds of miles within one day between shows, record store autograph sessions, and radio interviews.[43] Just days before the RCA contract was signed, Elvis was elected "Most Promising New C&W Artist" at the annual Disc Jockeys Convention in Nashville. *Billboard* continued to heap him with hillbilly honors, including "Most Promising Country and Western Artist."[44]

Although the deal with RCA was imminent, Parker hedged his bets, allowing Elvis to sign on November 12 for another year with *Louisiana Hayride* at $200 a show. After signing his movie deal with Paramount in April 1956, however, Elvis approached *Hayride* producer Horace Logan about being released from his commitments. "I'm gonna have to buy out of the rest of my contract, Mr. Logan," Elvis told the producer. "I really hate it 'cause ya'll been really good to me, but the Colonel says I got no choice." Within days, Logan received a check for $10,000 signed by Elvis.[45]

The wheels were turning faster and faster. Bob Neal, though he continued for a time to manage the more mundane affairs of Elvis's business as the Colonel painted the big picture, became irrelevant and bowed out entirely during the following year. Within weeks of signing Elvis, RCA reissued all five of his Sun singles under the sign of the dog and gramophone. *Billboard* trumpeted the RCA/Hill and Range contract in a headline reading, "Double Deal Hurls Presley into Stardom." The article noted, in the Walter Winchell press lingo of the period, that RCA Victor "plans to push his platters in all three fields—pop, R&B, and C&W"—but that producer Steve Sholes "plans to cut the warbler with the same backup—electric guitar, bass fiddle, drums and Presley himself on rhythm guitar—featured on his previous Sun recordings."[46]

As 1955 passed into 1956, Elvis arrived at the junction taking him to the career he may have dreamed of as early as Humes High School. The fare would ultimately be higher than Elvis had imagined, yet the singer remained true to his ambitions as he pushed ahead. The trickster who conducted him to the emerald cities of New York, Las Vegas, and Hollywood was a man whose authority he respected intuitively and, after the November contract, with good reason. Elvis was not the ignorant or naïve bumpkin of popular caricature, but neither was he a confident operator in the halls of wealth and power. The Colonel would be his intermediary.

As for the music, Elvis was never satisfied being the "Hillbilly Cat" or even the "King of Western Bop." He would soon be dubbed the "King of Rock and Roll," a crown he gladly wore even if it never encompassed the full realm of his dreams. An astute follower of the music industry, Elvis was aware that rock and roll had already been born up North, even if his Sun recordings represented a parallel evolutionary line. Some insiders would always view him as a usurper.

Notes

1. Probate Court of Shelby County, Tennessee (file A-655).
2. Albert Goldman, *Elvis* (New York: McGraw-Hill, 1981), pp. 131–152.
3. For conflicting accounts of Tom Parker's early life, see Alanna Nash, *The Colonel: The Extraordinary Story of Colonel Tom Parker and Elvis Presley* (New York: Simon & Schuster, 2003); James L. Dickerson, *Colonel Tom Parker: The Curious Life of Elvis Presley's Eccentric Manager* (New York: Cooper Square Press, 2001); and Dick Vallenga with Mick Farren, *Elvis and the Colonel* (New York: Delacourte Press, 1988).
4. Nash, *The Colonel*, pp. 38–44.
5. Nash, *The Colonel*, pp. 79–82.
6. Ralph M. Pabst, *Gene Austin's Ol' Buddy* (Phoenix, AZ: Augury, 1984), p. 172.
7. Eddy Arnold, *It's a Long Way from Chester County* (Old Tappan, NJ: Hewitt House, 1969), p. 46.
8. Nash, *The Colonel*, p. 96.
9. Nash, *The Colonel*, p. 99.
10. *Atlanta Journal*, January 22, 1997.
11. Arnold, p. 47.
12. The most likely candidate, Oscar Davis, had been Hank Williams's agent before becoming associated with Parker. "It was really Oscar who found Elvis," said Charlie Lamb, a carny turned country music advertising agent who worked for Parker. Nash, *The Colonel*, pp. 116–117.
13. AP story, November 20, 1957.
14. Nash, *The Colonel*, p. 117. There are many other reports of Parker shadowing Elvis in Texas from the fall of 1954 through January 1955, in Howard A. DeWitt, *Elvis: The Sun Years, The Story of Elvis Presley in the Fifties* (Ann Arbor, MI: Popular Culture Ink, 1993), p. 181.

15. Nash, *The Colonel*, p. 117.

16. DeWitt, p. 123.

17. Peter Guralnick, *Last Train to Memphis: The Rise of Elvis Presley* (Boston: Little Brown, 1994), pp. 163–165.

18. Peter Guralnick and Ernst Jorgensen, *Elvis Day by Day: The Definitive Record of His Life and Music* (New York: Ballantine, 1999), p. x.

19. DeWitt, p. 173.

20. *Billboard*, January 24, 1955.

21. Vellenga, p. 83.

22. Elaine Dundy, *Elvis and Gladys* (New York: Macmillan, 1985), pp. 260–262.

23. Report of Guardian Ad Litem re: the Estate of Elvis A. Presley, Deceased, Probate Court of Shelby County, Tennessee.

24. Arnold Shaw, *The Rockin' '50s* (New York: Hawthorn, 1974), p. 5.

25. DeWitt, pp. 194–195.

26. Pictured in DeWitt, p. 200.

27. Guralnick, *Last Train*, p. 208.

28. Quoted in the documentary *Mr. Rock & Roll*, 1999.

29. Shaw, *Rockin' '50s*, p. 6.

30. Shaw, *Rockin' '50s*, p. 7.

31. Shaw, *Rockin' '50s*, p. 8.

32. Guralnick, *Last Train*, pp. 216, 221–222.

33. Shaw, *Rockin' '50s*, p. 8.

34. DeWitt, pp. 217–218.

35. Jerry Hopkins, *Elvis: A Biography* (New York: Simon & Schuster, 1971), p. 113.

36. Shaw, *Honkers and Shouters*, p. 497.

37. "Folk Music Fireball," *Country Song Roundup*, September 1955.

38. Elvis may also have received a $6,000 signing bonus, minus percentages taken by Parker and Neal. Guralnick, *Last Train*, pp. 514–515.

39. Shaw, *Rockin' '50s*, p. 9. Hill and Range purchased 100 percent of every song Elvis recorded for Sun after the initial Arthur Crudup

and Bill Monroe single except "I Forgot to Remember to For-get," 50 percent of which had been acquired by Shaw for Marks Music.

40. Elvis Presley Music was affiliated with the American Society of Composers, Authors and Publishers (ASCAP), and Gladys Music with its competitor, Broadcast Music Incorporated (BMI). It was a shrewd business decision to spread the wealth of Elvis between both nonprofit organizations chartered to collect royalties on behalf of publishers and writers.

41. Along with the multigenerational audiences of *Louisiana Hayride* and the Hank Snow tours, anecdotal evidence suggests that Elvis had an audience in the segregated sections of the black South. One trade magazine noted that his records "have been spilling over" into the rhythm and blues field. *Cashbox*, December 3, 1955. Arthur Crudup recalled hearing Elvis's rendition of his song "That's All Right" on a jukebox in Forrest, Mississippi, as early as 1954. Chris Hodenfield, "Arthur Crudup May Get It Back," *Rolling Stone*, December 9, 1971.

42. Dave Marsh, *Elvis* (New York: Rolling Stone, 1982), p. 62.

43. DeWitt, p. 245.

44. *Billboard*, November 12, 1955.

45. Horace Logan with Bill Sloan, *Elvis, Hank, and Me: Musical History on the* Louisiana Hayride (New York: St. Martin's Press, 1998), pp. 174–175.

46. *Billboard*, December 3, 1955.

6

The King of Rock and Roll

On January 14–15, 1955, one year before Elvis's first journey to New York for his national television debut, a "Rock and Roll Jubilee Ball" was staged at New York's St. Nicholas Arena. The show, featuring sold-out performances by rhythm and blues stars such as Fats Domino, Ruth Brown, and Joe Turner, was organized by disc jockey Alan Freed. He has been called "the father of rock and roll" for naming the emerging genre of music and acting as the main bridge between a new generation of rhythm and blues performers and a young, multiracial audience.[1] Freed began by imagining rock and roll as black music that appealed to teenagers of all backgrounds. He never thought a white Southerner would be crowned as the music's king.

Freed claimed he began calling the music rock and roll as early as 1951.[2] In that year, the onetime classical music radio announcer began working the night shift on Cleveland's station WJW. His sponsor, local record storeowner Leo Mintz, convinced him to program rhythm and blues records on the strength of the reaction of white teenagers to the music they heard in his shop. Freed changed the name of his show to *The Moon Dog Rock 'n Roll House Party*, with Moon Dog referring to the rhythm and blues recording that became his theme song, Todd Rhodes's "Blues for Moon Dog." The term *rock and roll* was in the air, literally, on radio shows and jukeboxes playing such recent rhythm and blues hits as the Ravens' "Rock All Night," Roy Brown's "Good Rockin' Tonight," and Wyonie Harris's "All She Wants to Do Is Rock."[3]

Freed was not the lone white voice of rhythm and blues in the tract town wilderness of Eisenhower's America but soon became the loudest. Disc jockeys with idiosyncratic, hipster personalities were all the rage following World War II, a time when increasing numbers of stations began programming rhythm and blues to reach black audiences and the lower cost of radios meant that middle class teenagers could own their own receivers. Behind the closed doors of their bedrooms, the kids chose whatever they wanted to hear. Many opted for eccentric disc jockeys spinning strange records through the night on AM radio. The most influential disc jockeys tended to be white, whether Symphony Sid in Boston, Hunter Hancock in Los Angeles, or Dewey Phillips in Memphis.

A 50,000-watt giant, WJW's long reach gave Freed a wide radius for his manic on-air antics, and influence over the purchasing power of his young audience. Recruiting most of his talent from the East Coast, Freed began organizing rock and roll package shows as early as the summer of 1952. The following year he sold 18,000 tickets for his "Moon Dog Coronation Ball" at Cleveland Arena, a facility that seated half as many people. Angry ticket holders left outside the turnstiles rioted, linking rock and roll with violence in the public mind. Freed set an example for racial harmony in popular music but personal and professional irresponsibility left him vulnerable to opponents jealous of his success, uneasy about race mixing, and dismayed by the music he promoted. Freed died in 1965 at age 44, unemployed, ruined by alcoholism and a scandal surrounding "payola," the common and well-established practice in the record business of paying disc jockeys for airplay. Freed made a fortune from rock and roll in the 1950s but lost everything within a few short years.

Freed moved to New York in the fall of 1954, taking the key nighttime spot on WINS and rocketing the station's ratings skyward. "Alan Freed's Rock and Roll Party," as his show was soon called, stirred resentment among some African Americans who denounced the disc jockey at a meeting in Harlem. Black bandleader Lucky Milinder defended Freed, acknowledging his debt to black hipster culture but insisting, "in no way does he burlesque Negroes."[4]

In some respects African American music had no greater friend than Freed. He disdained white cover versions of black records; in the early years, the entertainers he lined up for his live shows were all black. The format of his radio program was widely imitated, especially after CBS began broadcasting him coast to coast. At the onset of 1956, it was Freed who defined rock and roll. Any controversy surrounding the music was muted and localized, since the audience was largely confined to black youths and white teenage hipsters in the North. All of this would change with the arrival of Elvis on the national stage, which coincided with the rise of "massive resistance" to desegregation in the South.

A New Generation

For Elvis, his rapid ascent from a regionally popular exponent of "rural rhythm" to the mover and shaker in a worldwide pop culture earthquake was a dream come true, but with social and personal consequences he could not have foreseen. The extent of Elvis's runaway success was made possible by exposure on network television and the power over promotions and distribution wielded by RCA, a major label with a sizable investment in his success. The mass marketing of Elvis, however, cannot entirely explain the response by young people in America and, soon enough, the world.

Although teenagers already understood themselves as a separate youth culture during the war years, the trend accelerated with the postwar economic boom that lifted all middle class boats, for children as well as parents. Distinct groups, especially those that feel misunderstood or disadvantaged, tend to embrace charismatic peers as exemplars. Elvis became the most popular exemplar of teen identity as he climbed onto the national stage through the medium of television. His rise was inseparable from shifts in economics. During the 1950s, the buying power of adolescents and young adults become widely recognized. In 1956 America's 13 million teenagers represented a combined income of $7 billion. Boys saved their allowance and after-school job money for cars. Girls purchased clothing, cosmetics, and the majority of 45-rpm singles sold in the United States.[5] As a result, a young female audience drove the careers of many singing stars in the 1950s.

Sex appeal was essential. Bill Haley, Elvis's white predecessor in associating rock and roll with youthful defiance, a singer who also crossed country with rhythm and blues, was a chubby, unassuming, married man pushing middle age. By contrast, Elvis was slender, dynamic, young, and available.

Race was also crucial. No black star from any of Freed's rock and roll revues, regardless of their magnetism, could have been widely embraced as a sex symbol by white American teenagers of the 1950s. From a mainstream national perspective, Elvis had the advantage over all contenders of being familiar yet exotic, Caucasian yet from a distinct Southern subculture. Many younger white teens had grown up in Northern suburbs with virtually no contact with African Americans and were unfamiliar with the roots of Elvis's music. For them, the strangeness of his sound and persona made him all the more thrilling. It was as if Elvis stepped off a flying saucer and into the homes of millions of Americans through the young medium of television.

Jackie Gleason, the producer of *Stage Show*, the program where Elvis made his national debut, was right to describe the singer as "the guitar-playing Marlon Brando."[6] No other sector of popular culture or show business was as important in setting the stage for the ascent of Elvis, and the mass popularity of rock and roll among teenagers, than Hollywood. Three movies prepared the way, *The Wild One* (1954), *Rebel Without a Cause* (1955), and *The Blackboard Jungle* (1955). Only the latter featured rock and roll in the soundtrack—and then almost as an afterthought. In *The Wild One*, Brando's motorcycle gang listened to bebop, and in *Rebel*, James Dean and Natalie Wood tuned the car radio to romantic rhythm and blues. The emergence of rock and roll was registering tectonic shifts already beginning to occur.

With his Method acting emotion and evident contempt for polite society, Brando jettisoned the glamorous veneer that Hollywood stars of previous generations found indispensable. He was as raw and supposedly "authentic" as the new music being embraced by youth, ostensibly more "honest" than the polished professionals he threatened to displace. Brando cast the die for the rebellion of white youth, and the rebel image Elvis would assume in part, as the motorcycle riding antihero of *The Wild One*, described by film critic Richard Schickel as "the first major movie to confront the seismic rift that slowly, surely opened between the generations in the 1950s."[7] *The Wild One* was ostensibly a "problem picture" about juvenile delinquency, a pattern of antisocial behavior associated with what psychiatrist Robert Lindner termed the "mutiny of the young" in a much reported 1954 lecture, "a profound and terrifying change in the new generation of adolescents." Lindner called them "rebels within the confines of conformity." They were not seeking to overthrow the existing order but lashed out at their emotional bruises and frustrations.[8]

The Wild One fulfilled Lindner's diagnosis. Wearing an insolent sneer and a leather jacket, Brando's Johnnie rode into town without the benefit of a political agenda, but with an urge to overturn the neatly planned world of postwar America. Johnnie replied, "Whaddya got?" when asked what he was rebelling against. Hiding his bashfulness under a crooked Robert Mitchum/Marlon Brando sneer, Elvis became Johnnie with a guitar.[9]

He rode a motorcycle, too. Elvis was featured on the cover of the May 1956 issue of *Harley Davidson* magazine, whose copywriter hailed him as "that rocket blazing a fiery trail across the musical sky" and gladly noted that the singer owned a 1956 KH model painted in bold tones of red and white. Elvis was pictured on the magazine's cover astride the bike, wearing outlaw jeans and leather jacket but tipping his hat in a gesture suggesting a Southern gentleman rather than a hooligan.[10]

For its white middle class teenage audience, *The Wild One* was a fantasy of rebellion. *Rebel Without a Cause* hit closer to home. Its antihero Jim Stark, played by James Dean, was a high school student beset by emotional turmoil and uncertain of his status with peers and the adult world. It was shot from the perspective of its adolescent characters, with the young people "always in the foreground and the adults . . . for the most part shown as the kids see them," according to director Nicholas Ray.[11]

The Blackboard Jungle was a direct descendent of the Dead End Kids movies of the 1930s with its jive-talking black, white, and brown delinquents from a troubled inner city high school. Like Johnnie's gang, they listened to bebop, but the last minute incorporation of "Rock Around the Clock" as the movie's theme song set a tone, connecting the scenario to the musical upheaval in the making. The song was picked after the movie was otherwise completed, culled from the record collection of Peter Ford, son of the film's adult star Glen Ford. "Rock Around the Clock" was meant to represent the latest in what kids were listening to. Despite its rhythmic roots in the swing era, the song became the first recognizable international rock and roll hit through its association with *The Blackboard Jungle*, "the 'Marseillaise' of the rock revolution."[12] "It was wide open," Haley later said of the musical moment, "and we offered a simple beat that the kids could dance to."[13]

Elvis strode into the generational cleavage represented by *The Wild One, Rebel Without a Cause*, and *The Blackboard Jungle*, becoming the towering symbol of what many parents feared and many children increasingly embraced. Like J. D. Salinger's Holden Caulfield or James Dean's Jim Stark, and perhaps filling the empty emotional space left by Dean's death in a reckless car wreck at the end of 1955, Presley was interpreted as another slouching embodiment of generational misunderstanding, yet he was always at odds with those expectations. Where many white, middle class youths who embraced rock and roll felt unfulfilled by the often recently won affluence of their parents, Elvis was uncomfortable with the poverty that was his legacy and chafed against its limits. He may have been alienated, yet he yearned for his place in the sun. Elvis never raised the flag of rebellion against his family, but lavished them with presents and lived with his kinfolk until his death. If Elvis rebelled against his parents at all in the early years of success, it was only because of the habitual frugality they maintained even after he became rich.

Elvis's impact on the South had been profound, not only on audiences but on the next wave of artists to emerge from that audience. Gene Vincent, who scored a national hit with "Be-Bop-A-Lula" (1956), claimed to be working out his own mix of "the sounds of the colored folk" with "the sounds of Hank Williams and Red Foley" when he heard Elvis on the radio. The rockabilly sound of Sun Records left a permanent mark.[14]

The New Singing Rage

The shock waves Elvis triggered traveled across the nation via television signals. What is sometimes overlooked is that the sensation he caused did not occur on his first TV appearance but gathered force cumulatively if rapidly. The singer had tasted the new medium as early as 1955 on a *Louisiana Hayride* telecast and other country music shows, but viewers were limited and regional.[15] He debuted on national TV on January 28, 1956, when swing era bandleaders Tommy and Jimmy Dorsey featured him in the first of six Saturday nights on their CBS variety program, *Stage Show*. The studio audience was sparse; teenagers rushed past Elvis's name on the CBS Studio 50 marquee for a nearby roller rink, ignoring a pitchman hawking free tickets.[16] Bill Randle, who continued to promote Elvis through his radio shows, was on hand to introduce the singer as "a young fellow who, like many performers—Johnnie Ray among them—came out of nowhere to be an overnight big star." Randle added, "We think tonight that he's going to make television history for you."[17]

Randle's verdict was slightly premature. Elvis bemused the studio audience with his animated, hip-shaking medley of Big Joe Turner tunes, and given *Stage Show*'s low ratings, the brief performance stirred little immediate attention nationwide. It deserves a footnote in history nevertheless as a steppingstone to Elvis's stardom. With his unfailingly lowbrow tastes, Colonel Parker was able to grasp the significance of television more firmly than better pedigreed observers. The Colonel seemed to understand that TV was displacing the older media from their central role in popular culture, and that a spot on even a minor network program could take his client further than a string of successful one-nighters on the concert road.

For his third *Stage Show* appearance on February 11, Elvis performed "Heartbreak Hotel" and "Blue Suede Shoes," a pair of songs he had just recorded for RCA Victor. A lot was riding on the success of those songs, both for Presley and his record label. While the performances that night with the Dorsey Brothers orchestra were not much admired, the RCA recordings would rapidly cement Elvis's status as "The New Singing Rage," as the ads in the music trade papers called him.

The two songs were recorded in the sessions that resulted in Elvis Presley's self-titled debut, albeit "Heartbreak Hotel" was not released on the LP. In keeping with standard industry practice in an era when albums were generally comprised of songs not considered commercial enough to be released as singles, "Heartbreak Hotel" was to receive promotional priority while the Elvis Presley album was deemed a secondary product. RCA was surprised when the LP became the label's first million-selling pop music album after spending 10 weeks at the top of *Billboard*'s pop album chart in 1956.

The first batch of recordings Elvis made for RCA Victor was made in two sessions during January 1956 in between a performance schedule that grew more hectic with the passing weeks. On January 10 and January 11, Elvis occupied the RCA studio in Nashville to begin work for his new label. The compressed time frame was not unusual in an age when musical acts often mastered their material in front of audiences and recordings were done live with the tape machine running. Overdubbing was uncommon. Second chances were usually granted only in cases of flubbed notes or other obvious mistakes.

Elvis brought his band with him, including Scotty Moore, Bill Black, and D. J. Fontana, along with a sheaf of songs that had been forwarded to him weeks earlier by Steve Sholes, a New Jersey-born former big band musician with a long and varied background at RCA. Sholes began working for the label as a messenger in the New York office and was later responsible for producing "V discs" to entertain the U.S. military with music during World War II. He recorded such important artists as Jelly Roll Morton, who argued that he was the inventor of jazz, and Dizzy Gillespie, who took jazz into the outer limits with bebop in the 1940s. After being put in charge of the label's country and western music division, Sholes transformed RCA into the dominant country music label, and was instrumental in turning Nashville, already home to the *Grand Ole Opry*, into the center for country recording. In that capacity, Sholes had discovered, signed, or recorded Hank Snow, Chet Atkins, Eddy Arnold, Porter Wagoner, Pee Wee King, and Homer and Jethro.[18] Despite his proven success in steering country acts to the top of the charts, Sholes was anxious over Elvis. The impressive deal Colonel Parker had negotiated for his client raised the stakes higher than ever, and he worried that Carl Perkins, a rockabilly who remained at Sun, might overtake Elvis with a rising hit single called "Blue Suede Shoes." "The money we paid which seems like peanuts today, was pretty big, and they called me in and wanted me to assure them that they would make their money back in the first year," Sholes recalled years later, speaking of his label's New York executives.

Apparently, Sholes's competitors were betting on his failure. "A story was going around Nashville that I was the biggest fool ever came down the pike," he continued, "because we would never be able to make the kind of records he made for Sam Phillips over in Memphis. The truth of the matter is we didn't. By the time we got around to making 'Heartbreak Hotel' for Victor, his style had evolved a lot. We were making a new sound that was different even from the original sound that Elvis had put together."[19]

Given the breadth of Elvis's musical tastes, he would never have been content to simply continue along the rockabilly lines drawn for him at Sun Records. Whether hedging his bets over Elvis's public or sensing the singer's catholic interests, Sholes had sent Elvis country, blues, rhythm and blues, ballads, and novelty numbers to select from for his RCA recording sessions.[20] Sholes focused on material owned by Hill and Range, the music-publishing giant that would exert a powerful gravitational pull on Elvis throughout his career. Elvis had already become intrigued with "Heartbreak Hotel," written by a 40-year-old English teacher from Jacksonville, Florida.

Mae Boren Axton first met Elvis a year earlier while working as a publicist for Colonel Parker during the rising star's Florida tour. An erudite woman who enjoyed opera, classical, and folk music, she moonlighted as a freelance feature writer and became interested in country music while on a magazine assignment in Nashville. When the *Grand Ole Opry*'s Minnie Pearl introduced her to powerful Nashville music publisher Fred Rose as a country songwriter, Axton produced a tune for his perusal within hours to cover up the case of mistaken professional identity.[21] Although the story sounds like an episode from *I Love Lucy*, her resourcefulness resulted in a songwriting side career that led to Elvis's breakout national hit.

His signature barely dry on his RCA contract, Elvis was approached by Axton at the November 1955 country music DJ convention, held at Nashville's Andrew Jackson Hotel, with a song she insisted would sell a million records. The annual event had already become an important networking opportunity for agents and artists, with record labels renting hospitality suites and free drinks all around. Supposedly, Elvis was so impressed when he heard the demo recording that he exclaimed, "Hot dog, Mae, play it again."[22] Perhaps the added incentive offered by Axton, who granted him coauthorship and one-third of the royalties, was less important to Elvis, who never fancied himself a songwriter and was already as rich as his childhood dreams, than the emotional impression the song left with him.

According to an often repeated story, the inspiration for "Heartbreak Hotel" came from an article in the *Miami Herald* about a suicide who left behind a one-line note: "I walk a lonely street." Songwriter Tommy Durden, a friend and collaborator with Axton, brought her the idea of a song based on this suicide note, a blues song they would pitch at Elvis. They enlisted Jacksonville entertainer Glen Reeves to tape a demo on Axton's home recorder in the "shaky" singing style of Elvis. Supposedly, Elvis's vocal performance for RCA closely copied Reeves, whose performance had been a copy of Elvis's recordings for Sun.[23]

The room where "Heartbreak Hotel" was recorded contributed to its dark, haunting sound. RCA rented the studio from the Methodist TV, Radio and Film Commission, and the room, true to its owner, boasted a high ceiling and arches like a church. The hallways and stairwells could be employed as echo chambers, which added a dark sonic dimension to Axton's song not unlike the eerie effect achieved by Chicago's Chess Records with the voodoo blues of Muddy Waters and Howlin' Wolf. Nashville studio musician and RCA country music executive Chet Atkins, who assisted Sholes in organizing the session, recalled that bass notes would "roll around for a long time" in the room.[24] The acoustical setting intensified Black's dour bass line. Floyd Cramer, who played piano behind Elvis on *Louisiana Hayride* and joined his band on tour during the previous year, added a darkness before dawn jazz club feel on piano. Scotty Moore's guitar break was searingly metallic for its time. For Elvis, articulating the lyric with deep resonance and emotional conviction, the song stretched his emotional range. It was no simple down-and-out blues number, though it derived from the genre. "Heartbreak Hotel" was almost surreal in imagery, world weary yet worldly. The brooding menace in Elvis's voice, which threatened to flare into defiance, lifted the lyric above mere resignation. The Nashville professionals were bemused, but the song would have a terrific impact on a younger generation of listeners. "When I heard it I dropped everything," said John Lennon.[25]

Not unlike Elvis himself, Sholes and Atkins wanted to put some flesh on the bare-boned Sun sound. In addition to Cramer's piano and

Fontana's drums, Atkins hired Gordon Stoker of the Jordanaires, a vocal quartet that had toured with Eddy Arnold, and Ben and Brock Speer of the Speer Family gospel quartet, for background harmonies on some numbers. At the same time, Sholes was concerned with not entirely losing the Sun ambiance. His engineers had no idea how Sam Phillips achieved his famous "slapback" echo, but figured out how to make their own reverberations.

Aside from "Heartbreak Hotel," Elvis's Nashville session yielded a pair of rhythm and blues songs that had been tested on his road shows, Ray Charles's "I Got a Woman" and Clyde McPhatter's "Money Honey." Presley's penchant for ballad singing found expression in a pair of songs by Tin Pan Alley writers. Ira Kosloff and Maurice Mysels's yearningly vulnerable "I Want You, I Need You, I Love You" could have been written for Elvis's pop-singing role model, Dean Martin. The doo-wop-influenced "I Was the One" was penned by Aaron Schroeder, who became a hit maker a few year's earlier with Rosemary Clooney's recording of his "At a Sidewalk Penny Arcade" and went on to write such hits for Elvis as "Stuck on You" and "It's Now or Never" before becoming a music publisher whose catalog included Jimi Hendrix's "Purple Haze" and Randy Newman's "Short People."

Although Elvis was accompanied at the Nashville session by "his kinfolk and hangers-on," as Atkins recalls, "he was quiet and subdued and worked very hard." The intensity of his regional popularity was already such "that he didn't want to go out of the house in the daytime." Atkins added that Elvis split the tight pants he wore to the session at the seat and had to have "one of his boys run over to the motel to get him another pair of trousers."[26]

The story of the split pants could have been a favorite tall tale of Atkins in the years to come, when asked, as he surely often was, about his encounter with Elvis. Likewise, Sholes's story about Elvis breaking so many guitar strings from playing so loudly that he was given a ukulele pick made from felt to soften his strokes. Both men agree that Elvis was entirely serious about his music and in control of the session's direction.

"If anyone made a mistake on a number, he would never point it out to them," Sholes recalled. "He'd just say, 'Let's try it again, I think I was a little flat on that one,' until the musician picked up on it himself . . . When you get an artist of Elvis's caliber, one who analyzes himself as closely as Elvis does, and is willing to keep working as hard as Elvis, you know that all these things added together are what made him successful."[27]

By the end of May, "Heartbreak Hotel" was number one on *Billboard*'s country and pop charts, and number three on its rhythm and blues chart. A little like Michael Jackson's album *Thriller* a quarter century later, it was the perfect crossover hit, dominating multiple sectors of the market. From 1956 through 1959, crossover hits would not be as uncommon as they would become in many future years. Carl Perkins's "Blue Suede Shoes" and Elvis's "Hound Dog" and "Don't Be Cruel" topped the country, pop, and rhythm and blues charts in September 1956. Between September 1957 and October 1958, 16 of the number one records on the rhythm and blues charts were by white performers.[28] Similarly, in 1959, the ordinarily white pop chart included 20 number one hits by black artists.[29] A convergence in popular taste took place for a few years in the late 1950s, a premature cultural desegregation resulting from the spillover of rhythm and blues into a younger white market that was spearheaded by the phenomenal success of Elvis.

The Power of Television

The early months of 1956 were a blur of road trips in between increasingly noticed appearances on *Stage Show*. "We were working near everyday," Scotty Moore said. "We'd pull into some town, go the hotel room and get washed up or go right to the auditorium or movie house, and after we played our shows, we'd get back in the cars and start driving to the next town." He claimed that they were largely unaware of the national excitement they were stirring, having no time to read about themselves in the press and seldom hearing their own records "because it was drive all night, sleep all day, and there wasn't much radio at night. There was a lot of crowd reaction, but we'd been seeing that for a year. How were we to know? All we knew was drive, drive, drive."

It was like being in a space capsule rocketing close to the speed of light. Back on the ground, the music trade press was noticing changes that the band was unable to see. *Billboard*'s country and western column noted that "Heartbreak Hotel" had "snowballed rapidly in the past two weeks, with pop and R&B customers joining Presley's hillbilly fans in demanding the disk."[30]

As with many country singers and truck drivers traveling on the lengthening ribbons of paved state and federal highways, the fast-pace journey from town to town was fueled by cheap amphetamines, "pep pills," touted as a miracle drug by pharmaceutical companies as far back as the late 1930s and more popular than ever after the U.S. military fed the drug to many servicemen during World War II to maintain wakefulness.[31] The cross-country hustle of 1956 may have been Elvis's first brush with dangerous pharmaceutical drugs.

Elvis's friend from Memphis, Red West, became the band's driver and roadie, to use a term that would be coined a decade later when rock concert tours became a distinct division of the entertainment industry. West remembered a disorienting schedule that involved Elvis and the band breaking from their tour to fly to New York for *Stage Show*, and then fly back to meet him at their next scheduled performance. This went on for several crucial weeks when the world of popular culture began to turn on its axis. "I was by myself," West said. "I drove straight through because we didn't have much time. There was a show the next night. I took No Doz and kept going. I'll never forget it. I was really fightin' it to stay awake. But the TV shows was what did it. That's what sent him on his way."[32]

Sam Phillips had given up Elvis Presley for money, and Sun Records, suddenly flush with operating cash, was not out of the rock and roll game just yet. Sun recording artist Carl Perkins broke nationally in January 1956 with his own song, "Blue Suede Shoes," whose slaphappy lyric defined youthful exuberance and style by elevating a particular sort of hipster footwear as a generational symbol. At Elvis's second RCA recording session, held in New York City on January 30 and January 31 in the label's state-of-the-art studio, Sholes insisted on recording a competing version of Perkins's number. It was standard practice in those years to rush out covers of hit songs on other labels as if to catch the sparks of a shooting star before it disappeared from the pop music firmament. Many music industry executives believed that consumers purchased records for the song, not the performer. Elvis must have disagreed. After 13 takes of "Blue Suede Shoes," he stopped, declaring that it would be hard to top Perkins's original anyway.[33]

The two-day stint in the studio, when combined with the Nashville recordings and some leftover tracks from Memphis, gave the label enough material for Elvis's long playing album debut. Many bases were touched. Elvis sculpted baroque vocal flourishes on a hopped-up rockabilly transformation of a rhythm and blues number previously recorded by Roy Hamilton, "I'm Gonna Sit Right Down and Cry (Over You)." The rollicking "One-Sided Love Affair" was boogie-woogie polished to a pop gleam and without the barrelhouse danger, a concept already familiar in the swing era. The only embarrassment for the man who soon would be king of rock and roll came on "Tutti

Frutti." Elvis sounds asleep when compared to the maniacal, off-the-scale energy of Little Richard's original.

Five previously unreleased songs recorded for Phillips and purchased by RCA along with Elvis's contract with Sun filled out the album. Like the freshly cut material, these songs pointed to the wide scope of Elvis's aspirations. Included were a pair of hillbilly weepers, "I'll Never Let You Go (Lil' Darlin')" and "I Love You Because," the latter by the prolific Leon Payne, who had also penned Hank Williams's classic "Lost Highway"; a spry rockabilly tune, "Just Because"; the upbeat country of "Trying to Get to You," which Elvis infused with an especially lusty, powerful vocal; and a spooky performance of Richard Rodgers and Lorenz Hart's lonesome "Blue Moon," a song that had been heard often in network radio shows and Hollywood movies during the 1930s.

Released in March, the long player, simply called *Elvis Presley*, became the first rock and roll album to climb to the top of *Billboard*'s pop album chart and the first rock album to earn a million dollars in sales. It was a remarkable achievement at a time when albums were considered the province of adults and their music, especially classical, jazz, show tunes, and great singers such as Frank Sinatra. Teenagers primarily purchased the less expensive 45-RPM singles. *Elvis Presley's* front cover represented the leading edge in commercial design with striking typography, a bold color scheme in pink and green, and a dynamic black-and-white photograph of Elvis singing and playing his heart out. A quarter century later the design inspired the cover of one of the great albums to emerge from Britain's punk rock scene, the Clash's *London Calling*.

Colonel Parker was conspicuously absent from the *Elvis Presley* sessions. Despite the charges that Parker interfered with the direction of Elvis's music, there is little evidence that he imposed himself on the creative process in the early years. Elvis put it this way about the division of labor, "He never butts into record sessions. I don't butt into business."[34]

The music seems to have been the least of the Colonel's concerns. The old carnie trusted no one, especially show promoters; he was tireless and focused on details, counting the pennies from every ticket sold to make certain they added up, and launching a line of cheap Elvis merchandise. He was determined by his own measure to give the crowd its money's worth. The Colonel bawled out Red West one night, blaming him for the band being late for a show. West claimed he could not pry Elvis out of bed with a woman he met at the previous night's concert. Whether or not his excuse was true counted for nothing in Parker's eyes.[35]

When he cast his eyes upward from the small details, the Colonel's longer vision involved promotion. Parker was more preoccupied with television than records, and his efforts were paying off. By his final appearance on *Stage Show* on March 24, Presley cut a more polished and carefully groomed figure than two months earlier, and could count on the adulation of his studio audience. Viewers across the country were also paying attention. After the show, Elvis and the boys drove through a snowstorm to visit the Delaware hospital where his rival in "Blue Suede Shoes," Carl Perkins, was laid up following a serious car accident. Perkins had been hurrying for New York to what would have been his national TV debut on *The Perry Como Show*. Although he recovered from his injuries, his career never regained momentum, taking a potential white Southern rival to Elvis off the playing field.

The next stop for Elvis was *The Milton Berle Show*. The show's variety format, as common in those days as situation comedy and reality TV in later eras, reflected some of the oldest show business conventions, especially from vaudeville and the circus, with its changing lineup of singers and dancers, jugglers and illusionists, and animal acts. It was the Colonel's natural habitat, broadcast in a new medium. Only a few years earlier Berle, a longtime radio vaudevillian, was known as "Mr. Television" for commanding an astonishing 80 percent of TV viewers. By 1956 Uncle Miltie was already old hat, clinging to tumbling ratings in his show's final season, now remembered chiefly for hosting a pair of Elvis performances on April 3 and June 5. Berle's over-the-top visual antics, honed years earlier in the Borscht Belt, including a skit in which he played Elvis's twin brother, Melvin, a rube wearing clown-size suede shoes in honor of Elvis's rendition of a song fast becoming more identified with Presley than Perkins. Although later eyes might interpret this as an old man's disrespect for a rising star, it was all part of Berle's shtick. He once greeted the dignified jazz artist Duke Ellington wearing an outrageously striped and checkered zoot suit. The fact that he insisted on booking occasional black acts was a sign that Berle was broad minded.[36]

Ecstatic Audiences

During Elvis's endless round of touring as spring turned into the summer, the crowds grew younger, larger, and louder, drowning out the music with the same sort of shrieking acclaim that would greet the Beatles a decade later. Amplification was still low volume in those years; electric guitar amps the size of suitcases were unable to overpower the tidal wave of adulation rising from the theater seats. Girls filled the majority of those seats and photographs show their eyes and mouths wide open in an emotional outburst somewhere near ecstasy. Those same pictures also reveal some male faces in the crowds. Although Elvis's audience is usually remembered as white, this was not the case everywhere he played. "A thousand black, brown and beige teen-age girls in the audience blended their alto and soprano voices in one wild crescendo of sound that rent the rafters," an African American columnist reported from Elvis's hometown of Memphis.[37] A good deal of anecdotal evidence indicates that Elvis was popular among young African Americans during his early years with RCA. While attending the historically black Morehouse College, Julian Bond, who became a civil rights leader in the 1960s and chairman of the NAACP, performed Elvis's "Teddy Bear" as part of a student revue.[38]

What was the audience so excited about? The photographs of Elvis in concert reveal a dynamism that was not unprecedented for fans of African American swing and rhythm and blues, but leaped out in contrast to the polite demeanor of his greatest rival on the teenage hit parade, Pat Boone, who covered many of the same rhythm and blues songs as Elvis. It was the new authenticity versus the old respectability. While Boone came across as the type to bring a date a pink corsage and some reassuring words for the parents about driving safely and returning before curfew, Elvis was a wild card, polite but primal, an uncertain element in an increasingly suburbanized America whose guardians demanded neatly trimmed lawns and expectations to match. Where Boone was conventionally handsome, Elvis was sexy with puckered lips, hooded eyes and falling locks of greased hair reminiscent in some photographs of Rudolf Valentino, the object of female fantasy in the 1920s.

Colonel Parker booked Elvis for a two-week engagement in Las Vegas starting the end of April. Although the city of flaming pink and incandescent yellow neon light became integral to Elvis's image before his death, he was not a good fit for the Venus Room of the New Frontier Hotel in 1956. For Elvis, the Nevada side trip was not entirely a waste of time, even though he neither drank nor gambled. He had the opportunity to meet one of his mother's favorite entertainers, Liberace, who responded to the new star with good humor. The casino audience, however, was unenthusiastic at best. "Las Vegas is a resort for old people," as Tom Wolfe would write in the 1960s, and it was already true in the 1950s. He added, "It is not by chance that much of the entertainment in Las Vegas . . . will recall for an aging man what was glamorous twenty-five years ago when he had neither the money nor the freedom of spirit to indulge himself in it."[39] Time would be Elvis's ally in the conquest of the high-rolling gambling resort. Meanwhile, with his loafers and sport coat and acoustic guitar, and his hillbilly accent, Elvis did not adhere to the Vegas tourists' notion of glamour. "Elvis Presley, coming in on a wing of advance hoopla, doesn't hit the mark here," the entertainment trade paper *Variety* reported.[40] *Variety* had already taken a stand against rhythm and blues and its editors were in no mood to tolerate rock and roll. Among the trade papers, they would be the most consistently hostile to Elvis.

The legacy of Elvis's premature booking in Las Vegas was his discovery of "Hound Dog," or rather, a peculiar version of the song that became his signature. As a rhythm and blues fan, Elvis must have heard the original 1952 recording by Big Mama Thornton, a woman's empowering rebuke of a no-good, sexually voracious man. While roaming the lounges along the strip, Elvis and his band stumbled across Freddie Bell and the Bellboys, performing "Hound Dog" with a more upbeat tempo and a shift in lyrics. According to D. J. Fontana, Elvis heard the Bellboys' "Hound Dog" at the Sands and "learned the lyrics from them. He came on stage one night and told us he was going to sing it."[41]

The "Hound Dog" recording session provided another example of Elvis's perfectionism and intuition. Thirty-five takes were recorded at RCA's Manhattan studio on a hot day with the air conditioning off to keep the whirring air from being heard on the recording. Elvis pondered the various performances at the end of the session in "deep concentration, absorbed and motionless," Steve Sholes recalled. Finally, "he slowly rose from his crouch [on the studio floor] and turned to us with a wide grin, and said, 'This is the one.'"[42]

Attacking Elvis

Elvis's hard-driving rendition was introduced to a wide public on his second *Milton Berle* appearance, one of the faltering program's best-rated episodes that season, overtaking the popular Phil Silvers comedy *Sergeant Bilko* for the first time. Berle was in usual form, kidding Elvis for his bumpkin ways, advising him to "stick to Heartbreak Hotel and stay away from the Waldorf." Elvis's performance of "Hound Dog" that evening touched off what soon became a wild fire of scorn and animosity in the press and segments of the public that threatened to consume his chances of rising higher in an entertainment industry wary of controversy.

The attacks came from all sides and perspectives. Some critics questioned his talent. *Variety* called him a "loose-jointed hillbilly" who was "making monkeys out of real singers."[43] Others supposed he would have an adverse effect on American culture and morals. In another jeremiad, *Variety* called rock and roll, whose public face increasingly resembled Elvis, "suggestive and vulgar, tinged with the kind of animalism that should be confined to dives and bordellos."[44]

Middle-aged critics, already anxious over concerns about juvenile delinquency and the uncertain mores of a society in rapid transition, feared that their children would be lost to a modern pied piper. Because of allegations that he corrupted America's youth, Elvis was brought to the attention of the FBI as early as the spring of 1956, when a Memphis businessman wrote the bureau's director, J. Edgar Hoover, urging him to curb the singer through enforcement of interstate commerce statutes. "There are minds who will scarcely stop short of complete indecency to exploit their wares upon the public, and youth is not able to discriminate between the right and wrong of it," he wrote. Hoover declined to take the recommended action, but the FBI began to maintain a file on Elvis.[45]

The Roman Catholic Church had long tried to impose moral guidelines on popular culture, especially regarding sensuality and the body. The adaptation by Hollywood of the Production Code in the 1930s resulted in part from concerns over the influence of Catholic clergy on censorship boards in cities with large Catholic populations. In 1928, Chicago's Catholic-dominated board snipped 6,000 scenes from Hollywood movies, creating an imperative for the industry to accommodate the Church's concerns.[46] The headline in the Catholic weekly *America*, "Beware Elvis Presley," summed up the argument of Church leaders who feared he was a bad influence on young people. According to the article, "If the agencies (TV and other) would stop handling such nauseating stuff, all the Presleys of our land would soon be swallowed up in the oblivion they deserve."[47] Condemnation came from the top of the American Catholic hierarchy. Francis Cardinal Spellman condemned Elvis's influence on youth from the pulpit.[48] Protestant fundamentalists also lent loud voices to the chorus of recrimination.[49]

The anti-Elvis media coverage was somewhat mollified by the singer's behavior with the press, whose members were as sensitive to their own prerogatives as they were in sensing a good story. He gladly submitted to lengthy interviews and was unfailingly polite and humble, even when flirting with female reporters. The reported contrast between Elvis on stage persona and in person, along with articles showing him as a dutiful son, planted seeds of acceptance in the minds of many older readers. His paradoxical image as a well-mannered rebel was already apparent in the early days of national media coverage.

America's intellectual elite remained unconvinced by Elvis's good manners. Their arguments against the emergence of Elvis and rock and roll were grounded in the work of the Frankfurt School, especially the influential social philosopher Theodor Adorno. The exiled German intellectual assumed that popular culture was the product of a manipulative and dehumanizing entertainment industry, seeking only to sell movies and records the way Detroit sold cars. He worried about the "filthy tide" of pop music and compared fandom to an "addiction."[50] For highbrow critics, this industrialized mass culture aimed for low common denominators in public taste; pop music was by definition moronic and conformist and should be opposed on principle. Because Elvis rose from the South, a region whose working class culture was regarded as a pestilential backwater, the singer was attacked with special umbrage.

The attitude cut across the liberal and conservative intelligentsia. With the example of Nazi Germany at hand, with its manipulation of popular culture in the pursuit of war and mass murder, liberal intellectuals, while keeping a careful profile in the McCarthy era, feared that popular culture could easily become a tool of the right wing. After all, Adorno had already equated popular culture with fascism. Elia Kazan's film *A Face in the Crowd* (1957) was essentially a parable about an evil Elvis, a guitar-playing Southern entertainer played by a malevolent Andy Griffith, whose television-based stardom attracted the interest of rightist politicians. The film echoed the anxiety of critic Dwight MacDonald, who wrote that "the masses are in historical time what a crowd is in space: a large quantity of people unable to express themselves as human beings." He added that their "morality sinks to that of the most brutal and primitive members, its taste to that of the least sensitive and most ignorant."[51]

The right wing feared that Elvis was a Trojan horse for desegregation, a white harbinger of degenerate black culture as the battle for civil rights became virulent. The White Citizens Councils, organized in the South to oppose federal enforcement of school desegregation rulings, attacked rock as "Negro music" that was "designed to force 'Negro culture' on the South."[52] Although Elvis had aroused little attention from the authorities in Jacksonville, Florida, when he twice performed in the city as a rural rhythm act in 1955, the attitude of the city fathers hardened in 1956 as a result of Elvis's new status as the standard-bearer for rock and roll. When he performed a two-day run at Jacksonville's Florida Theater in August, Judge Marion W. Gooding warned the singer not to swivel his hips and threatened to have him arrested for impairing the morals of minors. Elvis restricted his movements to wagging his little finger in subtle mockery of the judge. Elvis told reporters, "I can't figure out what I'm doing wrong. I know my mother approves of what I'm doing."[53]

Despite the upsurge of racist rhetoric and actions from white Southerners who felt threatened by the push to desegregate, the region was not of one mind on Elvis. In July he performed at a Memphis baseball park, crowded with fans despite heat in the high nineties. He was probably sincere in playing on Southern resentment against the East Coast elite. "You know, those people in New York are not gonna change me none," he reassured the audience."[54] That same summer the Mississippi-Alabama Fair and Dairy Show, where he sang in a talent show as a boy, proclaimed "Elvis Presley Day." Mississippi Governor J. P. Coleman, chairman of the Mississippi Sovereignty Commission, founded to stave off civil rights for its black citizens by any means possible, awarded him a "scroll of honor."[55]

The line of criticism that had the least impact at the time but has enjoyed the greatest longevity came from African American activists, charging Elvis with stealing his music from black artists. According to one Harlem columnist, "Bo Diddley should do something about Elvis Prisley [sic], a blond lad who has copied Bo's style to the letter."[56] Like many of Elvis's white foes, they did not appreciate that he was making something new from a variety of American influences.

Grumpiness on the part of the older generation watching their children have fun must have been a factor in the fusillade of complaints fired Elvis's way. Colonel Parker would have appreciated the sales pitch of a Cincinnati used car dealer who promised "to break 50 Elvis Presley records in your presence if you buy one of these cars today." The dealer sold five in one day, meaning that Elvis sold 250 records to an audience that despised him. The Colonel could not have benefited more if he had staged the promotion himself.[57]

"Hound Dog" was the tipping point of all this controversy, and the song's authors were not among the fans of Elvis's rendition. "I didn't like the way he did it," Jerry Leiber said years later. Leiber and his partner, Mike Stoller, began writing rhythm and blues as teenagers, including memorable songs from the 1950s such as "Kansas City," "Yakety Yak," "Poison Ivy" and, later, a number custom written for Elvis whose performance they did enjoy, "Jailhouse Rock." Leiber and Stoller were Jewish kids with East Coast roots who moved to California with their families in the westward migration triggered by World War II. They related to black culture as fellow outsiders in an anti-Semitic society, and grew up in schools where African and Latin American music seeped into their blood. Their experience in crossing the tracks was similar to Elvis's own adventures on Beale Street, yet they did not care for him at first.

"The song is not about a dog; it's about a man, a freeloading gigolo," Leiber explained. "Elvis's version makes no sense to me, and even more irritatingly, it's not the song Mike and I wrote." Leiber and Stoller were pleased, however, by the royalties they received from Elvis's version, and his hit would change the direction of their careers. "By virtue of the Presley cover, we were thrown into the biggest commercial revolution in American music: teenage rock and roll. . . . White teenagers had been listening to some of the rhythm and blues that Mike and I had written and produced. Elvis was the prime example. When the music was sung by one of their own, white teenagers liked it even more. That's understandable. And that's why, in gross terms, rock and roll became a mega-industry while R&B would lag behind," Leiber said.[58]

White teenagers from across the world embraced the incessant beat of Elvis's "Hound Dog." "I saw a cousin of mine dance when I was very young," said David Bowie, who grew up to be one of Britain's signature rock stars of the 1970s. "She was dancing to Elvis's 'Hound Dog' and I have never seen her get up and be moved so much by anything. It really impressed me. The power of music."[59]

The Last Steps to Stardom

"Hound Dog" would figure prominently in Elvis's next televised step into stardom, but this time, the controversy came from his fans, not his detractors. The morning after Elvis's July 1 performance on *The Steve Allen Show*, a new Sunday-night show that was launched as a younger, hipper challenge to the king of variety TV, Ed Sullivan, fans picketed the NBC studio in Rockefeller Plaza, shouldering signs reading "We Want the Real Elvis" and "We Want the Gyratin' Elvis." Their complaint was that the star had not been allowed to shake the night before and was pressed into a mold where he did not fit. By this time millions of young Elvis fans had formed a rebellious conception of him, based largely on television and the chorus of disapproval from parents and the press. Looking across the widening generational chasm, they blamed the old guard that controlled the entertainment industry and most everything else.

Steve Allen was caught in the middle. He wanted the ratings boost Elvis Presley could give him, but weeks before Elvis's scheduled appearance and before his brand new Sunday show had even debuted, he was already under pressure to cancel. "If he does appear, you can rest assured that I will not allow him to do anything that will offend anyone," he told reporters.[60] In those early days of television, a network program's corporate sponsor was the demigod no one could displease, and sponsors played by a cautious rulebook, determined, as Allen put it, not to offend anyone. The carnival subculture of Colonel Parker was a decade or more from overtaking the corporate culture of the networks, which treated their programs as guests in the homes of their targeted middle-class audience.

Allen had already pioneered the TV talk show as the first host of *The Tonight Show*; he was a witty and irreverent comedian and a prolific composer of jazz era pop music; he wrote for *Ebony* magazine and did more "to regularly showcase African American talent" than anyone on network television; yet at 35 he was a man of the previous generation and no friend of the new music called rock and roll.[61] He did not deserve the opprobrium that the first generation of rock critics heaped on him for dressing Elvis in a tuxedo for a skit in which he serenaded a dog with "Hound Dog."[62] From the perspective of the 21st century, the program looks insipid, but so does much of what passed for entertainment in television's early years. For a canny insider like Allen, his words of introduction that night registered his anxiety over displeasing his sponsors. "We want to do a show the whole family can watch and enjoy," he said. After all, television was intended in those days for families of decidedly conservative tastes. Years later, Allen explained: "We thought putting Elvis in formal wardrobe to sing the song was humorous. We also asked him to stand perfectly still, and we positioned a real hound dog on a stool next to him—a dog that had been trained to do nothing but sit and look droopy. I must say Elvis took it quite naturally, and good-naturedly."[63]

Elvis looked uncomfortable for portions of the broadcast, but shrugged off whatever displeasure he felt as just the sort of compromises entertainers made on their way to the top. "He always did the best he could with whatever situation he was given," recalled Jordanaire Gordon Stoker, who backed Elvis on *The Steve Allen Show*.[64]

The next stop on the way up was the gatekeeper of most American homes on Sunday evening, Ed Sullivan, a charmless man with the stiff body language of Richard Nixon who managed to parlay his position as a powerful gossip columnist for the *New York Daily News* and occasional vaudeville impresario into a commanding spot on television. Sullivan had publicly declared that Elvis was out of bounds for his top-rated CBS family show, saying, "He is not my cup of tea." He changed brands quickly when the upstart Allen stole 55 percent of the viewing audience that first Sunday in July, leaving Sullivan with a paltry 15 percent. Within weeks, Sullivan announced he was booking Elvis for three shows in the fall and winter of 1956–1957 for an unprecedented fee of $50,000. The contract represented a significant first step by rock and roll toward the mainstream of American life.

Recovering from an auto accident a month earlier, Sullivan was not on hand to greet Elvis on September 9, the first of the three scheduled performances. The evening's host was the great British actor Charles Laughton. The star of *Mutiny on the Bounty* and *The Hunchback of Notre Dame* was a witty and cultivated man who viewed the occasion with indulgent good humor. Anticipation for the show was phenomenal. Steve Allen, whose success with Elvis made Elvis on Sullivan possible, bowed out for the night. NBC aired a British movie in Allen's time slot. In an age when most homes had only one television set, the eyes of America would be on Elvis. On September 9, the Sullivan show reached 82.6 percent of the television audience or 54 million people, a record that would stand until 1964 when Sullivan presented the Beatles to America.

Elvis was fourth-billed on a program with acrobats, musical comedy, and Broadway singer Dorothy Sarnoff, as an insert patched into the New York-based broadcast by remote from Los Angeles. This time the performance was genuinely Elvis but in censored form. Hedging his bets, Sullivan showed Elvis only from the waist up, truncating his pelvic swivel but allowing much of his dynamism to shine through the fuzzy black-and-white signal. The studio audience went wild, signaling to the rest of America what it was missing on the small screen. Along with his latest number one record, the exuberant "Don't Be Cruel," written by the African American songsmith Otis Blackwell, Elvis performed a ballad from his forthcoming first movie, "something completely different from anything we've done," he told the audience, "Love Me Tender."

The critics and representatives of the old guard continued to despise him. As one high school music teacher wrote to the *New York Times*, "One shudders to contemplate the cultural level of the next generation."[65] Their opinions could not stop the rising tide. Elvis returned to *The Ed Sullivan Show* on October 28, this time with its namesake master of ceremonies presiding. "I can't figure this darn thing out. He just goes like this and everybody yells," Sullivan said, shaking his hip in a gesture of levity. With every vestige of camera fright long evaporated, Elvis was monarchial in confidence yet playful, as if he took the idea of being a rock and roll star in stride. "Teenagers are my life and triumph," he said afterwards. "Ever since I got to be a sort of name I've examined my conscience and asked myself if I led anybody astray even indirectly, and I'm at peace with my conscience."[66]

For his final appearance on *The Ed Sullivan Show*, January 6, 1957, the streets around the studio were closed for many blocks. "I'd say five thousand kids [were] standing around screaming. They had policemen on horses directing, trying to keep the crowd from getting out of control," said Neal Matthews of the Jordanaires. He added that by this time, Elvis employed doubles to distract the mob of fans. "[He would] Send a big black limousine up to the stage door, have somebody that sort of looked like him and dressed like him. All the kids would come over there and Elvis'd slip in the side door."[67]

Elvis shared the program with boxer Sugar Ray Robinson and Carol Burnett, then a rising 23-year-old comedian, but he was the main attraction. Resplendent in a gold lame vest and velvet shirt, Elvis showed a side of himself few outside the South had suspected by performing an old spiritual, "Peace in the Valley," along with rock and roll hits. It would be his last television performance until his return from the service.

The new medium of television was powerful for its ability to reach into homes, exposing millions of Americans to identical images simultaneously through the broadcasts of the three networks. The Colonel appreciated television's role as a promotional tool, yet he recognized that the prestige of being in movies was still greater than TV. Music writer Peter Guralnick speculated that as controversy over Elvis's performances intensified, Parker decided to isolate his client from the relentlessly negative publicity by breaking him into Hollywood. "Elvis's business was communication, after all, and what better way to communicate with his audience all around the world than from the silver screen, where the image always flickered, the candle burned but never flamed—and fame, carefully nurtured, need never go away?"[68]

If so, the Colonel could not have found a more willing partner than his sole client. Elvis was of the last generation to experience the magic of Hollywood's golden age, a time when options for mass entertainment were few. Aside from reading and radio, movies brought people out of their homes and into public spaces. The cinema was a special arena. Whether screened in ornate movie palaces or simple neighborhood bijous, movies were a chance to be alone in the crowd and in the dark, immersed in personal interpretations of the dream world unfolding on the big screen. The coming of television in the 1950s spurred the studios toward spectacles in panorama and colors brighter than reality and impossible to achieve on the small, primitive screens of America's living rooms. For decades Hollywood's stories provided many Americans with their surest guide to socialization in a world of change. The stars were role models. Elvis learned to dream, in part, from the many hours spent in the movie houses of Memphis. He crafted his image from the look of the stars. Elvis wanted to be a popular singer, like Bing Crosby or Dean Martin, and imagined he could reach their level someday. Singing was one thing. He had been doing that since he was a child. Being in movies was something else again, involving an alchemy of transformation, and he entertained dreams of following his favorite singers to Hollywood, where their talent as performers provided the raw material for movie stardom.

As early as March 1956, Parker began soliciting movie work for his client by placing ads in the trade papers. Less than a week after Elvis's debut on Milton Berle, Parker signed a three-movie contract with Paramount Pictures, reserving the right for Elvis to work for other studios. Signing for Paramount was Hal Wallis, the producer of *Casablanca*, who had worked more recently with Elvis's favorite, Dean Martin, in comedies with Jerry Lewis. Elvis's ideas on acting, as expressed just before leaving for Hollywood in August, were remarkably in line with the stance of Marlon Brando and other Method-inspired actors who prized emotional authenticity over polish. "I don't think that you learn to become an actor," he said. "I think you just, maybe you've got a little bit of acting talent and develop it. If you learn to be an actor, in other words, if you're not a real actor, you're false."[69]

Elvis made his cinematic debut with 20th Century Fox in a modest western with a post-Civil War theme, hastily re-titled *Love Me Tender* after the rewritten Civil War-era ballad Elvis sang in the film. The singer was given a supporting role as the youngest brother in a close-knit Southern family. Helming the picture was Robert Webb, considered a competent action director but not an A-List filmmaker. Elvis sang four songs in the otherwise forgettable movie under music director Lionel Newman, the composer for all of Marilyn Monroe's movies at Fox and uncle of songwriter Randy Newman.

Elvis entered Hollywood just as the old studio system was collapsing. During earlier decades, a handful of studios controlled the production and distribution of virtually all significant American movies and dominated the world market. Patterned after Henry Ford's Detroit, the studios were assembly lines with creative teams and staffs of actors who usually kept to a tight production schedule. Most of the movies were considered product, which did not preclude artistry or even personal vision from directors, actors, and writers willing to put their stamp on the vast industrial process.

The old system came to an end in the 1950s after studios were forced through antitrust action to divest their profitable chains of movie theaters, which had ensured a steady revenue flow and control over distribution. Elvis's role in the emerging "new Hollywood" would play out as a vestige of the old order. In the 18 months between coming to Hollywood and leaving for service in Germany, he made four pictures in rapid succession, which were released gradually to keep Elvis in the public eye while he was away in the army.

Elvis impressed everyone as a hard worker, actually memorizing the entire script of *Love Me Tender* before production began.[70] The movie's producer, David Weisbart, who had produced the epochal *Rebel Without a Cause*, compared Elvis's "smoldering appeal for teenagers" to James Dean, adding that he "often expresses the loneliness and yearning of all teenage kids as they break away from childhood and become adults."[71]

At night, Elvis palled around with actors of his generation, including Dennis Hopper, who played one of the hoodlums in *Rebel Without a Cause*, and *Rebel's* co-star, Natalie Wood, a child actor making a smooth transition into an ingénue. She clung to Elvis as they rode the streets of Los Angeles on his motorcycle, drawing curious crowds. She found him incredibly nice and sincere, without a trace of cynicism. "He felt he had been given this gift, this talent, by God," she recalled. "He didn't take it for granted. He thought it was something that he had to protect."[72]

Love Me Tender, which under normal circumstances might have filled the bottom half of afternoon matinees, earned half a million dollars in ticket sales during the first week of release in November. Beating

Elvis faces the dark side of stardom as he testifies in court following a fistfight with young men annoyed at his celebrity. (Library of Congress, Prints and Photographs Division, New York World-Telegram and Sun Newspaper Photograph Collection, LC-USZ62-117770)

it for the number one spot at the box office was a movie of more enduring significance, *Giant*, James Dean's final and posthumous film.

During 1956 several quickie movies were produced to exploit the phenomenon of rock and roll before the fad faded. *Rock Around the Clock* and *Don't Knock the Rock* were silly movies, but contained sterling if staged footage of Little Richard, Gene Vincent, and other early rock and roll stars. Colonel Parker and Hal Wallis had a more traditional career in mind for Elvis, one that referred to his roots in rock and roll as an everyman, American success story, but would not be dependent on a musical trend whose future was unwritten.

Loving You (1957) was his first film for Paramount, his first in color, and the first for which he played the lead role. Cast with reliable character actor Wendell Cory and sultry film noir heroine Lizabeth Scott, Elvis played a version of himself in a fictionalized but recognizable telling of his career story. Scott was an assertive manager of a country band led by Cory; Elvis was the singer who took the band over the top. The plot made allusion to several recent news stories, including an impatient Memphis filling station manager who took a swing at Elvis and a 19-year-old boy who picked a fight in a Toledo hotel, blaming the singer for the breakup of his marriage because his wife carried Elvis's picture in her wallet. An undercurrent of male resentment had become another of Elvis's woes, along with the impossibility of finding privacy. His motorcycle rides with Natalie Wood were fodder for UPI wire service stories. During his first Hollywood sojourn, Elvis turned to a nocturnal life style that would continue for years to come.

"The only time he could get out, really, was at night," said Jordanaire Neal Matthews. "He'd rent a skating rink or a movie house and rent it for the whole night . . . That's the only entertainment he had. He couldn't go out."[73]

From a filmmaking perspective, Elvis's most memorable movies were made before his military service. The plot of *Jailhouse Rock* (1957) reinforced a mythology of Elvis by portraying him as the sullen but good-hearted rebel, a young man from the lower ranks whose roots were in country but whose future was in rock and roll. The movie's showstopper was a riveting dance number choreographed around the Leiber-Stoller song "Jailhouse Rock." Shot on a multitiered stage set, Elvis's moves would be mirrored down the decades in Michael Jackson's famous moonwalk.

Colonel Parker essentially auditioned Leiber and Stoller for their role as purveyor of songs to the King of Rock and Roll. They were unimpressed with him. "He told dozens of canned jokes. I can't remember any of them except that they weren't funny. But it didn't matter that we didn't laugh, because the Colonel wasn't really conscious of us . . . he was more interested in putting on his own show than getting to know us," Leiber recalled.[74]

Meeting Elvis was another matter altogether. Leiber commented on his "physical beauty," finding his presence riveting, his "shy smile and quiet manner . . . were disarming."[75] Just as striking was his musical depth. "There wasn't any R&B he didn't know," said Stoller, who worked up an arrangement for the song during the recording session while Leiber gave Elvis vocal cues.[76]

Soon enough, Leiber and Stoller were given the sense that Parker wanted Elvis to keep his distance from them. Black, Moore, and Fontana had already begun to feel dispensable in the Colonel's eyes, a situation that would cause the band to separate from Elvis in 1957. "Don't take it personally," Stoller recalls a comment by one of Elvis's Memphis friends, part of the nucleus of what became the Memphis Mafia. "It's just that the Colonel doesn't want Elvis to develop a friendship with anyone but us."[77]

Elvis was granted a delay in reporting to the army, allowing him to complete work on his current Hollywood assignment, *King Creole* (1958). Although the movie included several Leiber-Stoller numbers, it

Teenage fans personalize an Elvis movie poster with their own messages to the star. (Library of Congress, Prints and Photographs Division, New York World-Telegram and Sun Newspaper Photograph Collection, LC-USZ62-114912)

was not another rock and roll production but was the closest Elvis ever came to making an A-List film. Michael Curtiz, who had helmed many of Warner Brothers' most beloved movies before leaving the studio over a salary disagreement, directed *King Creole*. The Hungarian-born filmmaker had worked in nearly every genre, directing *The Adventures of Robin Hood, Santa Fe Trail, Mildred Pierce, Angels with Dirty Faces, Yankee Doodle Dandy*, and most memorably, *Casablanca*. Set in the steamy old districts of New Orleans, *King Creole* is an unsentimental film noir concerning a young singer, played by Elvis, working his way up against the high odds of poverty and organized crime.

Walter Matthau, playing a crime kingpin, headed the first-rate supporting cast. Elvis favorably impressed him. "He was very intelligent," Matthau said. "Also, he was intelligent enough to understand what a character was and how to play the character simply by being himself through the means of the story."[78]

At the start of 1956, the music called rock and roll was still an inchoate concept, distinguished from its rhythm and blues roots largely on the say-so of promoters such as Alan Freed, hoping to market the music to a wider, younger, biracial audience. When first exposed to Elvis, Freed did not even consider him to be a rock and roll singer, saying that he "really sings hillbilly, or country-and-western style."[79] By year's end, Elvis had stolen everyone's thunder and had defined this nascent music according to his own image. He became the king of rock and roll largely through the Colonel's perceptive use of television and in the process, changed the music's direction. From now on it would not simply be rockabilly or rhythm and blues for white teenagers, but something that a Memphis columnist came close to defining as early as 1955 in a review of Elvis. "He has a white voice [and] sings with a negro [*sic*] rhythm which borrows in mood and emphasis from country style."[80] It was a sound that straddled several boundaries in American society.

The music, however, was only part of the message Elvis delivered. To the fans that watched on television, spellbound by a performance whose apparent authenticity amplified dissatisfaction against the anxiety and caution of postwar America, Elvis became a liberating symbol. He was able to reach even deeper emotional chords than James Dean or Marlon Brando through the power of music with an incessant beat.

Elvis enjoyed this music and appreciated the enthusiasm of fans who, voting with their dimes and dollars, made him the citizen king of youth culture, but like many of his critics, he seemed to believe that rock and roll was a fad, another Lindy hop or Hula-hoop craze, and would shed few tears as it passed. "When it's gone, I'll switch to something else. I like to sing ballads the way Eddie Fisher does and the way Perry Como does. But the way I'm singing now is what makes the money. Would you change if you was me?" he demanded.[81]

Notes

1. Arnold Shaw, *The Rockin' '50s* (New York: Hawthorne, 1974), p. 111.

2. Alan Freed, notes to *Alan Freed's Top 15* (End Records, n.d.).

3. Shaw, *Rockin' '50s*, pp. 105–106.

4. Shaw, *Rockin' '50s*, p. 108.

5. *Scholastic Magazine*'s Institute of Student Opinion, 1956, cited in Ed Ward, Geoffrey Stokes, and Ken Tucker, *Rock of Ages: The Rolling Stone History of Rock & Roll* (New York: Rolling Stone Press, 1986), p. 123.

6. Ed Ward, *Rock of Ages*, p. 116.

7. Richard Schickel, *Brando* (New York: Thunder's Mouth Press, 1999), p. 64.

8. Quoted in Max Lerner, *The Unfinished Country: A Book of American Symbols* (New York: Simon & Schuster, 1959), pp. 373, 375.

9. Glen Jeansonne and David Luhrssen, "Elvis: Rock 'n' Roll's Reluctant Rebel," *History Today*, August 2007, pp. 36–37.

10. "Who is Elvis Presley?" *The Enthusiast*, May 1956.

11. David Dalton and Ron Cayen, *James Dean American Icon* (New York: St. Martin's Press, 1984), p. 73.

12. Shaw, *Rockin' '50s*, p. 138.

13. Shaw, *Rockin' '50s*, p. 142.

14. Susan VanHecke, *Race with the Devil: Gene Vincent's Life in the Fast Lane* (New York: St. Martin's Press, 2000), p. 14.

15. Howard A. DeWitt, *Elvis: The Sun Years, The Story of Elvis Presley in the Fifties* (Ann Arbor, MI: Popular Culture Ink, 1993), pp. 295–296.

16. Chuck Crumpacker, jacket notes to *Elvis* (RCA, date LPM 1382). Crumpacker was the pitchman.

17. Peter Guralnick, *Last Train to Memphis: The Rise of Elvis Presley* (Boston: Little Brown, 1994), pp. 244–245.

18. *The Comprehensive Country Music Encyclopedia* (New York: Times Books, 1994), p. 352.

19. Jerry Hopkins, *Elvis: A Biography* (New York: Simon & Schuster, 1971, p. 121.

20. Guralnick, *Last Train*, p. 235.

21. Guralnick, *Last Train,* pp. 185–186.

22. Guralnick, *Last Train,* p. 229.

23. Albert Goldman, *Elvis* (New York: McGraw-Hill, 1981), pp. 170–171.

24. Chet Atkins with Bill Neely, *Country Gentleman* (Chicago: Henry Regnery, 1974), p. 186.

25. Jonathan Cott, *Back to a Shadow in the Night: Music Writings and Interviews, 1968–2001* (Milwaukee, WI: Hal Leonard, 2002), p. 349.

26. Atkins, pp. 188–189.

27. Hopkins, pp. 127–128.

28. "Chart Toppers of 1958," *Billboard*, December 15, 1958, p. 44.

29. "Hot 100 of the Year," *Billboard*, October 20, 1959, p. 78.

30. Guralnick, *Last Train*, p. 252.

31. For a lucid account of the development and proliferation of the drug, see Nicolas Rasmussen, *On Speed: The Many Lives of Amphetamine* (New York: New York University Press, 2008).

32. Hopkins, pp. 125–126.

33. Grelun Landon, "Elvis Presley: The Tape Keeps Rolling," RCA publicity material, 1984.

34. Joe Hyams, "The Highest Paid Movie Star Ever," *New York Herald-Tribune*, May 16, 1957.

35. Red West, Sonny West, and Dave Hebler as told to Steve Dunleavy, *Elvis: What Happened?* (New York: Ballantine, 1977, pp. 120–121.)

36. Michael Winship, *Television* (New York: Random House, 1988), p. 174 ff, p. 182.

37. *Pittsburgh Courier*, December 22, 1956.

38. Brian Ward, *Just My Soul Responding: Rhythm and Blues, Black Consciousness, and Race Relations* (Berkeley: University of California Press, 1998), p. 137.

39. Tom Wolfe, "Las Vegas (What?). Las Vegas (Can't Hear You! Too Noisy). Las Vegas!!!!" in *Smiling through the Apocalypse: Esquire's History of the Sixties*, ed. Harold Hayes (New York: McCall, 1970), pp. 211, 213.

40. "A Howling Hillbilly Success," *Variety*, April 30, 1956.

41. Robert Johnson, "These are the Cats Who Make Music for Elvis," *Memphis Press-Scimitar*, December 15, 1956.

42. Guralnick, *Last Train,* pp. 298–299.

43. "The Elvis Presley Story: He's Making Monkeys out of Singers," *Variety*, May 9, 1956.

44. "Rock'n'Roll Pros and Cons," *Variety*, June 13, 1956.

45. James L. Dickerson, *Colonel Tom Parker: The Curious Life of Elvis Presley's Eccentric Manager* (New York: Cooper Square Press, 2001), p. 77.

46. Mark A. Vieira, *Sin in Soft Focus: Pre-Code Hollywood* (New York: Abrams, 1999), p. 13.

47. "Beware Elvis Presley," *America*, June 23, 1956.

48. "Spellman in Plea to Save U.S. Youth," *New York Times*, October 1, 1956.

49. "Baptist Minister's Sermon vs. Elvis: 'He'll Hit the Skids,'" *Variety*, October 17, 1956.

50. Theodor Adorno, trans. E. B. Ashton, *Introduction to the Sociology of Music* (New York: Seabury Press, 1976), pp. 15, 22.

51. Dwight MacDonald, "A Theory of Mass Culture," in *Mass Culture: The Popular Arts in America*, ed. Bernard Rosenberg and David Manning White (Glencoe, IL: Free Press, 1957), pp. 69, 70.

52. "White Council vs. Rock and Roll," *Newsweek*, April 23, 1956.

53. "Elvis—A Different Kind of Idol," *Life*, August 27, 1956; *Jacksonville Journal*, August 10, 1956.

54. Robert Johnson, "Elvis Sings and Thousands Scream," *Memphis Press-Scimitar*, July 5, 1956.

55. Jerry Hopkins Collection, Special Collections, University of Memphis.

56. "Backstage with Clyde Reid," *Amsterdam News*, March 31, 1956.

57. Shaw, *Rockin' '50s*, p. 154.

58. Jerry Leiber and Mike Stoller with David Ritz, *Hound Dog: The Leiber and Stoller Autobiography* (New York: Simon & Schuster, 2009), pp. 94–95.

59. Quoted in Shaw, *Rockin' '50s*, pp. 152–153.

60. *New York Journal-American*, June 13, 1956.

61. Ben Alba, *Inventing Late Night: Steve Allen and the Original Tonight Show* (Amherst, NY: Prometheus, 2005), p. 96.

62. For an especially vitriolic attack, see Dave Marsh, *Elvis* (New York: Rolling Stone Press, 1982), pp. 102, 106.

63. Hopkins, p. 138.

64. Guralnick, *Last Train*, p. 294.

65. Henry Feldman, letter to *New York Times*, September 30, 1956.

66. Gordon Sinclair, "Sinclair Says Elvis 'Fine Lad,' Hopes to Last for 40 Years," *Toronto Star*, October 29, 1956.

67. Hopkins, p. 177.

68. Guralnick, *Last Train*, pp. 384–385.

69. Guralnick, *Last Train*, p. 323.

70. Harold Stone, "Meet Mr. Rock'n'Roll," *Top Secret*, November 1956.

71. Jules Archer, "Is This Unassuming Rocker America's Newest Rebel?" *True Story*, December 1956.

72. Goldman, pp. 220.

73. Hopkins, p. 170.

74. Leiber, p. 111.

75. Leiber, p. 111.

76. Leiber, pp. 112–113.

77. Leiber, p. 121.

78. Guralnick, *Last Train*, p. 451.

79. John A. Jackson, *Big Beat Heat: Alan Freed and the Early Years of Rock & Roll* (New York: Schirmer, 1991), p. 143.

80. Robert Johnson, "Suddenly Singing Elvis Presley Zooms into Recording Stardom," *Memphis Press-Scimitar*, February 5, 1955.

81. Kays Gary, "Elvis Defends Low-Down Style," *Charlotte Observer*, June 27, 1956.

7

G.I. Blues

Elvis Presley never forgot his family or his roots. The year 1956 was one of increasing momentum, a blur of incessant motion between concerts and television, recording sessions and movie sets. Despite the unceasing demands of celebrity and his enjoyment of the perquisites of stardom, Elvis remained anchored to his origins. He admitted that he called his parents daily, because "my mother is always worried about a wreck, or me getting sick."[1] His income allowed his father, Vernon, to retire at age 39 from the paint factory where he had worked on the production line. Vernon's role as major domo to his son began at this time. As Elvis explained in a television interview, "he can take care of all my business and look after things while I'm gone." In keeping with the most ancient economic precepts of family life, Elvis added, "Anything that is mine is theirs."[2]

By the end of 1955 he purchased a modest house in Memphis for himself and his parents; a few months later, in March 1956, Elvis scrambled up the next step of the ladder into the American dream by buying a single-story frame house on Audubon Drive, a subdivision on the east side of Memphis. It was not a palace but comfortably middle class, the sort of dwelling promoted as attainable and idyllic in glossy magazine spreads of the era, and constructed by the thousands in the postwar housing boom. Elvis was photographed lounging on a metal patio chair on the brick terrace near the pool, which he added after moving in. When he was in town, he occupied one of the three bedrooms, which was famously furnished in pink, from the wallpaper to the nightstand, to the bed skirts and even the telephone.

Elvis had houseguests, among them, an 18-year-old dancer from Brooklyn whom he met on a break in Las Vegas, Dottie Harmony.

She was one of a carousel of women Elvis dated in 1956 and 1957. Although she spent two weeks in Elvis's bedroom, he slept in a room down the hall. She recalled that he read the Bible with her every night and tried to convince her to give up smoking and drinking. Gladys was a friendly presence. Harmony remembered that she puttered in the tomato patch out back, and cooked Elvis's favorite dishes, a combination of Old South and *Ladies Home Journal*, including black-eyed peas, greens, and coconut cake. "It's a little hard to believe, but we mainly just hung around," Harmony said. We would go out to the airport and watch the planes take off. One night we stopped and helped an old man change a tire." Although he "was just the nicest guy," Harmony recalls that Elvis was jealous when she caught the eye of other men and ripped the phone from the wall during one angry outburst.[3]

Elvis had the lot ringed with an iron fence to keep out the curious, but nothing, not even the signs posted by the city declaring, "NO PARKING, LOITERING OR STANDING," could prevent hundreds of fans from gathering at the gate. According to one story, the disgruntled neighbors offered to pool their money to purchase the Presley house in order to restore quiet and rid themselves of their famous, if unwanted, neighbor. Elvis supposedly replied by offering to buy all of the surrounding properties.[4]

The problem became moot in spring of 1957 when Elvis decided to move to more secluded parts on the outskirts of town. The mansion called Graceland sat on over 18 acres in the town of Whitehaven, which would be annexed by Memphis in 1969. The house was a columned Georgian colonial, two stories tall, owned by a prosperous family of landowners and set back from the highway in a grove of towering oaks. Shortly after it was built in 1939, Graceland was described as possessing a "fine heritage from the past in its general feeling of aristocratic kindliness and tranquility."[5] The five-bedroom house was Tara on a modest scale, an embodiment in limestone of Margaret Mitchell's nostalgic, best-selling novel of the Old South, *Gone with the Wind*. For Elvis, becoming master of Graceland was probably less a fantasy of rising into the planter aristocracy, which may have been inconceivable to someone of Elvis's origins in the Southern class system, than a fantasy of emulating the old Hollywood stars who dwelled in gated mansions called Pickfair and Falcon Lair. Although fans would continue to gather outside the walls of Graceland, the estate was spacious enough to afford its owner the privacy he craved. Elvis's uncles, Travis and Vester, worked as guards at the gate, keeping female fans at bay.

The house itself was large enough to accommodate the singer's parents and beloved grandmother, Minnie May Presley.

Soon enough, Elvis began to put his own stamp on Graceland. "Every year he does somethin' different to it," said the Memphis Mafia's Alan Fortas years later. "When he originally bought it, it was just a reg'lar old house. He put in a floor in the basement, paneled the walls, all his gold records are hanging there. He's got a pool table, a record player, used to have a slot car track there, any kind of entertainment you want." Like a Hollywood star, he also installed a movie theater with a professional projector and screen. A swimming pool was added, the living and dining room walls were painted purple with gold trim, and he made his bedroom "the darkest blue there is, with a mirror that will cover one entire wall."[6] Like Michael Jackson's Neverland Ranch decades later, Elvis attempted to create a world largely self-contained, designed according to his ideas of high style and to accommodate his pastimes and the life he dreamed of as a child.

For a night out with girlfriends, his entourage, and visitors, Elvis would rent the Rainbow Rollerdrome to "play football on skates," Fortas recalled. He also reserved the Memphis Fairgrounds to ride the Ferris wheel and the rollercoaster, or to play "dodge-'ems," as the locals called bumper cars. The host treated his guests to all the hotdogs, hamburgers, and popcorn they could eat. "Elvis being from Memphis, it was a special favor to him through the Park Commission, I'm sure," Fortas said of the private nocturnal parties in the amusement park. "They would keep four or five operators there who could operate the different rides."[7] On other occasions, Elvis rented the Whitehaven High School football stadium for night games. "Sometimes he had about thirty players," said his old friend from Lauderdale Courts, Buzzie Forbes. "He had the team he sponsored here in one of the amateur leagues, plus Red West and some of the guys from Rick Nelson's team in Hollywood, people he'd bring back with him."[8]

Uncle Sam Calls

Months before Elvis accepted the deed to Graceland, and during all the nights of harmless if secluded fun with his associates, the singer labored under the knowledge that the life he had come to enjoy would almost certainly be put on hold. Like most American boys, Elvis had fulfilled his legal obligation by registering with the Selective Service upon reaching his 18th birthday, and along with millions of his peers, he was assigned a number in the draft lottery. By the end of 1956, his number came up. As early as January 4, 1957, shortly before his final appearance on *The Ed Sullivan Show*, Elvis drove past a cluster of waiting reporters and photographers to Kennedy Veterans Hospital in Memphis for a preliminary physical examination. He passed and was classified 1-A, immediately available for service.

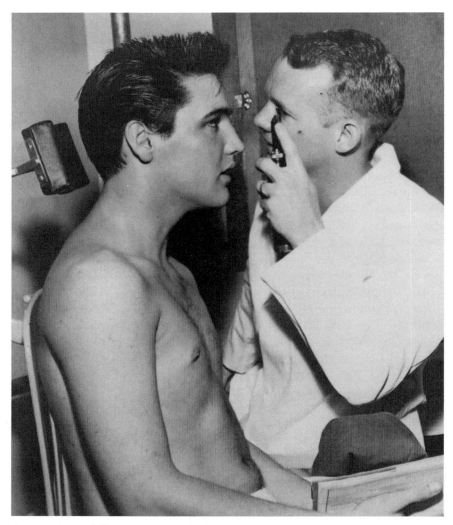

A bare-chested Elvis is deemed fit for service by U.S. Army physician Fred Jeff Burford. (Library of Congress, Prints and Photographs Division, New York World-Telegram and Sun Newspaper Photograph Collection LC-USZ62-117769)

Elvis was drafted at an unusual point in the history of American conscription, when compulsory service was neither a matter of national emergency nor the focus of dissent. Violence met the introduction of the draft during the Civil War in many parts of the country; police raids and vigilantism enforced conscription legislation in World War I. Isolationists opposed Franklin D. Roosevelt over reintroducing the draft in 1940, fearing it was another inexorable step toward American involvement in World War II, but after Pearl Harbor, objections came only from the political fringes.[9] The nation largely embraced the concept of the citizen soldier at war for democracy, never imagining that conscription would continue beyond the end of hostilities. However, the postwar necessity of garrisoning the defeated nations of Germany and Japan, and rising tensions with the onset of the Cold War, brought an extension of the draft. Conscription kept the ranks full during the Korean War (1950–1953), a conflict accepted by most Americans with resignation rather than enthusiasm. The draft continued after the armistice with North Korea, justified largely by the extensive network of American defense treaties and bases spread across the world like a picket fence to contain Communism. The antidraft protests of the Vietnam era were a decade in the future.

The bureaucracy that classified Elvis as 1-A was a familiar facet of American life in the 1950s, affecting choices in education, career, and family for millions of young men. The draft system derived from the Selective Service Act (1940) and its postwar amendments was based on the principle that military duty "should be shared generally in accordance with a fair and just system of compulsory military training and service," and was apportioned through a complicated set of quotas. The system was administered by local draft boards, appointed by the federal government from candidates proposed by governors and adjutant generals of the states. The boards enjoyed wide latitude in determining the fitness or deferment of individuals chosen by the national Selective Service lottery. An inductee must have reached the age of 19 and could be called to serve in the army for a tour of 21 months.[10]

Although many men classified as 1-A chose to volunteer for other branches of the service over being drafted into the army, military duty was more of a pervasive threat than an inevitability during the Eisenhower administration. In the 1950s, two-thirds of men registered for Selective Service avoided serving; from 1948 to 1953, draft boards rejected 52 percent of prospective inductees for failing achievement tests or physicals, and for other reasons.[11] Complaints were heard among politicians and pundits that "the draft pool had suffered a massive leakage of manpower through deferments" granted to individuals for educational, professional, and family reasons.[12] Moreover, the number of men required for active duty declined as Eisenhower reduced the size of the military through a mixture of fiscal conservatism and prioritizing strategic nuclear weapons. The army shrank in numbers from 1.5 million in 1953 to only 873,000 in 1960, Elvis's final year of service. In 1957, when Elvis was drafted, only 139,000 men were called up.[13]

The numbers lend superficial support to the charge that Elvis was singled out for the draft "to put him back in his place."[14] However, a closer examination undermines the notion of a conspiracy against rock and roll's biggest star. The lottery system by which Elvis's number was selected operated according to the mechanics of chance. Once his number was chosen, Elvis, regardless of whether he had remained a truck driver or became a controversial celebrity, was a prime candidate for the army. He suffered from none of the physical disabilities, such as flat feet, poor eyesight, or hearing, that won many candidates the rejected status of 4-F. He was sufficiently well educated to pass the achievement test. He was unmarried, childless, out of school, and uninvolved in any occupation deemed essential to the national defense.

Draft boards were usually filled with white men of conservative inclinations, culled from the ranks of the American Legion and the chamber of commerce.[15] The chairman of the board that drafted Elvis, Milton Bowers, was a Memphis industrialist, Democratic Party politician, and cog in Boss Crump's political machine. While one could suspect that Bowers and his fellow board members were happy to send Elvis to the army in the hope of "straightening out" a young man who for them symbolized cultural miscegenation and moral license, they were handed no other option under the Selective Service laws than to draft him. Elvis met all requirements for a 1-A classification. Some men in his situation requested deferment on one ground or another, and some local boards were generous. Elvis accepted his fate without public complaint.

Other than asking Elvis to pick up his induction papers in person rather than receive them in the mail, the Memphis board treated the singer no differently than any other young man caught in the Selective Service lottery. Like most 1-A's, Elvis was given many months' notice that his induction was likely. Having passed his preliminary physical in January, he finally received his letter from the president, welcoming him to the military, a few days before Christmas 1957.[16]

Elvis's reaction in December differed little from many Americans of his time, bifurcated between a public and genuine show of patriotism, and private thoughts of disappointment. To the press, he was grateful for "what this country has given me. And now I'm ready to return a little."[17] To his associates, he sang a different tune. According to his friend George Klein, Elvis was upset and anxious. "Damn, what are we going to do?" he reacted upon sharing the president's induction letter. "The Colonel says we might could [sic] get a deferment to make *King Creole*, but he says I probably got to go."[18]

Apparently, Elvis had endured months of waiting to hear from the draft board with the balm of denial, consoling himself that maybe he could still escape the demands of military service. He relied on Parker's judgment and, as was sometimes true, the Colonel's strategy for accepting the rulings of the Selective Service was not without justification. The contradictory attitude of the American public toward celebrities and the draft had been established during World War II, when "citizens wanted movies and baseball to continue, but no deferments for stars of screen or diamond."[19] The Colonel worried that even the appearance on Elvis's part of shirking his civic obligation would erupt in a firestorm hot enough to reduce his enterprise to ashes. He was even careful to avoid any perception that Elvis accepted special privileges from the military. While waiting final word from the draft board, the U.S. Navy approached the singer, proposing an "Elvis Presley Company" recruited in Memphis, and the U.S. Air Force wanted him to tour recruiting stations. The Colonel was insistent. Elvis would enter the army like any dutiful citizen called to the colors, trading without complaint his crown as King of Rock and Roll for a private's stripes, and his defiant hairdo for a regulation crew cut.[20]

Only one concession was requested. Both Paramount studio and Elvis asked for a 60-day deferment to finish work on *King Creole*. Elvis humbly insisted that he was ready to serve, but asked for the delay for the sake of the movie studio, "so those folks will not lose so much money, with all they have done so far." He concluded his letter with a polite Merry Christmas to Bowers and his colleagues. On December 27, the board unanimously granted Elvis's request.[21]

For the press, Elvis maintained a stoic front. "I'll do whatever they tell me, and I won't be asking no special favors," he said at a Hollywood party hosted by producer Hal Wallis to celebrate the completion of *King Creole*.[22] Back home, he told reporters only that his mother "hates to see her son go in service."[23]

For Elvis's fans, news of his induction came as a staggering blow.[24] Some politicians, pundits, and veterans complained that his deferment for *King Creole* amounted to favoritism for a young man who deserved no favors.[25] "With all due respect to Elvis, who's a nice boy, we've drafted people who are far, far more important than he is," said Bowers, deflecting criticism from both sides.[26] Many reporters could think of nothing cleverer than gleeful speculation on the effect of a military haircut on Elvis, as if, like Sampson, he could be shorn of his potency.

Just Another Soldier

Elvis's journey from stardom to soldier of Uncle Sam began March 24 on a chartered Greyhound bus with other Memphis recruits bound for Fort Chaffee, Arkansas. It turned into a parade of flashing camera bulbs, questions shouted by reporters, and the screams of young girls. The attention paid to the celebrity recruit was not unprecedented. When the King of Hollywood became Private Clark Gable at the Los Angeles Federal Building in 1942, "MGM and the War Department conspired to make it a front-page event, with more than a hundred reporters, photographers and newsreel cameramen covering."[27] Fans gathered when the bus stopped for lunch at the Coffee Cup diner in West Memphis, Arkansas. Accounts differ on whether dozens of girls surged at Elvis and tore his clothes, or a mob of two hundred prevented the recruits from leaving the bus, forcing the driver to bring food back from the restaurant.[28]

Although some soldiers at the Fort Chaffee boot camp jeered,[29] the military command did its best to accommodate the unusual attention paid to the army's new recruit. Elvis could have been placed in the Special Services, whose recent members included Eddie Fisher and Vic Damone, a pair of drafted pop singers who served their country as entertainers during the Korean War. As with Elvis, they were healthy and eligible, and there was nothing their well-connected managers could do to thwart Uncle Sam.[30] Elvis could have fulfilled his military obligation by singing at military bases, appearing at bond and blood drives, and in television recruiting ads, much as Fisher had done with a little help from his manager, Milton Blackstone.[31] The Colonel would hear none of it, insisting that his client did not want "the easy way out."[32] Elvis understood that Parker's decision was meant to dampen the firestorm of adult opposition, an angry chorus of recrimination that neither Fisher nor Damone had to endure. The Colonel thought that Elvis's long-term success would depend on the acceptance of what was then the adult market, never imagining how Elvis's fans in the rising baby boom generation would alter that market forever.

Greeting the Greyhound at the entrance to Fort Chaffee were hundreds of fans and curious military dependents who came for a glimpse of Elvis. The fans were not admitted to the post, but Colonel Parker and more than 50 reporters and photographers were already waiting. Elvis made his bed in the barracks several times for the benefit of photographers and treated the attention cheerfully, drawing the line only at signing autographs while "in ranks."[33] Elvis's first G.I. breakfast, an all-American repast of eggs, sausage, toast, and coffee, was thoroughly documented by photojournalists. The battery of tests administered to the recruits was off-limits, but the press remained to witness Elvis's first lunch.[34] The climax of the day for story-hungry reporters came at the base's barbershop, where Elvis's famous locks were shorn. The barber, a lean Oklahoman called James Peterson, obligingly posed for the photographers, holding his electric clippers aloft before going to work. Afterward, Elvis repaired to a phone booth to call his parents.[35]

Elvis was quickly posted to Fort Hood, Texas, a huge military reservation whose flat, open plain was ideal for the unit he would train with, the 2nd Armored Division, which General George S. Patton had led during World War II. At the inevitable press conference upon his arrival, Elvis emphasized that he was just another G.I. Fort Hood's commanding officer, General Ralph R. Mace, elaborated, "I feel the Army has shown that it is trying to make an ordinary soldier out of Mr. Presley, the same as all the other fine young men who are with us, and that he has been afforded no special privileges." The general added that Elvis "has conducted himself in a marvelous manner."[36]

The attention Elvis received from the media and fans was different only in degree from Eddie Fisher's basic training at Food Hood a few years earlier. "At mail call one guy got two letters, another guy got four; I got 4,500. My mail was delivered to the barracks in potato sacks," Fisher recalled. "I was constantly receiving long-distance telephone calls. Photographers were sneaking around trying to get pictures of me."[37]

Colonel Parker was surprised to learn that Fort Hood's public information officer was a woman of high rank. Lieutenant Colonel Marjorie Schulten became responsible for managing the circus Parker inevitably brought to town, to sort through the two thousand fan letters and numerous phone calls Elvis received during his first week on the base, and to cultivate the image of Elvis as a patriotic G.I. doing his duty no differently than any other conscript. There is no evidence that Elvis presented her with any public relations headaches. He was by all accounts an exemplary recruit, earning medals for marksmanship and occasionally serving as drummer boy when his company marched on the parade ground. He endured the increasingly good-natured ribbing of his barrack mates. "Maybe you'd like some rock'n'roll instead of reveille," was a typical remark.[38]

Killeen, where Fort Hood was located, was a typical army town. It was a short walk from the gates to the pawnshops, where many privates supplemented their slender pay of $78 a month, and to the bars, strip joints, and prostitutes where they spent their money. Elvis probably spent little time in the Killeen tenderloin. The army in accommodating its most famous conscript broke no regulations, yet the circumstances of his service bore only little resemblance to the lot of the average soldier. Elvis's wealth insured a way of life distinct from his fellow G.I.s. Army regulations permitted an enlisted man to live off base with his dependents, which usually meant his wife and children. Since Elvis's parents were dependent on him for their living, he was able to rent a trailer near the base and then a comfortable house in town, where he lived with Gladys, Vernon, and Minnie Mae during his three-month training. One of his close associates, Lamar Fike, also stayed with the family. Occasionally his steady girlfriend, Anita Wood, a teenage Memphis television personality, came to visit. On weekends Elvis, Fike, and other friends often tore off to the brighter lights of Dallas and Fort Worth. He returned to Graceland on a June furlough. The press reported that "Swarms of teen-age devotees had made elaborate plans to welcome the rock'n'roll singer on his first visit home" but that Elvis "for the most part played a game of hide-and-seek."[39]

Before Elvis could complete his stint at Fort Hood, Gladys fell ill with stomach complaints and was brought to a Memphis hospital, where she died on August 14, apparently of liver failure.[40] Elvis and Vernon were emotionally unprepared for her death. She was only 46 years old. Reporters found father and son at Graceland, and a poignant photograph was taken of them sitting on the steps of their home, weeping and trying to console each other. "Tears streamed down his cheeks," a reporter wrote of Elvis.[41]

Following the funeral, Elvis returned to Killeen with Vernon, Minnie Mae, Lamar Fike, and other associates. Red West recalled that everyone worked hard to cheer up Elvis, especially through singing and playing guitar.[42]

Elvis admires the pin on the dress of one of his younger fans, Judy McCreight. (Library of Congress, Prints and Photographs Division, New York World-Telegram and Sun Newspaper Photograph Collection LC-USZ62-117768)

Within a month, Elvis was on his way overseas. Crowds of fans gathered to watch the troop train carrying Elvis and more than three hundred other soldiers deployed to Germany in the regular rotation of troops assigned to the front gates of NATO in the Cold War. Colonel Parker and the U.S. Army arranged for a much-publicized farewell extravaganza at Brooklyn's sprawling Military Ocean Terminal, where Elvis boarded the troopship *General Randal* for his Atlantic crossing. Reporters with flashbulb cameras and the more cumbersome cameras of the newsreels and television networks recorded Elvis as he walked up the gangplank. Although his gear had already been stowed on board, the army thoughtfully supplied him with a spare duffle bag to stage a photogenic send-off for the press. The cooperative military brass even provided a pretty member of the Women's Army Corps, Mary Davies, for Elvis to kiss for the camera. At the press conference, Elvis told reporters that he would never sell Graceland "because that was my mother's home." He insisted once again that he was a good role model for his young fans. "I've tried to live a straight, clean life, not set any kind of bad example." Elvis also offered one of the best succinct explanations ever proposed for his remarkable success. "Well, sir, I've been very lucky . . . The people were looking for something different, and I was lucky. I came along just in time." The army band struck up an incongruous version of "Tutti Frutti" and other rock and roll hits as Elvis boarded the troopship to an uncertain future.[43]

Elvis was ordered to the 3rd Armored Division, which had taken part in the liberation of Germany from the Nazis, and by then had been integrated with a few black soldiers. He was stationed in the town of Friedberg, not far from Frankfurt, and was photographed often in uniform, usually looking distracted and faraway. Although posted to the army's Ray Barracks, Elvis recreated his life in Killeen by establishing a household near the base for Vernon, Minnie Mae, and his close friends, Lamar Fike and Red West. They maintained a familiar home life complete with Southern cooking and music. The round robin of women continued in Germany as it had back home.

When on duty, Elvis served as a jeep driver in a scout platoon. He spent stretches of his tour beyond the reach of the press on maneuvers at the Czech border, which would have been front line in the European theater of World War III. The motto on the 3rd Armored's unit patch, "SPEARHEAD," described the role it might have played in war. "We are at a training area for 50 days and believe me it's miserable," Elvis wrote Alan Fortas in one of the few surviving letters the singer ever penned. "It's cold and there is nothing at all to do up here . . . Boy it will be great getting out. I will probably scream so loud they'll make me stay 2 more years."[44] He brought no dishonor to his uniform.

Around Friedberg, he was accessible and easy to befriend. "How do you do, Ma'am. I'm always happy to meet someone from England," he said by way of introduction to Dorothy Lewis, a British clerical employee of the U.S. Army. She recalled: "A lot of people try to make out that he was stupid, but he was not. He was quite intelligent. He asked me a lot of questions about England . . . He had a very inquiring mind."[45]

The most important legacy of Elvis's German sojourn was his future wife, Priscilla Beaulieu, the stepdaughter of a U.S. Air Force captain stationed nearby. She was only 14 when she began dating Elvis. Priscilla claimed that her stepfather overcame his understandable hesitance over letting her date the world's most controversial entertainer only after Elvis called on their home in uniform with Vernon in tow. In her memoirs, they cuddled in his bedroom but he never touched her sexually. When she told him she was in love, Elvis supposedly replied, "Daddy keeps reminding me of your age and that it can't be possible," adding, "only time will tell."[46]

Anyone who thought that Elvis would fade into olive drab obscurity once he left his homeland for Europe was unaware of the excitement Elvis had already stirred overseas. He arrived in one of Europe's traditional ports of embarkation for America, Bremerhaven, at the start of October. He was met at the Columbus Quay, where tens of thousands of Europeans had sailed for America over the previous century, by fifteen hundred fans, along with television and newsreel cameramen, and reporters "representing virtually every major European periodical and newspaper."[47]

During this period the U.S. State Department sponsored international "goodwill" concert tours featuring American jazz artists such as Benny Goodman, Duke Ellington, Louis Armstrong, and even a leading figure from jazz's avant-garde, Dizzy Gillespie.[48] Granting official sanction to this music was a remarkable idea from the Foreign Service, mirroring the transparent glass design of postwar American embassies designed by modern architects such as Walter Gropius and Richard Neutra, to promote the image of America as an enterprising and open society, unlike its dour opponents in the Soviet bloc. The program generated controversy, as the musicians sometimes spoke out against U.S. policy. Louis Armstrong even cancelled his State Department concert dates in the Soviet Union, denouncing the government for "the way they are treating my people in the South."[49]

Elvis would not have been the State Department's ideal of a suitable ambassador of American culture, yet for many younger people around the world, he served just that purpose. "Our bomb shelter generation revolted against the stiff, straight old ways," said German disc jockey Werner Goetze, speaking of the generation whose childhood included the devastation of Allied air raids and the collapse of the Third Reich.

Like their peers in the United States, German teenagers were flush with newfound middle class prosperity, "the Economic Miracle" as the recovery from the war was called in Germany. They felt themselves to be distinct from their elders and embraced rock and roll as a generational totem. "They threw away their lederhosen for blue jeans and started standing and walking like cowboys," Goetze added.[50]

Of course, even Hitler had been an avid fan of cowboy novels by the German author Karl May, and the precedent for young Europeans adopting the latest musical fashions from the United States was well established. Ragtime was embraced in Great Britain and Continental Europe before World War I, eventually influencing composers such as Debussy and Stravinsky. The reaction by the old guard was similar to the opposition against rock and roll. British dramatist J. B. Priestly condemned ragtime as "the menace to old Europe, the domination of America, the emergence of Africa."[51]

In succeeding decades newer forms of African American music developed enthusiastic cults of fans and even became part of the cultural mainstream in many European nations. Dixieland jazz, swing, bebop, and cool jazz all found their adherents. In Britain, a composite of American folk, blues, and country influences called "skiffle" swept teenagers in the 1950s and laid the foundation for many rock bands that would dominate music a decade later, including the Beatles and Led Zeppelin. Not every young fan of African American music was enamored of Elvis; the tendency toward musical elitism that would characterize "underground" or "alternative" rock in future decades was already apparent in the teenagers who would become the Rolling Stones, who preferred actual black recordings to what they deemed as Elvis's copies.[52] The old guard European devotees of African American music were not, on the whole, pleased with the meteoric rise of Elvis, agreeing with a British magazine article by the esteemed American jazz critic Leonard Feather, who worried that music was "dragged down considerably by the success of Elvis Presley and his ilk."[53]

The BBC and most other state-supported broadcasting corporations were slow to admit rock and roll to their programming, but they had competition for the ears of younger listeners. Although the clarity of its signal in the United Kingdom varied with the weather, Radio Luxemburg sold air time to British record labels to program new rock and roll releases.[54] The half-dozen radio stations of the American Forces Network established in Germany after World War II to entertain U.S. servicemen garrisoning the occupied zone were audible as far away as London and southeast England. At first, the AFN focused on jazz.[55] As one G.I. stationed in Germany during the 1950s recalled of the network, "As the new rock'n'roll began to dominate the popular music charts in the States, it quickly gained a correspondingly larger portion of the programming time scheduled for popular music at AFN."[56]

Elvis's recordings reached a young audience throughout Europe and even into the Eastern Bloc, although he would never perform a concert on the continent.[57] The popularity of rock and roll among the "bulge generation," as baby boomers were known in the United Kingdom, has been attributed to "an audience hell-bent on emancipation from social responsibilities in the depressed and depressing aftermath of the war."[58] By 1956, England had its first rock and roll star, an ersatz Elvis called Tommy Steele,[59] followed by young singers with names such as Marty Wilde, Billy Fury, and Cliff Richard. France produced its Elvis in the form of Johnny Halliday. The first generation of European rock and roll has been generally dismissed as artificial and derivative, lacking genuine local roots and any understanding of the social and musical origins of rock in the United States. Elvis's presence in Europe during this period was incidental and had no influence on the future development of European rock. Great Britain would become the world center for the new music in the 1960s with barely more than a backwards nod to the King of Rock and Roll. In the United Kingdom, American rockabilly singers such as Eddie Cochrane and Gene Vincent left a more indelible impression than in the United States and rivaled Elvis for influence.

During his stint in the service, the Colonel and RCA managed Elvis's career in the States, supplying the hunger of fans by repackaging material that had already been released as singles on albums, and doling out new releases from a dwindling cache of leftover Elvis recordings. In March 1959, "A Fool Such as I" became his 19th consecutive million-selling recording, followed in June by "A Big Hunk o' Love," which became number 20. During that same summer, *King Creole* and *Love Me Tender* were rereleased in theaters as a double feature, and RCA assembled an elaborately packaged album of previously issued tunes, *A Date with Elvis*, complete with a 1960 calendar with Elvis's discharge date highlighted and a "personal message" from the singer. Parker worked to keep Elvis's name in the news, even when there was nothing new to report.

Even the older generation capitalized on Elvis's absence. The 1960 Broadway musical *Bye Bye Birdie* was a parody of Elvis in the form of Conrad Birdie, a swivel-hipped singer inducted into the army to the agony of his fans. The musical's author, Charles Strouse, had little understanding of rock and roll. The show produced one memorable pop song, "Put on a Happy Face," and introduced an unknown actor called Dick Van Dyke in the role of a music promoter. It was transformed into a 1963 movie, *Bye Bye Birdie*, which has survived as a staple in the repertoire of high school musicals and is occasionally revived on Broadway.[60]

When asked just before his induction if he would be able to regain his star status after his tour of duty, Elvis replied, "I wish I knew."[61] The survival of rock and roll was itself in doubt, written off for dead at a time when Elvis was in the army, Chuck Berry in prison, Buddy Holly had died in a plane crash, Little Richard returned to the church, and Jerry Lee Lewis was in disgrace for marrying his 13-year-old cousin. During his German sojourn, he expressed doubt. "I can't compete with these new singers," he would say when a performance on the radio or a jukebox caught his ear.[62] Elvis had no way of knowing the deep impression he had already made on the next generation of musicians and artists of all kinds, everyone from filmmaker David Lynch to actor Nicholas Cage, who would devote the best moments of his career emulating the image of Elvis from his early, pre-army movies as a brooding young man living within a code of honor.[63]

Notes

1. Carlton Brown, "A Craze Called Elvis," *Coronet*, September 1956.

2. From a 1956 television interview with *New York Herald Tribune* gossip columnist Hy Gardner, quoted in Patsy Guy Hammontree, *Elvis Presley: A Bio-Bibliography* (Westport, CT: Greenwood Press, 1985), p. 176.

3. Peter Guralnick, *Last Train to Memphis: The Rise of Elvis Presley* (Boston: Little Brown, 1994), pp. 361, 376.

4. Billy Smith, "The Audubon House," *The Record*, June 1979.

5. *Memphis Commercial Appeal*, October 27, 1940.

6. Jerry Hopkins, *Elvis: A Biography* (New York: Simon & Schuster, 1971), p. 188.

7. Hopkins, pp. 187–188.

8. Hopkins, p. 194.

9. See Glen Jeansonne, *Women of the Far Right: The Mothers' Movement and World War II* (Chicago: University of Chicago Press, 1996).

10. *U.S. Statutes at Large*, vol. 54 (September 13 and September 16, 1940), pp. 885–887; *Selective Service under the 1948 Act* (Washington, DC, 1951), p. 26.

11. George Q. Flynn, *The Draft, 1940–1973* (Lawrence: University Press of Kansas, 1993), pp. 141, 152.

12. Flynn, pp. 137–138.

13. U.S. Department of Commerce, *Historical Statistics of the United States* (Washington, DC, 1975), vol. 2, pp. 1141, 1143.

14. Dave Marsh, *Elvis* (New York: Rolling Stone Press, 1982), p. 122.

15. Flynn, p. 24.

16. Guralnick, *Last Train*, p. 443.

17. *Memphis Press-Scimitar*, December 21, 1957.

18. Guralnick, *Last Train*, p. 443.

19. Flynn, pp. 54–55.

20. Guralnick, *Last Train*, pp. 442–443; Hopkins, pp. 194–195.

21. *Memphis Commercial-Appeal*, December 28, 1957.

22. Vernon Scott, "Elvis at Home, Awaits Clippers," *New York World-Telegram*, March 15, 1958.

23. James H. White, "Elvis Back in Town with Sideburns Clipped and the Army on his Mind," *Memphis Commercial-Appeal*, March 15, 1958.

24. Hopkins, p. 196.

25. Hopkins, p. 197.

26. Hopkins, p. 197.

27. Warren G. Harris, *Clark Gable: A Biography* (New York: Harmony, 2002), p. 261.

28. Hopkins, p. 202; Guralnick, *Last Train*, p. 462.

29. Hopkins, p. 205.

30. Eddie Fisher with David Fisher, *Been There, Done That* (New York: St. Martin's Press, 1999), p. 41.

31. Fisher, p. 31.

32. Hopkins, p. 211.

33. *New York Journal-American*, March 25, 1958.

34. Hopkins, p. 205.

35. Hopkins, p. 206.

36. Hopkins, p. 207.

37. Fisher, p. 42.

38. Hopkins, p. 209; Alan Levy, *Operation Elvis* (New York: Henry Holt, 1960), pp. 59ff.

39. UPI, June 2, 1958.

40. Guralnick, *Last Train*, p. 473.

41. UPI, August 14, 1958; *Memphis Press-Scimitar*, August 14, 1958.

42. Red West, Sonny West and Dave Hebler, as told to Steve Dunleavy, *Elvis: What Happened?* (New York: Ballantine, 1977), p. 155.

43. Ren Grevatt, "On the Beat," *Billboard*, September 29, 1958; A recording of the press conference was released as *Elvis Sails*, RCA, 1958.

44. Patsy Guy Hammontree, *Elvis Presley: A Bio-Bibliography* (Westport, CT: Greenwood Press, 1985), p. 31.

45. Hammontree, p. 32.

46. Priscilla Beaulieu Presley with Sandra Harmon, *Elvis and Me* (New York: G. P. Putnam's Sons, 1985), pp. 22, 31, 35ff.

47. Guralnick, *Careless Love: The Unmaking of Elvis Presley* (Boston: Little Brown, 1999), p. 9.

48. See Penny M. Von Eschen, *Satchmo Blows up the World: Jazz Ambassadors Play the Cold War* (Cambridge, MA: Harvard University Press, 2004).

49. *New York Times*, September 19, 1957.

50. Hopkins, p. 221.

51. Michael Watts, "The Call and Response of Popular Music," in *Superculture: American Popular Culture and Europe*, ed. C. W. E. Bigsby (Bowling Green, OH: Bowling Green University Press, 1975), p. 125.

52. Philip Norman, *Sympathy for the Devil: The Rolling Stones Story* (New York: Linden Press/Simon & Schuster, 1984), p. 45.

53. Leonard Feather, "Boom Year for Jazz, Pops, R&R," *Melody Maker*, December 15, 1956.

54. Gordon Thompson, *Please Please Me: Sixties British Pop, Inside Out* (New York: Oxford University Press, 2008), p. 78.

55. Thompson, pp. 81, 174; Watts, p. 128.

56. Richard C. Helt, "A German Bluegrass Festival: The 'Country-Boom' and Some Notes on the History of American Popular Music in West Germany," *Journal of Popular Culture* 10 (Spring 1977), pp. 821–832.

57. Hopkins, p. 225.

58. Watts, p. 130.

59. Thompson, p. 11.

60. Charles McGrath, "50 Years Older, 'Birdie' Returns to the Nest," *New York Times*, October 11, 2009.

61. White, "Elvis Back in Town."

62. As recalled by Dorothy Lewis, Hammontree, p. 33.

63. Greil Marcus, *The Shape of Things to Come: Prophecy and the American Voice* (New York: Farrar, Straus & Giroux, 2006), pp. 106, 175.

8

Spinout

On March 3, 1960, two thousand fans waved goodbye to Sergeant Elvis Presley at the tarmac of Frankfurt's Rhine Main Airbase.[1] Upon returning to America at McGuire Air Force Base in New Jersey, he was greeted by thousands of fans, the Colonel, music publisher Jean Aberbach, and Nancy Sinatra, who bore a gift from her famous father of a pair of ruffled tuxedo shirts "along with Frank's regards."[2] The gift was probably Sinatra's way of telling the kid to clean up his act.

The Colonel had been busy while Elvis was in Germany. He forced RCA to accept new terms in fulfillment of contractual obligations through movie recordings. He also obtained an increased salary for Elvis plus a share of the profits from film producer Hal B. Wallis.[3] The Colonel stayed in constant communication with fan clubs and show-business people, burnishing Elvis's image in their eyes. And that improved image of a more mature young man who gained stature through the military service would help make possible a guest appearance on Sinatra's television program, which would stimulate the King's return to the large screen. A summit with Frank Sinatra, representing nothing less than a rapprochement between the generations, was the perfect place to start. The deal was announced with Elvis enroute from Germany.[4] In preparation for the television special, and to ensure fresh material was available as quickly as possible, Elvis headed into RCA Studio B in Nashville two weeks after his discharge, producing a number of worthy releases.

The first, "Stuck on You," was shipped to retailers within 72 hours of the March 20 session and sold most of its 1.4 million advance orders. Elvis was firmly in charge at the recording session, and especially relished "A Mess of Blues," a song written by a pair of Jewish, New York rhythm and blues songwriters, Doc Pomus and Mort Shuman. Lamar

Fike, who had met Pomus and Shuman, gave a demo for "A Mess of Blues" to the singer.[5]

Since leaving for the army, Elvis's voice had gained an octave in range, becoming an expertly polished instrument, but the *New York Times* panned as "drab and lackluster" his first post-army LP, *Elvis Is Back*, in May of 1960.[6] Elvis had changed during his service, and the question was whether the change was for better or worse. In 1977, upon hearing the news of his death, John Lennon would echo a common sentiment by saying, "Elvis died in the army."[7]

The coupling of Frank Sinatra and Elvis Presley raised many eyebrows and much curiosity. In 1957, during an interview with a Paris magazine, Sinatra had condemned rock and roll: "It is sung, played and written for the most part by cretinous goons . . . it manages to be the martial music of every side-burned delinquent on the face of the earth . . . it is the most brutal, ugly, desperate, vicious form of expression it has been my misfortune to hear."[8] Sinatra, who only a decade earlier had sent teenage girls into spasms of ecstasy, felt petulant as the train of history moved on and left him on the platform clutching the baggage of his past.[9] Elvis had replied respectfully and astutely to Sinatra's criticism. "He has a right to say what he wants to say. He is a great success and a fine actor, but I think he shouldn't have said it. He's mistaken about this. This is a trend, just the same as he faced when he started years ago."[10]

Why would Sinatra, the self-professed enemy of rock and roll, have agreed to Elvis's performance on his show? Some have speculated it was at the urging of his own little rock and roller, daughter Nancy. There was even a backdoor tie between Sinatra and Elvis through Nancy's fiancée, singer Tommy Sands, a Tom Parker client before the Colonel decided to concentrate exclusively on Elvis.[11]

More likely, the decision was made by his head, not his heart. After a promising start, ratings for Sinatra's previous 1957–1958 TV series dropped to a "pitiful low" and became "the least looked at network show in his time period," according to Hearst columnist Jack O'Brian.[12] It may have been ominous that the Sinatra program was used by Ford Motors to introduce the Edsel, an innovative car that became the automobile industry's most infamous failure in the market place. Sinatra's show had been cancelled, and after sitting out a year, in order to fulfill the remaining portion of his contract with ABC, he came back in 1959 with a series of bimonthly specials. More than likely, Sinatra agreed to host a "welcome home" party for the King of Rock and Roll at the urging of network executives and sponsors in response to his poor performance on the small screen. The Colonel arranged for Elvis's appearance to expose him to a wider audience, "safe and palatable for adult consumption," sans sideburns and pompadour.[13] The Colonel's agreement with the network called for Elvis to be paid $125,000, more than Sinatra himself.

ABC's Frank Sinatra Timex Special ("Welcome Home Elvis") aired on May 12, 1960, with such Rat Pack associates as Sammy Davis Jr., Peter Lawford, and Joey Bishop, and daughter Nancy Sinatra on hand.[14] According to Nancy, both her father and Elvis were initially nervous at the taping, but not intimidated. Sinatra was courteous, and Elvis was always courteous in public, especially with his elders. He was welcomed home by Sinatra while still in his army uniform, but by the show's end he would be in tuxedo, singing a duet with the host. Elvis joined the cast in the opening by joining in on "It's Nice to go Traveling." Later in the show, Elvis would sing his new releases "Fame and Fortune" and "Stuck on You." Those solo presentations were followed by the tuxedo-clad host and guest in a duet of each other's material. Sinatra sang "Love me Tender," while Elvis performed "Witchcraft." Although *Variety*, always hostile to Elvis, complained that the show "did not generate a quarter of a million dollars worth of excitement," Sinatra got the boost in ratings he wanted (a 41.5 percent share of the time slot viewers), and Elvis's presentation surpassed any expectations of the Colonel, RCA, and Hollywood.[15]

Back to Hollywood

From the start, Elvis wanted to be a movie star, playing a character he fashioned for himself from his comic books and the stories he absorbed in the darkness of the movie houses he haunted in Memphis. "When Elvis first went out to Hollywood, he was tremendously excited about being an actor. He wanted it more than anything. More than being a singer," recalled the Memphis Mafia's Marty Lacker.[16] Elvis carried the manner of movie idols such as Marlon Brando and Tony Curtis to the stage, making sure not to smile too much, or at least, fashioning the smile into a semi-sneer. "You can't be a rebel if you grin," he said.[17] For his part, Colonel Parker decided, correctly, that Elvis needed to be seen as well as heard to be truly appreciated. Television was too small for the King, and the Colonel made sure his fans would pay for the privilege. His first move after Sinatra was to restart Elvis's movie career.[18]

Elvis could have enjoyed a more artistically satisfying career in Hollywood had he been guided by a manager with a broader view of his potential. Even before his induction, the Colonel interfered with plans to cast his client in *A Walk on the Wild Side*, an A-List project based on Nelson Algren's novel and eventually filmed by director Edward Dmytryk.[19] According to rumor, Parker vetoed starring roles for Elvis in such esteemed films as *Thunder Road, West Side Story*, and *Midnight Cowboy*.[20] The Colonel is also supposed to have turned down a movie in which Elvis would have played his hero, James Dean.[21]

Instead of becoming the star of A-List films, Elvis occupied himself with a series of musicals that have been categorized as a genre unto itself, "the Elvis films."[22] Metro Goldwyn Mayer, Elvis's first movie home, saw great box office success in the 1940s through the 1950s with movie musicals such as *An American in Paris* and *Singing in the Rain*, a fact that would not have escaped Colonel Parker in the pursuit of a movie career for his client. Parker no doubt found a congenial partner in Elvis's producer, Hal Wallis. The more assertive Jerry Lewis castigated Wallis's narrow adherence to formulaic filmmaking and blamed him for the mediocrity of some of his Wallis-produced comedies with Dean Martin.[23]

Elvis's post-army movies drew the severest criticism yet made the most money. Wallis claimed that he used their reliable revenue stream to finance quality, dramatic productions with stars such as Richard Burton or Peter O'Toole. "In order to do the artistic pictures, it is necessary to make the commercially successful Presley pictures," he said.[24] In the case of Allied Artists, the money Elvis generated saved the studio from bankruptcy.[25] Of his 27 feature films during the 1960s, four could be categorized as westerns, the oldest recognizable genre in American film, and the remaining 23 were simply Elvis films, referred to by the singer as "travelogues," their content confined to a rigid formula.

The formula was grounded on tried and true Hollywood elements, repeated and varied only according to each movie's geographic or historical setting. Versions of Vernon and Gladys Presley turned up in many of the parental roles; the figure of the Colonel could also be perceived. Several of the movies were set at fairs or carnivals with Elvis as a performer or carnie, settings and situations comfortable to Parker. Most Elvis films featured their star as a single man, full of Southern charm, chased by girls, and rarely tied down. He was a bit of a troublemaker, but with a golden heart. There was often a fistfight in which Elvis defended someone's honor; his character is proven innocent of wrongdoing and all conflicts are brought to a positive resolution.

The protagonist was working class but ascending in prosperity, often through his love of music. There was usually an adult woman, self-employed or in a managerial capacity, along with a woman-child in the mode of Priscilla.

During the 1960s, Elvis films were produced on an assembly line with low budgets, tight deadlines, and a quota of three movies a year. The arrangement made millions of dollars for Elvis, the Colonel, and Jean and Julian Aberbach, owners of Hill and Range, the publisher of the songs Elvis sang in the movies. His scripts were marked with placeholders for the tunes and sent to Hill and Range's staff of writers, "who competed with each other to fill as many slots as they could."[26]

Contrary to popular misconception, Elvis worked with many reputable people in Hollywood during the 1960s. Norman Taurog, who directed many of the musicals starting with *G.I. Blues* (1960), was a Hollywood veteran, an Oscar winner for *Skippy* (1931). Clifford Odets, one of the American stage's leading dramatists in the 1930s, wrote the screenplay for the Elvis romp *Wild in the Country* (1961). Dolores Del Rio, visible since the 1920s as exotic or ethnic women in Hollywood pictures, played Elvis's mother in *Flaming Star* (1961). The screenwriter of *Girls! Girls! Girls!* (1962), Edward Anhalt, went on to win an Oscar for *Becket* (1964). Director George Sidney enjoyed a long career in MGM musicals from *Anchors Aweigh* (1945) and *Show Boat* (1951) through *Bye Bye Birdie* (1963) before directing *Viva Las Vegas!* (1964). The musical director for *Kissin' Cousins* (1964), composer Fred Karger, had been Marilyn Monroe's singing coach. Many but not all of the artists working with Elvis were in the autumn, if not the winter, of their careers. He had few opportunities to collaborate with the rising generation of new talent in filmmaking.

Elvis's first movie after returning from the service, *G.I. Blues*, was a transition film, a fantasy account of his previous two years. Already, Elvis bristled at the image being fashioned for him by the Colonel with the help of Hal Wallis. The soldier he played in *G.I. Blues* was not the outcast or rebel Elvis wanted to play on screen, but "cheerfully domesticated, a conventionally bland Hollywood stick figure."[27] As with all of his forthcoming movies, the plot surrendered pride of place to the notion of Elvis as the embodiment of hoary American ideals of social mobility coupled with the post-*Playboy*, prefeminist notion of the male libido unleashed. In his 1960s musicals, Elvis embodied a populist vision of Hugh Hefner's swinging bachelor. His characters could be found in hot spots such as Acapulco and Hawaii, but lacked the urbanity of James Bond or the jazz aficionado playboys of Hugh

Hefner's early years. Cast as a tank crewman in Germany, Elvis participates in a bet to win a date with a hard-to-get nightclub singer played by Juliet Prowse, who in real life was Frank Sinatra's girlfriend. Paramount's press department eagerly spread rumors of an Elvis-Prowse-Sinatra love triangle.[28]

Financially, if not artistically, *G.I. Blues* was unassailable. It reached number two in *Variety's* weekly ranking of top-grossing movies and was number fourteen at the box office for 1960. The soundtrack went to number one and spent 111 weeks on the *Billboard* charts.

Elvis's next movie was a socially conscious western, *Flaming Star* (1960). Cast as a victim of bigotry, a half-breed caught between white and Indian worlds, Elvis was granted a serious role originally written for one of his heroes, Marlon Brando. Beginning in the 1950s, the image of American Indians in westerns became more positive and often contained a progressive message as "the conflict between cowboys and Indians became a covert commentary on race relations."[29] *Flaming Star* was significant at a time when the civil rights movement made nightly headlines. Elvis was pleased with his role, telling a press conference at Graceland that he hoped his next movies "won't be rock and roll pictures, 'cause . . . you can only get away with that for so long. I'm thinking in terms of, I'd like to do a little more of a serious role. Because my ambition is to progress as an actor."[30]

Respected critics nodded in approval over his performance in *Flaming Star*. "It is the depth of feeling he reveals that comes as such as surprise," according to the *Saturday Review*.[31] Director Don Siegel, whose resume included the 1950s science-fiction classic *Invasion of the Body Snatchers*, and writers Nunnally Johnson, who had authored the screenplay for *The Grapes of Wrath*, and Clair Huffaker devised a sophisticated set of variations on western genre conventions. Elvis sings, but *Flaming Star* is no musical; his brief performance is integrated into the story and comments on his character's subtle marginalization as a mixed-race person in America. Like the sort of roles he loved to play, Elvis was an outcast in this film.

When *Flaming Star* proved less popular at the box office than *G.I. Blues*, the Colonel decided to push musicals at his client. The genre seemed an economically efficient way to merge Elvis's dual careers as singer and actor by focusing his recordings on soundtrack albums for his movies. The arrangement might have worked better had Parker shown any taste or sensitivity in the material he chose. Instead, Elvis grew increasingly alienated from his own career. A note of cynicism was heard in Elvis's voice as early as 1960, when he said of his movies, "All they're good for is to make money."[32]

Viva Las Vegas (1964) was the standout among the two-dozen Elvis musicals of the 1960s. Much of its success can be credited to costar Ann-Margret, who graduated from a screen role in *Bye Bye Birdie*, which spoofed Elvis, to playing opposite the real King. In *Viva Las Vegas* she was vixen, vamp, and, in all respects, a female Elvis Presley, "his alter ego," a cast member recalled.[33] The chemistry worked. "An electricity from the two charges the crew with alertness," *McCall's* magazine reported from the set in Las Vegas.[34] The press reported "romance off-stage between the couple."[35] *Time* magazine called *Viva Las Vegas!* "wholesome mindless spontaneity."[36]

As always, the Colonel was counting pennies, disturbed by the expense of making a Hollywood movie with some aspirations of quality. Elvis's movies were rigidly budgeted to ensure maximum profitability for the Colonel and his client. *Viva Las Vegas* went over budget and, lacking the ability to distinguish one picture from another unless they were faces on U.S. currency, Parker was determined to prevent Elvis from ever making another expensive film.[37]

The music was of higher caliber than the norm of Elvis films, largely because of songwriter Doc Pomus's contributions, including the frenetic rock number "Viva Las Vegas" and one of Elvis's finest jobs as a ballad singer, the jazz-tinged "I Need Somebody to Lean On." Along with the sexuality of Ann-Margret and Elvis, *Viva Las Vegas* worked because, like the city that was both its setting and a virtual character, the movie aptly depicted "every American fantasy of innocence and lust, flawless beauty and easy money, good times and charmed lives."[38] In a light-hearted way, Elvis and the movie proclaimed Las Vegas as the gaudy ideal of a nation suffused with consumerism and a hunger for money and distraction.

Biographer Bobbie Joe Mason's remark on Elvis's military service, "Long stretches of dull . . . routine alternated with adolescent binges," also applies to his post-army movie career.[39] Elvis came to dislike Hollywood for its association with his sinking self-esteem as an entertainer, which only caused his outsider's insecurity as a country boy in the city of dreams to flare up. He felt most at home in Memphis with his people, and while shooting movies, brought along his family, whether kinfolk or the surrogates of the Memphis Mafia, who provided a little bit of home. Not willing to be confrontational, he would present a Cadillac, motorcycle, or ring as an apology for bad behavior with friends. He disliked firing inept or even dishonest individuals. On the other hand, he sometimes promoted conflict within the Memphis Mafia to combat the frustration and boredom he often felt with his career and his circle of companions.[40]

Many of Elvis's movies depict the struggle of upward mobility into a higher economic, if not social class, paralleling the singer's own experience. Reflected in the fun house mirror of Hollywood fantasy was the rising postwar economic tide that lifted many poor, rural, or otherwise marginalized Americans. The view of economic uplift, with individuals moving up through hard work and a pinch of luck, was as old as Horatio Alger and fundamental to the American mythology of Elvis and his fans. However, the individual autonomy suggested by these myths was compromised by the Colonel's controlling hand, especially as Elvis retreated from the outside world and behind the fences of Graceland.

Court of the King

Originally a reaction to the dark side of celebrity with its mob scenes of fans and incessant intrusion by the press, his isolation only increased during the 1960s. If Elvis needed something, it was delivered; the role of his surrogate family, like the retinue of a feudal baron, was to entertain and to serve. He had easy access to amphetamines and barbiturates for stimulation and rest, and provided them to his followers like a well-meaning but irresponsible pharmacist. Elvis's personal physician, George Nichopoulos, was amazed at his patient's knowledge of the contents of the *Physicians Desk Registry*.[41] Like many doctors and patients then and now, Elvis minimized the side effects and gave no thought to the body's reaction to cocktails of pharmaceuticals. In the absence of his mother, many boundaries on his behavior had fallen away. Elvis took up drinking, breaking with the strictures of his childhood religion.

When he returned to the United States, Elvis brought the 17-year-old Priscilla to Memphis. In her account, he once again won over her reluctant parents by promising he would watch over her and see that she finished Catholic high school. "He said I'd always be chaperoned and that he'd take care of me in every way. Declaring his intentions honorable, he swore that he loved and needed and respected me."[42] She was the unsullied virgin he would marry, set aside for his own as he pursued any other woman who caught his eye. In keeping with the playboy ideal of the 1960s, Elvis was liberated from consummating sex only in marriage, but the women who fulfilled his desires too easily were condemned to be discarded like yesterday's toys.

Elvis has a little fun with his image as master of ceremonies at a charity event, 1961. (Library of Congress, Prints and Photographs Division, New York World-Telegram and Sun Newspaper Photograph Collection LC-USZ62-117771)

Unknown to the public, Priscilla lived in Graceland, cared for by Vernon and Elvis's grandmother, while Elvis attended to his career. When he was home, she rode on the back of his motorcycle, watched movies late at night in rented cinemas, and went shopping with him on

Union Avenue after the stores were closed to the public. To the press, Elvis said she was "just a friend."[43] Their relationship was kept quiet while Elvis waited for Priscilla to grow up, molding her into his "ideal woman" with a spooky determination reminiscent of James Stewart's character in the Alfred Hitchcock classic of male obsession, *Vertigo*. In the words of one biographer, it appeared that he was trying to "make her resemble himself, as though he could fabricate his missing twin."[44] Elvis kept the promises he made to her parents. He proposed to Priscilla at Christmas time in 1966 and married her in the fantasy setting of Las Vegas's Aladdin Hotel on May 1, 1967; their only child, Lisa Marie, was born on February 1, 1968.

Elvis purchased a 160-acre cattle ranch near Graceland, across the state line in Walls, Mississippi. Naming it the Flying Circle G, the property became a retreat for Elvis and Priscilla as well as friends and family. He bought everyone a house trailer, and played at being a cattle rancher, a cowboy like one of his characters in the movies. The Circle G was an expensive hobby, worrisome to his bookkeeper, Vernon, who complained of his son's spendthrift ways, and to the Colonel, who murmured darkly that they would all go broke.[45] As the 1960s raced to its conclusion. Elvis's movies were not selling tickets as briskly as before.

For his stays in Hollywood, Elvis leased a Frank Lloyd Wright dwelling in Bel Air, designed in an Oriental style and owned by the Shah of Iran.[46] According to Lamar Fike, "It was very modern, which Elvis liked . . . He hated antiques of any kind. He said, 'I grew up with antiques.'"[47] Elvis furnished the women's dressing room with a two-way mirror, evidence of his growing fascination with voyeurism.[48]

Bel Air was the site of what was perhaps the most storied encounter in popular culture. If Elvis's appearance with Frank Sinatra was his summit with the past, he met the future in the form of the Beatles. The Colonel and the Beatles' manager, Brian Epstein, were determined that the King of Rock and Roll and the young usurpers would meet. While the Beatles were excited by the prospect, Elvis had been postponing the moment. Certainly, the publicity would harm neither of them; the Beatles would be able to pay homage to an early influence, and the King could benefit from some residual fan carryover.

It was an uncomfortable group of people that converged on the afternoon of August 27, 1965, at Elvis's Bel Air house, especially Elvis, who behaved with sullen indifference. According to legend, John Lennon good naturedly tweaked him with the question, "Why don't you go back to making rock'n'roll records?" Elvis distractedly replied, "It's my movie schedule. It's so tight."[49] Envy must have colored Elvis's response to the new stars. The critics even praised the Beatles for their movies. He was also aware that his days of dominating the charts had ended. Elvis's last number one record was "Good Luck Charm" (1962). Of the 48 number one songs from 1964 through 1965, 21 were by British artists, 10 of them by the Beatles.[50]

Evidence of Elvis's growing disgust with the direction of his career can be discerned in his movie performances. He became less concerned with even a superficial attempt at lip-synching. Fake musicianship resulted in discrepancies for anyone with an ear for music. In *Blue Hawaii* (1961), the crying sound of a steel guitar was heard in a performance scene, but no steel guitar was visible. Worst of all were scenes in which Elvis played a four-string bass guitar instead of the six-string lead guitar the plot called for. Sound and visuals were disconnected. A Hollywood low point was averted when Elvis finally put his foot down during the filming of *Harum Scarum* (1965). According to Lamar Fike, he refused Parker's orders to add a talking camel to the story.[51]

Elvis's usual response to the Colonel was to sullenly defer to him as an authority figure, the way lower class Southern whites had been taught for generations to defer to their bosses. Occasionally, Elvis acted against Parker's wishes. He supplemented the cheaply produced soundtrack albums the Colonel insisted upon with recordings for RCA that allowed him to explore his desire to become a great pop singer in the manner of Dean Martin. Elvis even wrote one of the songs he sang, the lovelorn "You'll Be Gone." Jordanaire Gordon Stoker, who sang backup on many sessions in the 1960s, recalled that Elvis maintained his professionalism even when the songs the Colonel sent to Elvis were threadbare. "He always tried to make the best out of any situation," Stoker said. "Sometimes he'd walk over to us and say, 'Man, what do we do with a piece of shit like this?'"[52]

In 1959, the Colonel decided that Elvis would not accept a role in the movie version of the Broadway musical *Lil' Abner*. He did not want Elvis sharing the spotlight with other singers.[53] Perhaps more importantly, he had no ownership in the production, which was based on Al Capp's syndicated comic strip, a familiar feature in American newspapers since the 1930s. Five years later, he allowed Elvis to star in a takeoff on *Lil' Abner*, *Kissin' Cousins* (1964). The movie appeared in the context of a plethora of popular television shows in the 1960s featuring hillbillies and rural Southern settings, such as *Green Acres* and *Petticoat Junction*, in which pockets of the South were depicted as an American Brigadoon where time had ceased. Like *Lil' Abner*, these comedies were part of a longstanding American tradition of treating the less-developed South as the butt of humor, yet finding virtues among the region's backward denizens lacked by the more sophisticated Yankees and city dwellers.

In *Kissin' Cousins*, Elvis played both an air force officer trying to convince the hillbillies of Tatum Mountain to sell their land for a missile base and his opposite number, a girl-chasing local bootlegger wary of Uncle Sam. The eventual understanding between the factions of American society represented by Elvis's two characters, in which the old-school conservatives let their hair down a little and backwoods populists accommodate themselves to contemporary reality, has been interpreted as an allegory of the "new conservatism" born in the 1960s, which "[cut] across class lines and geographical boundaries to stand against a then-burgeoning counter-culture."[54]

The irony is that despite his role in helping ferment the rebelliousness of the baby boomer generation, the rebellion eventually left Elvis behind, standing disconcertedly on the opposite side of the barricade. Radical student leader Abbie Hoffman acknowledged the new decade's debt to Elvis but declared him hopelessly out of touch.[55] For his part, Elvis dismissed the Rolling Stones and other British groups as "a bunch of arrogant jerks" and continued through the height of the British Invasion to stay the course the Colonel had set. The rising counterculture questioned the value of the Protestant work ethic, to which Elvis subscribed. He had difficulty understanding what the younger generation wanted. In America you had everything you needed, you just had to work for it. Why were they complaining?

Among the differences between Elvis and his contemporaries from the 1950s and the next generation of rock stars was that the latter came to consider themselves as artists. Therefore, they behaved the way they thought artists should, with open inquiry, attitude, and free expression. Elvis considered himself an entertainer, and beyond that dividing line was a new world of popular music he did not understand. As the new generation's hair got longer, his became shorter, an expression of his view of the maturity an entertainer should have. He had forgotten what the ducktail had done for him, and that criticism by parents is not necessarily such a bad thing.

During the Hollywood years, Elvis became hooked on diet pills while trying to control his increasing tendency to put on weight. By 1962 he had already reached 200 pounds.[56] Dexedrine was carelessly prescribed in Hollywood in those years to help the stars maintain their ideal appearance. Even as he grew more dependent on pills, he was angered when he heard Bob Dylan's hit "Rainy Day Women # 12 and 35," assuming that the refrain, "Everybody must get stoned," was a call to drug use.[57]

Searching for Meaning

Perhaps the dissatisfaction Elvis felt with the direction of his career caused him to consider in more profound ways the meaning of his life. While the Beatles garnered much publicity in 1968 for going to India, asking questions for which the Western verities they inherited had no good answers, no one outside his inner circle suspected that Elvis was already studying the foundational texts of transcendental meditation. When the Beatles called on Elvis in Bel Air, George Harrison, the band member with the most serious interest in Eastern spirituality, found himself sharing a joint with Larry Geller, the Los Angeles hairdresser who led Elvis onto a path of searching and questioning as early as 1964.[58]

It was not the first instance of Elvis's interest in disciplines and beliefs that seemed exotic to most Americans of his time and background. As early as November 1958, while stationed in Germany, Elvis began taking instruction from Jürgen Seydel, "the father of German karate."[59] Elvis remained fascinated with martial arts through the end of his life. His interest raised no eyebrows among the macho company he kept. Spirituality divorced from physical combat, however, was beyond the pale. The Memphis Mafia, content to lead unreflective lives at the trough of their master, were disturbed by Geller's nightly visits, especially his long rap sessions with Elvis about philosophy, theology, and the cosmos. The discussions seemed to kindle dormant sparks in Elvis's imagination, causing him to consider rising above the emotional and creative valley he was trapped in. The Colonel and the Mafia were not happy. "To me it was almost like he was brainwashing Elvis," said the singer's factotum, Joe Esposito. "We were having fun, and now all of a sudden Elvis is outside looking at the stars all night or reading these books."[60]

The books Geller introduced to Elvis included Paramahansa Yogananda's *Autobiography of a Yogi*, Krishnamurti's *First and Last Freedom*, and Joseph Benner's *The Impersonal Life*, reading material that was also favored by the 1960s counterculture Elvis despised. He was an avid pupil, "requesting a new book almost every other day," Geller recalled. "It was never enough for him to simply read a book; he had to absorb it, think about it, question it."[61]

Unlike the Beatles, Elvis was never comfortable sharing his interests with fans or the wider world. He might have worried that his working class audience would not understand his journey. Suffering from the sense of cultural inferiority that always dogged him, he could also have worried that the media and academic elite would simply laugh at him.

After meeting Geller and absorbing himself in spiritual studies, Elvis reasserted himself. He returned to the Native American theme of *Flaming Star* in *Stay Away, Joe* (1968), where he played a Navajo struggling to prove that an Indian could raise cattle as well as the white man. Elvis felt he was playing "a more grown up character" for the first time in years.[62] One year later, he revisited the western genre for his final film, *Charro!*, as an outlaw going straight.

Meanwhile, Elvis insisted on recording material unrelated to his formulaic movie soundtracks. A session in Nashville, starting on May 25, 1966, helped rejuvenate Elvis musically. The singer went beyond the Hill and Range workshop for gospel and rhythm and blues material, although favorable publishing deals were eventually inked for most of the songs he recorded. Elvis even recorded Bob Dylan's "Tomorrow Is a Long Time," a song he learned from one of his favorite albums, a recording by African American folk blues singer and civil rights activist Odetta. Elvis was fully engaged and in charge, insisting on augmenting the Jordanaires with a trio of female backup singers and a gospel quartet, the Imperials, to achieve the sound of a gospel choir. RCA's Nashville chief, Chet Atkins, wisely assigned a younger man to produce the sessions. Felton Jarvis had been an Elvis fan since seeing a performance by the singer in 1955. As a producer, Jarvis had previously scored a rhythm and blues hit for Gladys Knight and the Pips and cracked the pop charts with Tommy Roe's "Sheila." Since coming to RCA in 1965, Jarvis had produced country as well as blues. He was an empathetic collaborator for Elvis and coaxed him toward a more contemporary sound.[63]

After gradually resuming more control over his career, Elvis openly forced his hand by returning to a concert setting with 1968's live television format of his "comeback special." This would be a vehicle to show the public his true identity. Ironically, Elvis's career would be reinvigorated by television, the medium the Colonel had deemed too small after it gained him the stardom he sought.

Notes

1. "The Girl He Left Behind," *Life.* March 14, 1960.

2. Nancy Sinatra, *Frank Sinatra: My Father* (Garden City, NY: Doubleday, 1985), p. 148.

3. Peter Guralnick, *Careless Love: The Unmaking of Elvis Presley* (Boston: Little Brown, 1999), p. 27.

4. *New York Times*, March 1, 1960.

5. Alex Halberstadt, *Lonely Avenue: The Unlikely Life and Times of Doc Pomus* (Cambridge, MA: Da Capo, 2007), p. 120.

6. John S. Wilson, "Elvis Returns . . .," *New York Times.* May 8, 1960.

7. Roy Coleman, *Lennon* (New York: McGraw-Hill, 1984), p. 533.

8. The interview was originally published in *Western World*, an English language magazine in Paris, and was quoted in "The Rock is Solid," *Time*, November 4, 1957.

9. For insights into Sinatra's almost obsessive hatred of Elvis Presley in the late 1950s as recalled by a member of Sinatra's staff, see George Jacobs and William Stadiem, *Mr. S.: My Life with Frank Sinatra* (New York: HarperEntertainment, 2003), p. 125.

10. *Los Angeles Times*, October 29, 1957.

11. Sinatra, p. 148.

12. Quoted in Arnold Shaw, *Sinatra: Twentieth-Century Romantic* (New York: Holt, Rinehart & Winston, 1968), p. 233.

13. Alanna Nash. *The Colonel: The Extraordinary Story of Colonel Tom Parker and Elvis Presley* (New York: Simon & Schuster, 2003), p. 189.

14. *New York Times,* May 12, 1960.

15. Shaw, p. 271.

16. Nash, *Elvis Aaron Presley: Revelations from the Memphis Mafia* (New York: Harper Collins, 1995), p. 86.

17. Guralnick, *Careless Love*, p. 133.

18. Douglas Brode, *Elvis Cinema and Popular Culture* (Jefferson, NC: McFarland, 2006), p. 5.

19. Guralnick, *Last Train to Memphis*, p. 448.

20. David Hajdu, "Hustling Elvis," *New York Review of Books*, October 9, 2003.

21. Roy Blount Jr., "Elvis," *Esquire*, December 1983.

22. Steven Zmijewisky and Boris Zmijewsky, *Elvis: The Films and Career of Elvis Presley* (Secaucus, NJ: Citadel Press, 1976), p. 80.

23. Jerry Lewis and James Kaplan, *Dean and Me (A Love Story)* (New York: Doubleday, 1982), p. 157.

24. "Elvis Helped in Success of Burton-O'Toole Movie," *Las Vegas Desert News and Telegram*, April 20, 1964.

25. Guralnick, *Careless Love*, pp. 187–188, 203.

26. Halberstadt, p. 143.

27. Guralnick, *Careless Love*, pp. 73–74.

28. Shaw, *Sinatra*, p. 271.

29. Peter Biskind, *Seeing Is Believing: How Hollywood Taught Us to Stop Worrying and Love the Fifties* (New York: Pantheon, 1983), p. 229.

30. Jerry Osborne, *Elvis: Word by Word* (New York: Gramercy Books, 1999), p. 151.

31. Arthur Knight, "Flaming Star," *Saturday Review*, December 1960.

32. Jean Bosquet, "Parker Learned Name—Fast," *New York Journal-American*, June 13, 1960.

33. Guralnick, *Careless Love*, p. 150.

34. Quoted in Ann-Margret with Todd Gold, *Ann-Margret: My Story* (New York: G. P. Putnam's Sons, 1994), p. 110.

35. Bob Thomas, "It Looks Like Romance for Elvis Presley and Ann-Margret," *Memphis Press-Scimitar*, August 6, 1963.

36. *Time*, May 29, 1964.

37. Guralnick, *Careless Love*, pp. 152–153.

38. Howard Hampton, "Elvis Dorado: The True Romance of *Viva Las Vegas!*" *Film Comment*, July-August 1994.

39. Bobbie Joe Mason, *Elvis Presley* (New York: Viking, 2003), p. 90.

40. Nash, *Elvis Aaron Presley*, p. 274.

41. Guralnick, *Careless Love*, p. 255.

42. Priscilla Beaulieu Presley with Sandra Harmon, *Elvis and Me* (New York: G. P. Putnam's Sons, 1985), p. 111.

43. *Memphis Press-Scimitar*, April 2, 1962.

44. Mason, p. 100.

45. Guralnick, *Careless Love*, pp. 251–252.

46. Guralnick, *Careless Love*, p. 80.

47. Nash, *Elvis Aaron Presley*, pp. 189–190.

48. Alan Fortas, *Elvis: From Memphis to Hollywood* (Ann Arbor, MI: Popular Culture Ink, 1992), pp. 139, 191; Red West, Sonny West, and Dave Hebler, as told to Steve Dunleavy, *Elvis: What Happened?* (New York: Ballantine, 1977), p. 279.

49. Coleman, p. 264.

50. *Billboard Charts* (http://billboard.com/charts), retrieved October 11, 2009.

51. Nash, *Elvis and the Memphis Mafia*, p. 326.

52. Guralnick, *Careless Love*, p. 122.

53. Brode, p. 100.

54. Brode, p. 102.

55. Abbie Hoffman, "Too Soon the Hero," *Crawdaddy*, November 1977.

56. *Memphis Press-Scimitar*, April 3, 1963.

57. Guralnick, *Careless Love*, p. 223.

58. Guralnick, *Careless Love*, p. 211.

59. Guralnick, *Careless Love*, p. 47.

60. Guralnick, *Careless Love*, p. 176.

61. Larry Geller and Joel Spector with Patricia Romanowski, *"If I Can Dream": Elvis's Own Story* (New York: Simon & Schuster, 1989), pp. 99–100.

62. Joseph Lewis, "Elvis Presley Lives," *Cosmopolitan*, November 1968.

63. Guralnick, *Careless Love*, pp. 228–233.

9

If I Can Dream

Elvis's displeasure with his movie career and his increasing boredom, depression, and indulgent hedonism had become so noticeable toward the end of 1967 that even the Colonel became concerned. Along with noting the declining sales for his movies and soundtrack albums, Parker realized that his client was dissatisfied with the direction of his career and needed to be placated. The Colonel decided to shift direction and met with NBC vice president Tom Sarnoff to discuss Elvis's first TV special since the Sinatra show.[1] Sarnoff and producer Bob Finkel brought in Steve Binder, a 21-year-old wunderkind who, after an apprenticeship with Steve Allen, had produced the popular TV rock show *Hullabaloo* and the outstanding concert film *The T.A.M.I. Show* (1965) along with the television special in which white singer Petula Clark embraced black singer Harry Belafonte, a controversial gesture in a racially divided America. Binder was a fan of 1960s rock and had little regard for Elvis, but after beginning discussions with him in May of 1968, he formed an amenable working relationship with the singer. Binder impressed Elvis with the idea that the television show should be an imaginative and vivid reflection of his life, produced with an emotional and creative freedom comparable to his early recordings. "Scared to death," Elvis replied when asked what he thought, but he was obviously intrigued.[2]

Binder and his audio engineer, Bones Howe, who had worked on several of Elvis's early RCA recordings, met with Parker in the manager's memorabilia cluttered office. After treating them to a scrapbook of his years as a dogcatcher in Tampa, the Colonel declared, "We're not going to tell you boys what to do creatively, because that's what we hired you for, but if you get out of line, we're going to let you know."

His main concern at that point was that Elvis's publishing companies secure all rights to the songs performed in the special.[3]

Binder and Howe began to conceive the show as an opportunity to capture Elvis's personality that had been hidden within a glut of mediocre movies. They wanted fresh concepts. Binder called on fashion designer Bill Belew, who submitted a costume with a Napoleonic stand-up collar and a black leather suit that evoked the Marlon Brando roots of Elvis's early image. The designer's objective was to fashion an in-the-moment look opposite to the out-of-step appearance of network television in the late 1960s.[4] Belew would later create the jumpsuits based on bull fighting costumes that became Elvis's concert garb in the last years of his life. Agreeing with the basic concepts, Elvis left for Hawaii to get in shape, leaving Binder and Howe to work out the details.

Music became a point of contention with Elvis's handlers. Howe brought in an extensive lineup of musicians, including Elvis's early colleagues Scotty Moore and D. J. Fontana to replicate the spontaneity of a jam session. Binder and Howe also fought with the Colonel on the show's final song. Parker wanted something conventional, a Christmas song to conclude a holiday special, but Binder and Howe pushed for an original composition, Earl Brown's "If I Can Dream." As if touched by the lyric's articulation of his own feelings, Elvis held his ground against all opposition. "We're doing it," he said, ending the discussion.[5] "If I Can Dream" climbed to number 12 on the charts, his highest-ranking single since 1965.

NBC worried that Howe was a troublemaker and Binder had to keep him out of sight for stretches of the production.[6] Elvis supported Binder in hiring music director Billy Goldenberg, who brought a full orchestra. Even though their tastes were different, Elvis and Goldenberg connected musically. Goldenberg recalled Elvis rehearsing "Guitar Man" over and over until he fully connected with the song, which was a key musical motif of the special. "He was so involved and excited and emotionally charged," Goldenberg said, recalling the singer's preparation.[7]

The program's structure was scripted around Maurice Maeterlinck's familiar 1909 stage play *The Blue Bird*, whose theme of searching for happiness through travel set a road metaphor Binder would use throughout the show. Just prior to filming, Elvis got cold feet, but Binder convinced him he had to go on. In the end, the familiar musical environment must have been a comfort to the singer. Fontana played drumsticks on an overturned guitar case, remembering the value of simplicity in his *Louisiana Hayride* days. "I heard Scotty, Bill [Black], and Elvis one night, and knew that I couldn't mess up that sound," he said.[8] Several members of Elvis's entourage were recruited for the band including Charlie Hodge on vocals, Alan Fortas, beating on a guitar back with his hands, and Lance LeGault, on tambourine. Elvis's charm and vulnerability took over as the cameras caught a self-mocking, but assured performer. "This is supposed to be an informal section of the show where we faint or do whatever we want to do, especially me," he told the intimate studio audience of some two hundred.[9] Wisely, ad-libs between the group and Elvis were uncensored. "It was a jam session . . . the director said: 'There's the stage. Don't worry about the cameras, just do what you want to do,'" Moore later remarked.[10]

It would be the last time Elvis performed with his erstwhile partners Moore and Fontana, and their presence seemed to stir memories of their early shows together. Elvis paced, panted, and toyed with the fans, performing raw and spirited renditions of "That's All Right" and "Heartbreak Hotel." He forgot the words to the latter, which only seemed to underline the bond-breaking joy of his performance.

Afterward, Elvis summoned the Colonel into his dressing room and told him he wanted to go on tour again.[11] When the Colonel later announced a "comeback tour" at a press conference, Elvis was unhappy with the choice of words. "He's making it sound like I'm a has-been."[12] The four hours of tape at Burbank studios was edited down to 50 minutes for the TV show. Elvis loved the final screening, viewing it numerous times with Binder, and promised the director he would never again do anything he did not believe in. Unfortunately, Binder was never allowed to work with Elvis again. The Colonel, viewing the young director as an interloper, knew how to close the doors.[13]

Incongruously sponsored by the leading maker of sewing machines, *Singer Presents Elvis* aired on December 3, 1968. The Colonel's conventional expectations of a large set with dance sequences and big production numbers had been undermined by Binder and Howe, who wanted more intimate performances, using a gospel medley and "Guitar Man" in retelling the search for the "Blue Bird" on the road. Both the sit-down and stand-up sessions were raw, and showed Elvis in control of his material and audience. The "Comeback Special" became a forerunner of MTV's "Unplugged" series, showing how a familiar act could shine in a new format.

In later years rock critics recognized Elvis's performance on the special as a pinnacle. Robert Palmer described the interplay between Elvis, Moore, and Fontana as telepathic, exclaiming "this is rock and roll as good as it gets."[14] Critical response at the time was mixed. The

Looking young, dangerous, and sexy, Elvis returns to form on his TV comeback special, 1968. (Photofest)

New York Times praised the show,[15] but writers without a connection to rock and roll were left scratching their heads. The *Hollywood Reporter* declared, "it looked as though someone had accidentally taped the rehearsal,"[16] while Elvis's old foe, *Variety*, recalled the earliest condemnations of the singer by denouncing "Presley's suggestion of simple, unthinking, illiterate sex."[17] The public responded warmly to the revitalized Elvis, sending the "Comeback Special" soundtrack to number eight. The special captured a 42 percent audience share and NBC's highest rating of the year. Eight years earlier, Elvis's first comeback special with Frank Sinatra was almost quiet and demure, but the 1968 special was an aggressive all-out attack on those he viewed as usurpers of the throne. Within days of the telecast, Elvis received offers from other TV producers and the London Palladium, but the Colonel was already working out a deal in Las Vegas.

Viva Las Vegas

As far back as 1957, *New York Times* critic John S. Wilson wrote that Elvis would eventually "settle into the mainstream," noting his potential was far from limited.[18] Wilson's forecast was proven accurate in the aftermath of the "Comeback Special." The Colonel was in touch with investor Kirk Kerkorian, whose newly constructed International Hotel was the largest in the world, boasting a 2,000-seat showroom. Parker negotiated a fee for Elvis of $400,000 for four weeks of two shows per night, with Mondays off and separate suites for Elvis and the Colonel. Meanwhile, Memphis mobsters George Klein and Marty Lacker convinced Elvis to reclaim his potency as a recording artist after a spotty track record in the 1960s by recording at Chip Moman's American Studios in Memphis rather than RCA Nashville.[19] American had been a hit factory in recent years for Dionne Warwick, Dusty Springfield, Wilson Pickett, and the Box Tops.

Elvis was nervous at the start of his January 1969 session at American, but soon found his way into a number of soon-to-be signature tunes, such as Eddie Rabbitt's "Kentucky Rain" and Mac Davis's "In the Ghetto." One of Moman's staff writers, Mark James, offered another future hit, "Suspicious Minds." Moman freed Elvis from his dependence on mediocre songs and, more than any producer since Sam Phillips, helped the singer forge a fresh sound from his many influences. Elvis's session at American transcended the categories of country, rock, rhythm and blues, and gospel. When Moman talked to Elvis during the sessions, he did not speak from the control room through talkback mikes, but would "walk out into the room and go into the booth with him personally."[20]

Moman was drawn into rock and roll as a teenager, playing on the road with Gene Vincent and Johnny Burnette. Later, he was a key figure at Stax, a legendary label for 1960s soul music. In 1967 and 1968, Moman's studio work included 80 hit singles over a 12-month period, while cowriting some of Aretha Franklin's hits.[21] Moman's studio produced the most successful run of singles for Elvis since the army. When they finished recording in February 1969, Elvis declared, "we have some hits, do we, Chips?" [22]

The session and the brisk sales and airplay for "In the Ghetto," "Suspicious Minds," and "Kentucky Rain" left him reinvigorated and excited about his Las Vegas opening. Elvis took responsibility for choosing the musicians that would back him. His best decision was calling on Shreveport guitarist James Burton, already a virtuoso at age 14 in the *Louisiana Hayride* stage band.[23] Burton went on to play second guitar on Dale Hawkins rockabilly classic "Suzie Q" (1957) and became Rick Nelson's lead guitarist. Elvis had complete confidence in his new bandleader. "At the first rehearsal, he came in and we shook hands, and talked like we had known each other for years," Burton recalled.[24] He remained as Elvis's stage band director through the singer's final concert tour.

Elvis also called on Bill Belew for a new set of costumes. The designer produced karate-themed two-piece Cossack suits, with bright macramé belts and high collars.[25] After the Imperials and the Sweet Inspirations were hired as backup singers, rehearsals began on July 18, 1969.

Although he suffered through a panic attack prior to the show, Elvis returned to the stage at the International Hotel on July 31 with a celebrity-packed audience. Within the first week the Colonel renegotiated for $125,000 per week, and two engagements per year for five years, writing the contract on a tablecloth during a meeting with hotel president Alex Shoofey. The four-week run in the summer of 1969 was seen by 101,500 patrons and broke all Las Vegas engagement records.[26] After his final show, he attended Nancy Sinatra's Las Vegas opening, and with Priscilla in tow, a party at Frank Sinatra's home. The casino city that had spurned him earlier in his career would now be the rock on which he built his career, but not without dissension. Lamar Fike later recounted a discussion where Elvis complained he would be playing "Vegas till he dies" because the Colonel owed so much money to the casinos. According to Fike, the Colonel's gambling debts were moved from one casino to another, using Elvis as a bargaining chip to diminish his markers.[27]

On the Road

Preparations began in January 1970 for his second engagement at the International. "Elvis didn't rehearse the way most musicians do," recalled his pianist, Glen D. Hardin. "We'd just go over and sometimes work all night, play all kinds of different songs." With his catholic tastes, Elvis expected his band to play almost anything during the four-week run beginning January 26.[28]

On February 28, he did two shows at the Houston Astrodome for the Texas Livestock Show, his first concert outside of Las Vegas since 1961. The Astrodome shows also heralded the first use of "Also sprach Zarathustra" from *2001: A Space Odyssey* to set a grandiose mood for the star's entrance.[29]

The next step was a full-fledged concert tour, consisting of six shows during September 1970 in Phoenix, St. Louis, Detroit, Miami, Tampa, and Mobile. The success of those dates led the Colonel to set a November tour for eight shows in the western United States. Soon multiple city tours, with the Colonel as advance man, became the norm.[30] Elvis would spend much of his last decade on the road in a whirlwind of activity that only seemed to detach him from everyday life. Unable to sleep after the adrenalin rush of performing, Elvis became dependent on sleeping pills, dangerously mixing the "downers" with the "uppers" used to control his weight. He shopped around for doctors willing to write prescriptions and exercised little restraint on his drug use despite the warnings of his personal physician, George Nichopoulos.

Although many tens of thousands of Elvis fans would have the opportunity to see the king in person over the next decade, and enjoy the live performances on albums, the Colonel wanted to reach audiences on an even grander scale. In the spring of 1970, Parker, after much hard bargaining, negotiated Elvis's return to the big screen in the form of a concert documentary, a vehicle to show an Elvis concert to millions of fans that had never seen him live. Already, he was not the lithe figure from the "Comeback Special" but had not yet turned into the hulking, unhealthy figure of a few years hence. The best part of the film, *Elvis: That's the Way It Is*, concerned what took place behind the scene, especially Elvis singing gospel with backup singers in hotel suites and rehearsal halls.

Richard Nixon extends a hand to Elvis during his Oval Office visit. (National Archives)

That's the Way It Is was filmed during a five-day period in August 1970 at the International in Las Vegas. During the engagement, the hotel received a kidnapping threat, which Elvis and the police took seriously. The singer went around armed with pistols.[31] At the end of the run, in recognition of attendance records, the hotel bestowed upon Elvis a mock-up of a prize fighter's belt, which he frequently wore in coming years.[32]

In December 1970, Elvis indulged one of his compulsive fantasies at a Los Angeles gun shop in a $20,000 shopping spree for himself and his entourage. His closest associates, including George Nichopoulos and Sonny West, received a Mercedes for Christmas.[33] Spending was only one manifestation of erratic behavior, turning the reality of his life into grist for the tabloids. At dawn on December 21, 1970, Elvis appeared at the gates of the White House and passed a handwritten note to a guard. He wanted to see the president, Richard M. Nixon. The message was taken to White House advisors, who saw Elvis as an opportunity to brighten Nixon's rather staid image. Hours later Elvis was ushered into the Oval Office, clad like a superhero in purple velvet with a high collar and cape.

Nixon was taken aback. "You dress kind of strange, don't you?" said Nixon. Elvis held his ground. "You have your show and I have mine," he replied. The conversation warmed when Elvis declared that he was "just a poor boy from Tennessee" who wanted to help the president turn back the influence of the 1960s counterculture, with its legion of villains in the form of hippies, drug dealers, student radicals, and black revolutionaries. He indulged in a fantasy of fighting wrongdoers that was rooted in his adolescent love of Captain Marvel. Nixon gratified Elvis with an appointment as an honorary agent in the Bureau of Narcotics and Dangerous Drugs, predecessor to the Drug Enforcement Agency.[34]

Elvis seemed in earnest about his role as a crime fighter. On December 30, he returned to Washington for a visit to the National Sheriffs Association, and while there, tried to arrange a meeting with FBI director J. Edgar Hoover. Hoover was out of town, but Elvis and his entourage were given a tour of the bureau, including an opportunity to fire guns on the practice range. Commenting on his respect for the FBI and calling Hoover the "greatest living American," Elvis also advised the agents who shepherded him that Jane Fonda, the Smothers Brothers, and other industry people "of their ilk have a lot to answer for in the hereafter." A few days later Hoover wrote him a brief note, expressing his thanks for visiting the bureau.[35]

Despite a death threat during his January run of 28 shows at the Las Vegas Hilton, as the International was renamed, 1971 was a year of honors. The U.S. Junior Chamber of Commerce named him among the Ten Most Outstanding Young Men of the Nation, his Tupelo birthplace was opened to the public, the city of Memphis renamed the portion of Highway 51 running past Graceland as Elvis Presley Boulevard, and the National Academy of Recording Arts and Sciences granted him the Bing Crosby Award for lifetime achievement.

From July 20 through August 2 he was in concert at the Lake Tahoe Sahara, where a young female fan, invited back to his room, overdosed and spent several days in intensive care. He did not visit her but made sure she was provided with a ticket home.[36] From August 9 through September 6, he was back at the Las Vegas Hilton. Elvis was on the road through November on a 12-city tour from Minneapolis to Salt Lake City. During this year, with the upheaval of the 1960s still playing out, Elvis performed what he considered an act of national healing with a medley by successful country songwriter Mickey Newberry called "An American Trilogy." One part, "The Battle Hymn of the Republic," represented the North; another, "Dixie," represented the South; and the spiritual "All My Trials" stood for African Americans.

Elvis and Priscilla in happier days at the wedding of Elvis's friend George Klein. (Corbis)

All three songs had their origins in the Civil War era, which for Elvis and many white Southerners retained a romantic poignancy.[37]

January 26 through February 23, 1972, saw the annual run at the Las Vegas Hilton. Shortly after Priscilla and daughter Lisa Marie arrived for a performance, Priscilla informed Elvis she was leaving him. On

February 23, the couple separated. He spent the next weeks in severe depression, calling and trying to win her back.[38] March and April were reserved for recording sessions on the road and RCA's Hollywood studio. The roadwork continued relentlessly, with an April 1972 tour of 15 stops in the Midwest, South, and Southwest. Always barking after the scent of money, the Colonel threatened to bolt the Hilton for Kerkorian's newest venture, the MGM Grand. His hard negotiating earned a weekly increase in fees for Elvis; for himself, he won an additional $50,000 per year for three years as consultant to the Hilton.[39]

Elvis ready to rock at the International Convention Center Arena, 1973. (Corbis)

While many fans enjoyed his over-the-top productions of the 1970s as the King's return to a rightful throne, others viewed the spectacle as the death of rock and roll. At his first-ever concert hall performance in New York City, his series of four Madison Square Garden shows in June 1972, he bounded onstage in a white sequined outfit complete with a series of tableau poses. Energizing the audience with a mélange of early material and recent hits, his 45-minute show drew mothers and daughters, along with laments by some critics that despite the breadth of his talent, Elvis the rocker had become Elvis the crooner.[40] For the 80,000 fans that witnessed his New York concerts, he was "a visiting Prince from another planet."[41] The June tour that followed included seven cities in the Midwest and Southwest, prior to a month-long August stay at the Las Vegas Hilton.

During this eventful year, he was introduced to a new girlfriend, Linda Thompson, who reigned as Miss Tennessee. He would also begin dating another beauty queen, Memphis actress Cybill Shepherd.[42] On August 18, he filed for divorce from Priscilla on grounds of irreconcilable differences. On a more positive note, in October the Colonel prodded RCA to advance Elvis $4 million against 65 percent of the gate from all tours for 1972 and 1973.[43] The star's need for money seemed insatiable.

On November 1, *Elvis on Tour* was released in theaters and would win a 1972 Golden Globe Award for "Best Documentary of the Year," the only Elvis film to win a prize. The movie was the work of Robert Abel and Pierre Adidge, the team behind another successful rock concert movie of the era, Joe Cocker's *Mad Dogs and Englishmen*. In his *New York Times* review, Vincent Canby commented that the film showed a private person indistinguishable from the public one, suggesting, "there is no real Elvis left. The person and image have become one. For better or worse the camera has sanctified him."[44] He finished the year with a seven-city tour ending in Honolulu.

After two days of rehearsal in Hawaii, *Elvis: Aloha from Hawaii Via Satellite* was simulcast to over 40 countries and half a billion people as a benefit show for the Kui Lee Cancer Fund, from the Honolulu International Civic Arena. It was one of the Colonel's grandest projects, and was the first telecast of its kind beamed around the world via satellites. Suggesting people pay what they could afford, the concert raised $75,000 for charity. It was not broadcast to the United States on its original date of January 14, 1973, primarily because it conflicted with Super Bowl VII. NBC rebroadcast an expanded version later in April. From Hawaii he returned to the mainland for his February 1973 engagement at the Las Vegas Hilton, noted for three shows cancelled due to illnesses.

The April 1973 tour consisted of eight cities on the West Coast, followed by a June through July tour stopping at 12 cities throughout mid-Atlantic and Southern states, broken by two weeks at the Lake Tahoe Sahara. The 1973 Nassau Coliseum show on Long Island was an example of the large-scale production Elvis was mounting, a vision of the Colonel's own circus rolling from town to town. It was "slick as oil, with big band and back-up singers . . . an affected routine involving scarves thrown to the audience after being handed to Presley by a musician, as much butler as guitarist."[45] At a week of sessions at Memphis's Stax Studios, prior to a month-long engagement in August at the Las Vegas Hilton, the musicians were surprised at how corpulent Elvis had become.[46]

The Divorce

Priscilla, who stood by faithfully as the bride-in-waiting for years, assumed that once she got Elvis to the altar, their marriage and life together would be a fairytale romance. Instead, her husband preferred the company of the boys in his entourage and felt his wife's place was at home. Her private world behind the closed gates of Graceland did not change after the wedding. It was not what she had bargained for, and it culminated with a divorce on October 9, 1973. In an unusual move, and at the Colonel's suggestion, the same law firm represented Elvis and Priscilla.

The divorce papers decreed shared custody of Lisa Marie. Priscilla received $750,000 in cash; $720,000 over ten years; 5 percent of Elvis Presley Music, Inc., and White Haven Music, Inc.; half of the $500,000 sale of a California house; $4,200 monthly alimony; and $4,000 monthly child support. Elvis agreed to pay her attorney's fees of $75,000.[47] One week after the divorce was decreed, Elvis was admitted to Baptist Memorial Hospital in Memphis for hypertension and headaches. By mid-December he was back in the studio at Stax.

In 1974, the Colonel established Boxcar Productions to promote various lines of Elvis products, a lucrative source of income since the singer's earliest days of stardom. Parker received 40 percent of all profits, while Elvis, and the Colonel's partners—Tom Diskin, George Parkhill, and Freddy Bienstock—each received 15 percent.[48] Concerned by the mid-1970s with Elvis's behavior and commitment to obligations, Parker negotiated a new "partnership agreement," which exploited a client who no longer seemed interested in the business side of music. The Colonel would continue to take his 25 percent management fee, but would now also receive a 50/50 cut of the profits with Elvis, with a revamped RCA recording contract to run through 1980.[49] The Colonel's chief concern was to ensure a steady revenue stream with an increasing amount of cash flowing directly into his own pockets.

The Final Tours

February 1974 brought the annual month-long run at the Las Vegas Hilton, delayed one day so as not to not conflict with Frank Sinatra's comeback at Caesars Palace.[50] A March tour took in 18 cities in the mid-Atlantic and South, with two shows in Memphis recorded for album release. In a very busy year, he also played 32 concerts from May through October, crisscrossing the United States. The 10-day stint at the Lake Tahoe Sahara in May and four days in October at least gave Elvis an opportunity to stand still. The year 1974 was the start of the three busiest years in his career, revisiting many cities and venues, and repeating many of the same shows.

Unfortunately, cancellations became more frequent, as were digressive personal monologues on stage. Too many sleeping pills was the chief cause of his confusion on stage. His weight went up despite his use of diet pills, worsening his health. In October he stayed at the home of one of Las Vegas's physicians to the stars, Elias Ghanem, in a guest suite added for special patients. Elvis underwent the doctor's controversial "sleep diet," which involved keeping sedation to suppress appetite.[51]

In January 1975, Elvis turned 40 amid a flurry of rumors of worsening health and drug use.[52] He was especially hurt when Johnny Carson made his birthday the butt of a monologue, calling him "fat and forty."[53] Elvis spent his birthday in seclusion at Graceland, awakened at 3:00 P.M. when Vester phoned birthday greetings from the guardhouse at the mansion's gate.[54]

On January 29, 1975, Elvis was admitted to Baptist Hospital after his girlfriend, Linda Thompson, found him struggling for breath. The local press reported he suffered from a "liver problem which has nothing to do with alcohol,"[55] but in reality, the hospitalization was an attempt by Nichopoulos to get control over Elvis's use of prescription drugs. Health problems did not keep him off the road for long. Although many fans blamed Nichopoulos for Elvis's death, he maintained that he tried to set his celebrity patient on a straight path even as he was drawn into Elvis's nocturnal lifestyle as a member of his entourage.[56]

March brought a brief session at RCA Hollywood, and a two-week run at the Las Vegas Hilton. Despite many off moments, the fans continued to cheer. In 1975 he performed 42 dates between April and October in the south and mid-Atlantic. Show cancellations increased during this period. He took time out on June 18 to undergo a facelift at the Mid-South Hospital in Memphis. Elvis was excited to play opposite Barbara Streisand in the role of the fading rock star ruined by alcohol in the remake of *A Star Is Born*. His involvement fell through because of the Colonel's demands for a profit percentage and salary.[57] The role went instead to Kris Kristofferson. At the end of August 1975, Elvis was again admitted to Baptist Hospital for hypertension and an impacted colon. Two weeks in early December were spent in concert at the Las Vegas Hilton, and on December 31 Elvis performed for 60,000 fans in Pontiac, Michigan.[58] For the Colonel it was a triumph, breaking records on revenue for a one-night performance by a single artist, grossing more than $800,000.

Elvis's behavior as he reached his 41 birthday was an unstable mix of grandeur and humility. He usually stayed up late and slept through the day. Elvis had grown strangely averse to the studio, leaving RCA and the Colonel desperate to shore up the sagging recording career of one of the world's biggest, if fading, stars. A January 1976 recording date was held at Graceland using an RCA mobile unit. Elvis turned up in the uniform of a Denver police captain after hastily returning from the funeral of an officer in Colorado. He had been befriended by the Denver police department and allowed to participate in drug raids as an observer.[59] Elvis appeared disinterested in recording music, preferring to discuss his plan to sweep drug pushers off the streets of Memphis. The local police had supplied him with photographs of alleged dealers.[60] In his final years Elvis was virtually unheard on the increasingly important album-oriented FM rock radio and was absent from the pop charts, but his albums and singles maintained a strong presence in the country and adult contemporary charts. Elvis's "Moody Blue" was one of the top country records of 1976.

From March through December 1976, Elvis performed in 77 cities, crisscrossing the United States, along with his usual two-week stint in Las Vegas. "There were nights he was so tired or so down I felt I had to hit the drums much, much harder than I had before," said percussionist Ronnie Tutt.[61] In mid tour, long-time entourage members Red West, Sonny West, and Dave Hebler were fired by Vernon to cut back

They once were great friends: Elvis joins the wedding party of bodyguard Sonny West. (Corbis)

on expenses. Elvis did not put up a fight.[62] Mistrust had began to pervade his view of the Memphis Mafia; Elvis and the Colonel communicated less than ever, and smaller venues and cities had by now crept into the tour schedules.[63] Reviews become more critical, and while diehard fans continued to support live performances, he was by now a caricature of himself in concert, just as he had become in his movies. A reviewer described an August show in Houston as an "incoherent, amateurish mess served up by a bloated, stumbling and mumbling figure" who broke the reviewer's heart.[64] A Memphis reporter covering

Elvis's closing night in Las Vegas wondered, "how much longer it can be before the end comes."[65]

His appetite for women remained almost as insatiable as it had since he first tasted the fruit of his sexual attraction on early tours of the South during his days with Sun Records. Toward the end of the year he was introduced to 19-year-old Miss Mid-South Fair, Ginger Alden, whom he dated in addition to Linda Thompson. Memphis mobster George Klein served as Elvis's matchmaker.

The 1977 tours of the South, Midwest, and Southwest between February and June included 53 concerts. For the first time since he returned to Las Vegas, there were no shows in the neon city on the desert; as the downward spiral continued, more shows were cancelled at the last minute. In June he walked out midway through a show in Baltimore.[66] His final concert was held in Indianapolis's Market Square Arena on June 26. Some members of the Memphis Mafia, painfully aware of declining performance skills and health, were encouraged by the good show he put on at the last stop of his tour. Elvis appeared excited about fasting, getting back in shape, and reenergizing himself for the next schedule of concerts due to start in August.[67]

Death of a King

The bitterness felt by Red and Sonny West and Dave Hebler after being cut from Elvis's payroll was converted into the currency of betrayal with the compilation of their tell-all book, *Elvis: What Happened?* The title amplified the public murmuring over the decline of one of America's most significant entertainers, the first enduring star of rock and roll. Written with the aid of tabloid reporter Steve Dunleavy, the assertions made in this best-selling paperback must be weighed cautiously against the anger of its authors, yet the overall picture of Elvis's decline into a pharmaceutical malaise is true enough.

Although it was published in the United States at the beginning of August, *What Happened?* appeared in serial form in Great Britain and Australia in late spring and rumors of its sordid content reached the United States. It only deepened the paranoia and delusion of Elvis's last months. When his major domo, George Klein, was indicted by a federal grand jury, Elvis called President Jimmy Carter for help. Unlike his earlier chat with Richard Nixon, the discussion ended leaving Elvis empty handed.[68] Elvis continued to find stimulation in long discussions with Larry Geller and the books Geller recommended, and George Nichopoulos put him on a liquid protein diet to reduce his weight, but the mood at Graceland was uneasy. He often wore a pair of handguns concealed in the waistband of his Drug Enforcement Agency tracksuit.[69]

Elvis had not resigned himself to death on the morning of August 16, 1977, when he was discovered by Ginger Alden unconscious in his bathroom at Graceland. He was scheduled to leave Memphis for yet another tour that night, his baggage including a parcel of prescriptions, an irresponsible cocktail of sedatives and pain relievers, including Seconal, Placidyl, Valmid, Tuinal, and Demerol. He was pronounced dead that afternoon at Baptist Memorial Hospital. Shelby County coroner Jerry Francisco reported that preliminary findings indicated the cause as "cardiac arrhythmia." Francisco discounted any direct connection between drugs and Elvis's death. Nichopoulos later claimed that his patient suffered degenerative arthritis, which explained his need for painkillers, along with glaucoma, high blood pressure, liver damage, and an enlarged colon.[70] Many of his ailments could only have been aggravated by drug abuse.

The 1968 "Comeback Special" had been a rejuvenator for Elvis, along with recording sessions with a new producer and his conquest of Las Vegas, the domain of the stars he admired, Frank Sinatra and Dean Martin. He rose when given new challenges but was discouraged at almost every turn by Colonel Parker and his Memphis companions from following his inclinations as a musician and an actor. Elvis was never secure in his role as King of Rock and Roll; his self-confidence allowed him to rebel against Parker's stifling expectations but only on occasion. Fundamentally conservative politically and socially and distrustful of the educated and the elite, his discomfort with many aspects of the changing world coupled with his need for privacy forced him into a secluded, nocturnal existence not unlike that of the reclusive tycoon Howard Hughes. Unlike Hughes, Elvis was the victim of a greedy, self-interested manager and needed to continue working to maintain his life style. Often afraid of standing up for himself and surrounded by people afraid to stand up to him, Elvis's physical, emotional, and mental health deteriorated on the incessant grind of the road.

Notes

1. Peter Guralnick, *Careless Love: The Unmaking of Elvis Presley* (Boston: Little Brown, 1999), p. 283.

2. Guralnick, *Careless Love*, p. 296.

3. Mississippi Valley Collection, University of Memphis.

4. Guralnick, *Careless Love*, pp. 298–299.

5. Guralnick, *Careless Love*, pp. 308–309.

6. Guralnick, *Careless Love*, p. 299.

7. Guralnick, *Careless Love*, p. 308.

8. Craig Morrison, *Go Cat Go!* (Urbana: University of Illinois Press, 1998), p. 117.

9. "The Complete Comeback Special" DVD.

10. Interview with Scotty Moore, March 29, 1998, with Elvis Australia, http://www.elvis.com.au, retrieved November 1, 2009.

11. Guralnick, *Careless Love*, p. 317.

12. Kathleen Tracy, *Elvis Presley: A Biography* (Westport, CT: Greenwood Press, 2007), p. 127.

13. Alanna Nash, *The Colonel: The Extraordinary Story of Colonel Tom Parker and Elvis Presley* (New York: Simon & Schuster, 2003), p. 246.

14. Robert Palmer, "Elvis Presley: Homage to a Rock King," *New York Times*, November 19, 1984.

15. Robert Shelton, "Rock Star's Explosive Blues Have Vintage Quality," *New York Times*, December 4, 1968.

16. *Hollywood Reporter*, December 5, 1968.

17. *Variety*, December 5, 1968.

18. John S. Wilson, "Elvis Presley: Rocking Blues Shouter," *New York Times*, January 13, 1957.

19. *Variety*, June 18, 1969.

20. Interview with Chips Moman, 2001, http://www.georgiarhythm.com, retrieved December 20, 2009.

21. Palmer, "Chips Moman's Views on World of Recording," *New York Times*, May 9, 1984.

22. James Kingsley, "Relaxed Elvis Disks 16 Songs in Hometown Stint," *Memphis Commercial Appeal*, January 23, 1969.

23. Alanna Nash with Billy Smith, Marty Lacker, and Lamar Fike, *Elvis Aaron Presley: Revelations from the Memphis Mafia* (New York: HarperCollins, 1995), p. 321.

24. Interview with James Burton, 1970, http://www.james-burton. net/interviews, retrieved November 30, 2009.

25. Mississippi Valley Collection.

26. Peter Guralnick and Ernst Jorgesen, *Elvis: Day by Day* (New York: Ballantine, 1999), pp. 259–261.

27. Nash, *Mafia*, p. 471.

28. Quoted in Patsy Guy Hammontree, *Elvis Presley: A Bio-Bibliography* (Westport, CT: Greenwood Press, 1985), p. 63.

29. Guralnick, *Day by Day*, p. 269.

30. Guralnick, *Day by Day*, p. 279.

31. Guralnick, *Careless Love*, pp. 392–393.

32. Guralnick, *Day by Day*, p. 279.

33. Wendy Sauers, *Elvis Presley: A Complete Reference* (Jefferson, NC: McFarland, 1984), p. 24.

34. Glen Jeansonne and David Luhrssen, "Elvis: Rock 'n' Roll's Reluctant Rebel," *History Today*, August 2007.

35. David Johnston, "The FBI and the King: Both Had Suspicious Minds," *New York Times*, August 17, 1997.

36. Tracy, p. 131.

37. For Greil Marcus, Elvis's medley "signifies that his persona, and the culture he has made out of blues, Las Vegas, gospel music, Hollywood, schmaltz, Mississippi, and rock'n'roll, can contain any America you might want to conjure up." *Mystery Train: Images of America in Rock'n'Roll Music* (New York: E. P. Dutton, 1975), p. 142.

38. Tracy, p. 132.

39. Guralnick, *Day by Day*, p. 308.

40. Don Heckman, "Presley, Talents Richly Intact, Shifts Emphasis to Rock/Gospel," *New York Times*, June 11, 1972.

41. Chris Chase, *New York Times*, June 18, 1972.

42. Guralnick, *Day by Day*, p. 310.

43. Guralnick, *Day by Day*, p. 313.

44. Vincent Canby, *New York Times*, June 17, 1973.

45. Ian Dove, "Presley Mixes Early Hits with More Recent Safe Songs," *New York Times*, June 25, 1973.

46. Guralnick, *Day by Day*, p. 327.

47. Sauers, p. 27.

48. Guralnick, *Careless Love*, p. 244.

49. Guralnick, *Careless Love*, pp. 248–250.

50. Guralnick, *Day by Day*, p. 332.

51. Stanley Booth, "The King is Dead! Hang the Doctor!" in *The Complete Elvis*, ed. Martin Torgoff (New York: G. P. Putnam's Sons, 1982), p. 74.

52. "Elvis the Pelvis Turns 40, But He Isn't All Shook Up," *People*, January 13, 1975.

53. Nash, *Memphis Mafia*, p. 507.

54. *Memphis Commercial Appeal*, January 9, 1975.

55. *Memphis Commercial Appeal*, January 30, 1975.

56. Booth, p. 71.

57. Guralnick, *Careless Love*, pp. 563–564.

58. Guralnick, *Careless Love*, p. 587.

59. *Denver Post*, January 29, 1976.

60. Guralnick, *Careless Love*, pp. 594–595.

61. Rose Clayton and Dick Heard, eds., *Elvis up Close: In the Words of Those Who Knew Him Best* (Atlanta: Turner, 1994), p. 307.

62. Red West, Sonny West, and Dave Hebler with Steve Dunleavy, *Elvis: What Happened?* (New York: Ballantine, 1977), pp. 322–323.

63. Guralnick, *Day by Day*, p. 362.

64. Bob Claypool, *Houston Post*, August 29, 1976.

65. Bill Burk, *Memphis Press-Scimitar*, December 12, 1976.

66. M. Bennett, "What's with Elvis: Walks out Midway at Show in Baltimore," *Variety*, June 1, 1977.

67. Guralnick, *Day by Day*, pp. 374–379, and Sauers, pp. 16–32.

68. In "Talk of the Town," *New Yorker*, August 18, 1977.

69. Guralnick, *Careless Love*, pp. 644–645.

70. Alan Higginbotham, "Doctor Feelgood," *The Observer*, August 11, 2002.

10

Always on My Mind

The day after Elvis's death, a crowd of 50,000 gathered outside Graceland. Eventually thousands of people were admitted to view the body. One man died of a heart attack, a woman in labor was rushed to the hospital, and hundreds were treated in the afternoon heat. Two young women were killed when a teenage driver lost control and careened into the crowd. The florists of Memphis ran out of flowers as offerings piled up around the palace of the King.[1]

Psychologists might attribute the outpouring to mass hysteria, voyeurism, nostalgia, or suppressed sexual yearnings. The fans who came said only that they loved him. The phenomenon was not confined to Memphis or the United States. In Europe tens of thousands grieved, driving home the idea he was more appreciated abroad.[2]

Mourners at the August 18 funeral included such rivals for Elvis's affection as Priscilla and Ann-Margret, professional associates Chet Atkins and the Colonel, and stars from outside his galaxy such as James Brown and George Hamilton. Caroline Kennedy covered the event for *Rolling Stone*. He was buried at Forest Hill Cemetery in Memphis, but after an attempt by four men to steal the body on August 28, Vernon removed the remains of Elvis and Gladys to the safety of Graceland's meditation garden.[3]

Scandals involving money began even before Elvis was buried. His third cousin, Billy Mann, accepted $18,000 to photograph Elvis in his casket. The lurid picture was published on the cover of *National Enquirer*.[4] In his will, Elvis named Vernon as his executor, listing his father, daughter, and grandmother as beneficiaries. After the deaths of Vernon and grandmother Minnie Mae, Lisa Marie would be the sole heir to the estate, held in trust until her 25th birthday.[5] After Vernon's death in 1979, control of the estate eventually passed to Lisa Marie. A string of law suits over the estate ended in 1983; the Colonel was forced to cede most of his shares in Elvis's catalog of recordings to RCA and the Presley family in exchange for a cash settlement. The Colonel was left with many years to enjoy his investment in Elvis's career. He died in Las Vegas in 1997.

With her mother advising her, Lisa Marie capitalized on her father's legacy through a company called Elvis Presley Enterprises (EPE). Graceland was expensive to maintain and came with high taxes, but the mansion turned a profit when opened to the public in 1982. EPE also acquired the strip mall across from Graceland in order to regulate the products being hawked at the King's doorstep. Graceland Plaza caters to all things Elvis, selling authorized merchandise to the tourist trade. After looking to Mount Vernon and other historic sites for inspiration, Priscilla, whose influence over the estate was pronounced, decided to restore Graceland to its original appearance as a Southern plantation. Some fans resented the changes, wanting the mansion preserved exactly as Elvis had left it. Second only to the White House as the most-visited American residence, it was placed on the National Register of Historic Places in 1991 and designated a National Landmark in 2006.[6]

Elvis Presley Enterprises rigorously pressed courts to issue cease-and-desist orders to fan clubs using the name and image of Elvis without permission. EPE became the guardian and arbiter of an American symbol, one of the most popular brands on earth. The struggle to regain control of his name and image was led by Priscilla, whose court battles helped redefine American publicity law and the marketing of dead celebrities.[7] The increase of the estate's value is remarkable considering EPE did not have Elvis's greatest asset, his recordings.[8]

Princess of Rock and Roll

Lisa Marie bore a striking physical resemblance to her father. Only four years old when her parents separated, Lisa Marie's disciplined childhood with her mother in Beverly Hills was relieved by frequent visits to Graceland, where she was pampered for weeks at a time and able to do whatever she wanted. Elvis was an "electrifyingly powerful, grand, beautiful presence" in her childlike eyes.[9]

She married musician Danny Keough in 1988, the union resulting in two children and divorce in 1992. In 1994, the daughter of the King of Rock and Roll stunned the world by announcing her marriage to the King of Pop, Michael Jackson. In a statement issued by Jackson's production company, she declared: "My married name is Mrs. Lisa Marie Presley-Jackson. I am very much in love with Michael. I dedicate my life to being his wife. I understand and support him. We both look forward to raising a family and living a happy, healthy life together."[10]

The union was not entirely successful. After Jackson's sudden death in the summer of 2009, Lisa Marie commented on her marriage and the similarity between her father and her ex-husband. "Our relationship was not 'a sham' as is being reported in the press," she wrote on her blog. "It was an unusual relationship yes, where two unusual people who did not live or know a 'normal life' found a connection. . . . As I sit here overwhelmed with sadness, reflection and confusion at what was my biggest failure to date, watching on the news almost play by play the exact scenario I saw happen on August 16th, 1977 happening again right now with Michael (A sight I never wanted to see again) just as he predicted."[11]

Following her divorce from the King of Pop, Lisa Marie's own career as a rock singer, songwriter, and recording artist began in earnest. "Lights Out," the first single from her 2003 debut album reached 18 on *Billboard*'s Hot Adult Top 40, and the album climbed to an impressive number five on *Billboard*'s Top 200 album chart.[12]

Tragic Hero

The Elvis cult touches many nerves of American popular culture: rebel; ascent of a working class boy to fame; white man with a black soul; the melting of musical influences; transformation from sexiest man in America into older, overweight parody; the legend of a hitchhiking ghost on the back roads of America. "For a dead man, Elvis Presley is awfully noisy," as one wag put it.[13] Paul Simon's song "Graceland" (1986) suggested that Elvis's home became a place of pilgrimage for anyone seeking a glimpse of American ideals manifested in a life. A 2002 poll suggested that 7 percent of Americans believed he was still alive.[14] The continuing popularity of Elvis and the folklore that grew around him became the subject of parody as long ago as the 1980s, notably in Mojo Nixon's college radio hit, "Elvis Is Everywhere."

Elvis did not endure as a hero to everyone. The influential rap group Public Enemy castigated him in their 1989 hit "Fight the Power," calling him a "straight up racist." Some cultural critics continued to see Elvis as a highwayman who waylaid black rhythm and blues, and strutted into town wearing the victim's clothes. Aside from Elvis's evident lack of race prejudice, the problem with that argument is that no culture, unless totally isolated, is self-contained. The black musicians who in part influenced Elvis were in part influenced by the white society around them. Cultural apartheid has always been largely impossible. This was especially true in the pre-civil rights South, where blacks and whites were segregated in closer proximity than blacks and whites in the supposedly enlightened North.

Rock critics who, conversely, praise Elvis for bringing black and white together, often have it partly wrong. Black and white music had been coming together for decades before Elvis set foot in Sun Studio. What Elvis accomplished was to awaken an increasingly somnolent America to the vibrancy of the nation's parallel black culture. His early TV appearances were pivotal events; nothing in popular culture has been the same since. A fortuitous collision of Elvis's own charisma with the carny skills of Colonel Parker and a generational mood pregnant with expectation turned a talented young singer from Memphis into a cultural hero.

With the musical and sociological foundation of rock and roll already in place, Elvis's ascent was powered by network television, which repeatedly beamed his provocative image into homes. Behind Elvis's rise was the marketing and distribution of a corporate behemoth, RCA. He enjoyed an advantage that was lacking in early black rock and roll stars such as Little Richard on the one hand and white singers like Pat Boone on the other. Elvis was white but distinctly different from the college-bound middle class boys next door. He tapped the same vein of gritty authenticity mined by Marlon Brando and other actors after World War II.

Tom Green, a popular Elvis impersonator in the upper Midwest during the 1980s and 1990s, articulated what many Americans felt about the King of Rock and Roll. "Elvis typified the American dream," he explained. "A guy in high school wishing he could do something so the world would take notice. He was from the lower middle class. He worked hard and created something that changed the world."

Green was not disappointed by Elvis's career development. "As I saw him on TV, in movies and followed his records, he turned into something I wanted to emulate," Green continued. "He helped bring me up, clean-cut wise. He helped form my mores. To be like Elvis wasn't that bad in the late '60s, an era of drugs and bad influences I stuck to the values I learned from my parents and Elvis."[15]

Revelations about prescription drug abuse do not undercut Green's point. To many of his fans, it mattered less what Elvis did than how he was perceived. As the polite rebel, Elvis was able to become the role model for individuals as disparate as Tom Green and Iggy Pop. As a Southerner beamed to the far corners of America and the world by TV, radio, and records, fans from outside the region where he grew up seldom understood his cultural context. Chivalry and deference were intrinsic to Southern folkways. Rebellion was also a Southern birthright. Elvis's seemingly contrary personality is a facet of being Southern as old as Reconstruction. He updated the stance, drawing from the look of juvenile delinquent movies from the early 1950s and the black performers he admired.

The legend continued to be fanned through Elvis fan clubs, conventions, and collectors. More than one hundred merchandizing licenses have been issued through EPE since 2002 for furniture, seasonings, apparel, chocolate, games, comic books, statuettes, musical equipment, pictures, pillows, and plates.[16] A collectors' market exists for memorabilia handled by the King. Autographs, because he generously signed anything handed him, are not as valuable. In 1994, collectors paid $41,500 for his American Express Card, and $101,500 for a cream-colored jumpsuit.[17]

Elvis was inducted into the Rock and Roll Hall of Fame in its initial year, 1986. He was also admitted to the Rockabilly Hall of Fame (1997), Country Music Hall of Fame (1998), and Gospel Music Hall of Fame (2001). In 1984, he was given the W. C. Handy Blues Award. That the gatekeepers of so many genres claim a piece of Elvis shows his widespread influence. His status as a national hero was confirmed when his likeness from the Sun Records' era appeared on a 1993 U.S. postage stamp.

His contribution to people's lives was visceral and visual, a link between individuals and an idea of American culture, burning in memory, cherished like a photo or keepsake, to be taken out as needed. Many children of the 1950s have vivid memories of seeing him on TV for the first time. While many of Elvis's critics dismissed most of his career after returning from the army, Greil Marcus suggested, "it may be that he never took any of it seriously, just did his job and did it well, trying to enjoy himself and stay sane."[18] He wrote those words several years before Elvis's death and the full extent of his declining physical and emotional health was known.

Prior to the late 20th century, literature played the leading role in explaining the American myth and dream. There was no greater dream than to write the great American novel. *The Adventures of Huckleberry Finn, The Grapes of Wrath, On the Road,* or *To Kill a Mockingbird* explore the American imagination by crossing frontiers both physical and personal, and investigate ideas of social advancement and the myth of the hero. Such stories were also told visually in the films of John Ford and Frank Capra. As technology made recorded music increasingly pervasive, and music seized the high ground of popular culture after World War II, the impulse driving American writing moved from pen and screen to the microphone.

In the preface to the 1885 edition of *Leaves of Grass*, Walt Whitman wrote that the proof of a poet is "that his country absorbs him as affectionately as he has absorbed it." By that definition, Elvis Presley was a poet, even if he was not a lyricist. Already in the 1920s Zelda Fitzgerald foretold the rising power of vernacular lyrics when she wrote, "we live our lives by the philosophies of popular songs."[19] This was never so true as in the second half of the 20th century when rock was embraced as the anthem of several postwar generations. Rock singers became, as poet Ezra Pound said of artists, "the antennae of the race."[20] The pressure placed on the shoulders of those artists by fans was great. Rock singers were expected to live by the philosophy of their songs; the fans expected their antennae to always be tuned in. According to U2's Bono, "we want our idols to die on a cross of their own making, and if they don't we want our money back."[21]

As generations pass, however, it already has become increasingly difficult for people who were not moved by Elvis when he was alive to take him entirely seriously. For many younger people, Elvis was an eccentric, isolated relic, a figure of pure black velvet kitsch found dead in his bathroom from drug use. For them, his songs remain a hit at karaoke bars, but his artistry has been eclipsed by his image. "Of the three towering icons of music, the Beatles, Johnny Cash, and Elvis Presley, Elvis is the least relevant to our generation," according to music critic Evan Rytlewski. "Everyone listens to the Beatles and Johnny Cash's rebel image resonates with us. I don't know too many people who are into Elvis."[22]

The boundless creative imagination of the Beatles, which laid the seeds for so many genres, is generally acknowledged as the foundation for the rock music of recent years by younger generations, not the man who once reigned as the King of Rock and Roll. Johnny Cash, who began his recording career at Sun Records in the wake of Elvis's success, has become the symbol of authentic Americana. His image as the stoic man in black is regarded as cool, unlike Elvis's latter-day image of sequined jump suits and mugging the microphone.

Elvis was a cultural hero to baby boomers around the world, especially in America, where many fans who came of age in the 1950s and

1960s identified with his ascent from obscurity to the zenith of stardom. Soon enough his flaws became apparent. Unlike many tragic heroes, however, he was not undone by hubris. Elvis was often self-deprecating as a public figure and remained generally humble in private life. Although intelligent and a seeker after knowledge, Elvis lacked an education that could help him make sense of the world and his place in it. Like many poor Southerners of his time, he bristled against authority but ultimately fell in line. Although he embarked on his career with an awareness of the music business, Elvis delegated full responsibility for the business of his stardom to an authority figure, Colonel Parker, who interfered with his development as an actor and recording artist. Forever uncertain of himself and his potential, Elvis transcended his sense of narrow limits when he sang songs with emotions he shared. After the image of his last years fades from public memory and only the recordings of his music remain, Elvis will be counted among the great musical artists of the 20th century, not only for his influence on popular culture in the 1950s but for the performances etched in memory.

Notes

1. Molly Ivins, "Presley Fans Mourn in Memphis," *New York Times*, August 18, 1977; Molly Ivins, "Elvis Presley Entombed: Two Mourners Killed by Car," *New York Times*, August 18, 1977.

2. Molly Ivins, "Why They Mourned for Elvis," *New York Times*, August 24, 1977; Jonathan Kandell, ". . . And Europe Grieves," *New York Times*, August 18, 1977.

3. Ivins, "Elvis Presley Entombed"; "4 Accused of Plot to Take Presley Body," *New York Times*, August 30, 1977.

4. *National Enquirer*, September 6, 1977; Jerry Hopkins, *Elvis Presley: The Biography* (London: Plexus, 2007), p. 386.

5. "Presley Will Names Father as Executor," *New York Times*, August 23, 1977.

6. National Historic Landmark summary listing, National Park Service, http://nps.gov.

7. S. C. Gwynne, "Love Me Legal Tender," *Time*, August 4, 1997.

8. Lisa Marie sold the controlling interest in EPE to Robert Sillerman (SFX Entertainment) in 2005, receiving cash, stocks, and

debt forgiveness totaling $100 million. Sillerman also acquired 50 percent of the estate's publishing rights. Lisa Marie was criticized by fans for her "disloyalty," but stressed her father would be pleased for the financial stability the deal afforded his family. Lisa Marie, with her mother as advisor, continues to own 15 percent of EPE and 100 percent of Graceland along with Elvis's personal effects. Chris Heath, "Lisa Marie Presley," *Rolling Stone*, May 17, 2003.

9. Heath.

10. Richard Perez-Pena, "Elvis Presley's Daughter Confirms She Wed Michael Jackson," *New York Times*, August 2, 1994.

11. Available at blogs.myspace.com/index.cfm?fuseaction=blog.view &friendId=42291868&blogId=497035326.

12. *Billboard* chart list for September 24, 2003.

13. Gilbert B. Rodman, *Elvis after Elvis: The Posthumous Career of a Living Legend* (London: Routledge, 1996), p. 1.

14. "Long Live the King," *New York Times*, August 16, 2002.

15. Dave Luhrssen, "Return to Sender: On the Campaign Trail with Elvis," *Shepherd Express*, May 14, 1992.

16. *Billboard*, June 15, 2002.

17. Monika Guttman, "To Collectors, the King's Alive," *U.S. News & World Report*, August 8, 1984.

18. Greil Marcus, *Mystery Train: Images of America in Rock and Roll Music* (New York: E. P. Dutton, 1975), p. 143.

19. Nancy Milford, *Zelda: A Biography* (New York: Harper Perennial, 1983), p. 300.

20. Ezra Pound, *ABC of Reading* (New York: New Directions, 1960), p. 73.

21. Bono, "What Elvis Left Behind," *Rolling Stone*, April 15, 2004.

22. Interview with Evan Rytlewski, February 2010. After starting as a music critic with the *Daily Cardinal* as an undergraduate at the University of Wisconsin, Rytlewski became arts editor of Madison, Wisconsin's alternative *Core Weekly* (2004–2006) and music editor of Milwaukee's alternative weekly, the *Shepherd Express* (2006–present).

Selected Bibliography

Adorno, Theodor. *Introduction to the Sociology of Music*. Trans. E. B. Ashton. New York: Seabury Press, 1976.

Alba, Ben. *Inventing Late Night: Steve Allen and the Original Tonight Show*. Amherst, NY: Prometheus, 2005.

Anderson, Nancy. "Elvis by His Father Vernon Presley." *Good Housekeeping*, January 1978.

Anderson, Robert Mapes. *Vision of the Disinherited: The Making of American Pentecostalism*. New York: Oxford University Press, 1979.

Ann-Margret. *Ann-Margret: My Story*. With Todd Gold. New York: G. P. Putnam's Sons, 1994.

Archer, Jules. "Is This Unassuming Rocker America's Newest Rebel?" *True Story*, December 1956.

Arnold, Eddy. *It's a Long Way from Chester County*. Old Tappan, NJ: Hewitt House, 1969.

Atkins, Chet. *Country Gentleman*. With Bill Neely. Chicago: Henry Regnery, 1974.

Bennett, M. "What's with Elvis: Walks out Midway at Show in Baltimore." *Variety*, June 1, 1977.

Bertrand, Michael T. *Rock, Race, and Elvis*. Urbana: University of Illinois Press, 2000.

Bigsby, C. W. E., ed. *Superculture: American Popular Culture and Europe*. Bowling Green, OH: Bowling Green University Press, 1975.

Biles, Roger. *Memphis in the Great Depression*. Knoxville: University of Tennessee Press, 1986.

Biskind, Peter. *Seeing Is Believing: How Hollywood Taught Us to Stop Worrying and Love the Fifties*. New York: Pantheon, 1983.

Bliven, Bruce. "The Voice and the Kids." *New Republic*, November 6, 1944.

Blount, Roy, Jr. "Elvis." *Esquire*, December 1983.

Bono. "What Elvis Left Behind." *Rolling Stone*, April 15, 2004.

Booth, Stanley. "A Hound Dog to the Manor Born." *Esquire*, February 1968.

Bosquet, Jean. "Parker Learned Name—Fast." *New York Journal-American*, June 13, 1960.

Brode, Douglas. *Elvis Cinema and Popular Culture*. Jefferson, NC: McFarland, 2006.

Broven, John. *Rhythm and Blues in New Orleans*. New York: Pelican, 1978.

Brown, Carlton. "A Craze Called Elvis." *Coronet*, September 1956.

Brown, Peter Harry, and Pat H. Broeski. *Down at the End of Lonely Street: The Life and Death of Elvis Presley*. New York: Dutton, 1997.

Burk, Bill. *Early Elvis: The Tupelo Years*. Memphis, TN: Propwash Publications, 1994.

Cantor, Louis. *Dewey and Elvis: The Life and Times of a Rock'n'Roll Deejay*. Urbana: University of Illinois Press, 2005.

Capparell, Stephanie. *The Real Pepsi Challenge: The Inspirational Story of Breaking the Color Barrier in American Business*. New York: Wall Street Journal Press, 2007.

Carr, Roy, Brian Case, and Fred Dellar. *The Hip: Hipsters, Jazz and the Beat Generation*. London: Faber & Faber, 1986.

Cash, Johnny. *Johnny: The Autobiography*. With Patrick Carr. New York: Harper Paperbacks, 1997.

Clayton, Rose, and Dick Heard, eds. *Elvis up Close: In the Words of Those Who Knew Him Best*. Atlanta: Turner, 1994.

Coleman, Roy. *Lennon*. New York: McGraw-Hill, 1984.

Cott, Jonathan. *Back to a Shadow in the Night: Music Writings and Interviews, 1968–2001*. Milwaukee, WI: Hal Leonard, 2002.

Country Music magazine, eds., *The Comprehensive Country Music Encyclopedia*. New York: Times Books, 1994.

Dalton, David, and Ron Cayen. *James Dean American Icon*. New York: St. Martin's Press, 1984.

Daniel, Pete. "Rhythm of the Land." *Agricultural History* 68, no. 4 (1994): 1–22.

Denisoff, R. Serge. "The Evolution of Popular Music Broadcasting, 1920–1972." *Popular Music and Society* 2 (Spring 1973): 202–226.

DeWitt, Howard A. *Elvis: The Sun Years, The Story of Elvis Presley in the Fifties.* Ann Arbor, MI: Popular Culture Ink, 1993.

Dickerson, James L. *Colonel Tom Parker: The Curious Life of Elvis Presley's Eccentric Manager.* New York: Cooper Square Press, 2001.

Dobbs, Dale. "A Brief History of East Tupelo, Mississippi." In *Elvis Presley Heights, Mississippi, Lee County, 1921–1984.* Tupelo, MS: Elvis Presley Heights Garden Club, 1984.

Doll, Susan M. *Understanding Elvis: Southern Roots vs. Star Image.* New York: Garland Publishing, 1998.

Dove, Ian. "Presley Mixes Early Hits with More Recent Safe Songs." *New York Times,* June 25, 1973.

Doyle, Peter. *Echo and Reverb: Fabricating Space in Popular Recording, 1900–1960.* Middletown, CT: Wesleyan University Press, 2005.

Dundy, Elaine. *Elvis and Gladys.* New York: Macmillan, 1985.

Escott, Colin. *Good Rockin' Tonight: Sun Records and the Birth of Rock'n'Roll.* With Martin Hawkins. New York: St. Martin's, 1991.

Feather, Leonard. "Boom Year for Jazz, Pops, R&R." *Melody Maker,* December 15, 1956.

Federal Writers Project. *Mississippi: The WPA Guide to the Magnolia State.* New York: Viking, 1938.

Fisher, Eddie. *Been There, Done That.* With David Fisher. New York: St. Martin's Press, 1999.

Flynn, George Q. *The Draft, 1940–1973.* Lawrence: University Press of Kansas, 1993.

Fortas, Alan. *Elvis: From Memphis to Hollywood.* Ann Arbor, MI: Popular Culture Ink, 1992.

Friedman, Josh Alan. *Tell the Truth until They Bleed: Coming Clean in the Dirty World of Blues and Rock'n'Roll.* New York: Backbeat, 2008.

Gary, Kays. "Elvis Defends Low-Down Style." *Charlotte Observer,* June 27, 1956.

Geller, Larry, and Joel Spector. *"If I Can Dream": Elvis' Own Story.* With Patricia Romanowski. New York: Simon & Schuster, 1989.

Gillett, Charlie. *The Sound of the City: The Rise of Rock and Roll.* 3rd ed. New York: Da Capo, 1996.

Goff, James R., Jr. *Close Harmony: A History of Southern Gospel.* Chapel Hill: University of North Carolina Press, 2002.

Goldman, Albert. *Elvis.* New York: McGraw-Hill, 1981.

Gray, Michael. *Hand Me My Travelin' Shoes.* London: Bloomsbury, 2007.

Guralnick, Peter. *Careless Love: The Unmaking of Elvis Presley.* Boston, Little Brown, 1999.

Guralnick, Peter. *Last Train to Memphis: The Rise of Elvis Presley.* Boston: Little Brown, 1994.

Guralnick, Peter. *Lost Highways: Journeys and Arrivals of American Musicians.* Boston: David R. Godine, 1979.

Guralnick, Peter, and Ernst Jorgensen. *Elvis Day by Day: The Definitive Record of His Life and Music.* New York: Ballantine, 1999.

Guttman, Monika, "To Collectors, the King's Alive." *U.S. News & World Report*, August 8, 1984.

Gwynne, S. C. "Love Me Legal Tender." *Time*, August 4, 1997.

Hajdu, David. "Hustling Elvis." *New York Review of Books*, October 9, 2003.

Hajdu, David. *The Ten-Cent Plague: The Great Comic Book Scare and How It Changed America.* New York: Farrar, Straus & Giroux, 2008.

Halberstadt, Alex. *Lonely Avenue: The Unlikely Life and Times of Doc Pomus.* Cambridge, MA: Da Capo, 2007.

Halberstam, David. *The Fifties.* New York: Villard Books, 1993.

Hammontree, Patsy Guy. *Elvis Presley: A Bio-Bibliography.* Westport, CT: Greenwood Press, 1985.

Hampton, Howard. "Elvis Dorado: The True Romance of *Viva Las Vegas!*" *Film Comment*, July-August 1994.

Harris, Warren G. *Clark Gable: A Biography.* New York: Harmony, 2002.

Hayes, Harold, ed. *Smiling through the Apocalypse: Esquire's History of the Sixties.* New York: McCall, 1970.

Heath, Chris. "Lisa Marie Presley." *Rolling Stone*, May 17, 2003.

Heckman, Don. "Presley, Talents Richly Intact, Shifts Emphasis to Rock/Gospel." *New York Times*, June 11, 1972.

Helt, Richard C. "A German Bluegrass Festival: The 'Country-Boom' and Some Notes on the History of American Popular Music in West Germany." *Journal of Popular Culture* 10 (Spring 1977): 821–832.

Hemphill, Paul. *Lovesick Blues: The Life of Hank Williams*. New York: Viking, 2005.

Higginbotham, Alan. "Doctor Feelgood." *The Observer*, August 11, 2002.

Hodenfield, Chris. "Arthur Crudup May Get It Back." *Rolling Stone*, December 9, 1971.

Hoffman, Abbie. "Too Soon the Hero." *Crawdaddy*, November 1977.

Hoover, J. Edgar. "Youth Running Wild." *Los Angeles Times*, June 27, 1943.

Hopkins, Jerry. *Elvis: A Biography*. New York: Simon & Schuster, 1971.

Hopkins, Jerry. *Elvis Presley: The Biography*. London: Plexus, 2007.

Horn, Maurice, ed. *World Encyclopedia of Comics*. New York: Chelsea House, 1976.

Howard, Edwin. "In a Spin." *Memphis Press Scimitar*, July 28, 1954.

Hyams, Joe. "The Highest Paid Movie Star Ever." *New York Herald-Tribune*, May 16, 1957.

Ivins, Molly. "Elvis Presley Entombed: Two Mourners Killed by Car," *New York Times*, August 18, 1977.

Ivins, Molly. "Presley Fans Mourn in Memphis." *New York Times*, August 18, 1977.

Ivins, Molly. "Why They Mourned for Elvis." *New York Times*, August 24, 1977.

Jackson, John A. *Big Beat Heat: Alan Freed and the Early Years of Rock & Roll*. New York: Schirmer, 1991.

Jacobs, George, and William Stadiem. *Mr. S.: My Life with Frank Sinatra*. New York: HarperEntertainment, 2003.

Jeansonne, Glen. *Women of the Far Right: The Mothers' Movement and World War II*. Chicago: University of Chicago Press, 1996.

Jeansonne, Glen, and David Luhrssen. "Elvis: Rock 'n' Roll's Reluctant Rebel." *History Today*, August 2007.

Jennings, Robert. "There'll Always Be an Elvis." *Saturday Evening Post*. September 11, 1965.

Johnson, Robert. *Elvis Presley Speaks!* New York: Rave Publications, 1956.

Johnson, Robert. "Elvis Sings and Thousands Scream." *Memphis Press-Scimitar*, July 5, 1956.

Johnson, Robert. "Suddenly Singing Elvis Presley Zooms into Recording Stardom." *Memphis Press-Scimitar*, February 5, 1955.

Johnson, Robert. "These Are the Cats Who Make Music for Elvis." *Memphis Press-Scimitar*, December 15, 1956.

Johnston, David. "The FBI and the King: Both Had Suspicious Minds." *New York Times*, August 17, 1997.

Kandell, Jonathan. ". . . And Europe Grieves." *New York Times*, August 18, 1977.

Kingsley, James. "At Home with Elvis Presley." *Memphis Commercial Appeal, Mid-South Magazine*, March 7, 1965.

Kingsley, James. "Relaxed Elvis Disks 16 Songs in Hometown Stint." *Memphis Commercial Appeal*, January 23, 1969.

Knight, Arthur. "Flaming Star." *Saturday Review*, December 1960.

Laird, Tracey E. W. Louisiana Hayride: *Radio and Roots Music along the Red River*. New York: Oxford University Press, 2005.

Lee, George W. *Beale Street: Where the Blues Began*. New York: Robert O. Ballou, 1934.

Leiber, Jerry, and Mike Stoller. *Hound Dog: The Leiber and Stoller Autobiography*. With David Ritz. New York: Simon & Schuster, 2009.

Leider, Emily W. *Dark Lover: The Life and Death of Rudolph Valentino*. New York: Farrar, Straus & Giroux, 2003.

Leland, John. *Hip: The History*. New York: HarperCollins, 2004.

Lerner, Max. *America as a Civilization: Life and Thought in the United States Today*. New York: Simon & Schuster, 1957.

Lerner, Max. *The Unfinished Country: A Book of American Symbols*. New York: Simon & Schuster, 1959.

Levy, Alan. *Operation Elvis*. New York: Henry Holt, 1960.

Lewis, George. *Massive Resistance: The White Response to the Civil Rights Movement*. New York: Oxford University Press, 2006.

Lewis, Jerry, and James Kaplan. *Dean and Me (A Love Story)*. New York: Doubleday, 1982.

Lewis, Joseph. "Elvis Presley Lives." *Cosmopolitan*, November 1968.

Lewis, Selma A. *A Biblical People in the Bible Belt: The Jewish Community of Memphis, Tennessee, 1840s–1960s*. Macon, GA: Mercer University Press, 1998.

Lichter, Paul. *The Boy Who Dared to Rock: The Definitive Elvis*. Garden City, NY: Dolphin, 1978.

Loewen, James W., and Charles Sallis. *Mississippi: Conflict and Change*. New York: Pantheon, 1974.

Logan, Horace. *Elvis, Hank, and Me: Musical History on the* Louisiana Hayride. With Bill Sloan. New York: St. Martin's Press, 1998, p. 141.

Luhrssen, Dave. "Return to Sender: On the Campaign Trail with Elvis." *Shepherd Express*, May 14, 1992.

Marcus, Greil. *Mystery Train: Images of America in Rock and Roll Music*. New York: E. P. Dutton, 1975.

Marcus, Greil. *The Shape of Things to Come: Prophecy and the American Voice*. New York: Farrar, Straus & Giroux, 2006.

Marsh, Dave. *Elvis*. New York: Rolling Stone Press, 1982.

Mason, Bobbie Joe. *Elvis Presley*. New York: Viking, 2003.

McGrath, Charles, "50 Years Older, 'Birdie' Returns to the Nest." *New York Times*, October 11, 2009.

McKee, Margaret, and Fred Chisenhall. *Beale Black and Blue: Life and Music on Black America's Main Street*. Baton Rouge: Louisiana State University Press, 1981.

McIlwaine, Shields. *Memphis Down in Dixie*. New York: E. P. Dutton, 1948.

Milford, Nancy. *Zelda: A Biography*. New York: Harper Perennial, 1983.

Miller, Edwin. "Elvis the Innocent." *Memories*, May 1989.

Miller, Jim, ed. Rolling Stone *Illustrated History of Rock & Roll*. New York: Rolling Stone Press, 1976.

Miller, William D. *Mr. Crump of Memphis.* Baton Rouge: Louisiana State University Press, 1964.

Morrison, Craig. *Go Cat Go! Rockabilly and Its Makers.* Urbana: University of Illinois Press, 1996.

Myrdal, Gunnar. *An American Dilemma: The Negro Problem in a Modern Democracy.* 20th anniversary ed. New York: Harper & Row, 1962.

Nash, Alanna. *The Colonel: The Extraordinary Story of Colonel Tom Parker and Elvis Presley.* New York: Simon & Schuster, 2003.

Nash, Alanna. *Elvis Aaron Presley: Revelations from the Memphis Mafia.* With Billy Smith, Marty Lacker, and Lamar Fike. New York: HarperCollins, 1995.

Norman, Philip. *Sympathy for the Devil: The Rolling Stones Story.* New York: Linden Press/Simon & Schuster, 1984.

Osborne, Jerry. *Elvis Word for Word.* New York: Gramercy Books, 2006.

Pabst, Ralph M. *Gene Austin's Ol' Buddy.* Phoenix, AZ: Augury, 1984.

Palmer, Robert. "Chips Moman's Views on World of Recording." *New York Times*, May 9, 1984.

Palmer, Robert. *Deep Blues.* London: Macmillan, 1981.

Palmer, Robert. "Elvis Presley: Homage to a Rock King." *New York Times*, November 19, 1984.

Palmer, Robert. *Rock & Roll: An Unruly History.* New York: Harmony, 1995.

Pareles, Jon, and Patricia Romanowski, eds. *The Rolling Stone Encyclopedia of Rock & Roll.* New York: Summit, 1983.

Pegg, Bruce. *Brown Eyed Handsome Man, The Life and Hard Times of Chuck Berry.* New York: Routledge, 2002.

Perez-Pena, Richard. "Elvis Presley's Daughter Confirms She Wed Michael Jackson." *New York Times*, August 2, 1994.

Petkov, Steven, and Leonard Mustazza, eds. *The Frank Sinatra Reader.* New York: Oxford University Press, 1995.

Polk, William T. *Southern Accent: From Uncle Remus to Oak Ridge.* New York: William Morrow, 1953.

Ponce de Leon, Charles L. *Fortunate Son: The Life of Elvis Presley.* New York: Hill & Wang, 2006.

Porteous, Clark. "Prison Singers Find Fame with Record They Made in Memphis." *Memphis Press-Scimitar*, July 15, 1953.

Pound, Ezra. *ABC of Reading*. New York: New Directions, 1960.

Presley, Priscilla Beaulieu. *Elvis and Me*. With Sandra Harmon. New York: G. P. Putnam's Sons, 1985.

Quain, Kevin, ed. *The Elvis Reader: Texts and Sources on the King of Rock'n'Roll*. New York: St. Martin's Press, 1992.

Raiteri, Charles. "Eddie Bond: A Reluctant Rockabilly Rocker Remembers." *Goldmine*, August 1, 1986.

Rasmussen, Nicholas. *On Speed: The Many Lives of Amphetamine*. New York: New York University Press, 2008.

Rijff, Ger, ed. *Long Lonely Highway: A 1950's Elvis Scrapbook*. Ann Arbor, MI: Pierian Press, 1987.

Roberts, John Storm. *The Latin Tinge: The Impact of Latin American Music on the United States*. 2nd ed. New York: Oxford University Press, 1999.

Rodman, Gilbert B. *Elvis after Elvis: The Posthumous Career of a Living Legend*. London: Routledge, 1996.

Rolling Stone, ed. *Rolling Stone: The Decades of Rock & Roll*. San Francisco: Chronicle Books, 2001.

Rosenberg, Bernard, and David Manning White, eds. *Mass Culture: The Popular Arts in America*. Glencoe, IL: Free Press, 1957.

Rosenblum, Martin Jack, and David Luhrssen. *Searching for Rock and Roll*. Mason, OH: Thomson, 2007.

Rowe, Mike. *Chicago Blues: The City and the Music*. New York: Da Capo, 1975.

Sauers, Wendy. *Elvis Presley: A Complete Reference*. Jefferson, NC: McFarland, 1984.

Schickel, Richard. *Brando*. New York: Thunder's Mouth Press, 1999.

Scott, Vernon. "Elvis at Home, Awaits Clippers." *New York World-Telegram*, March 15, 1958.

Scrivener, Mildred. "My Boy Elvis." *TV Radio Mirror*, March 1957.

Shaw, Arnold. *Black Popular Music in America*. New York: Schirmer, 1986.

Shaw, Arnold. *Honkers and Shouters: The Golden Years of Rhythm and Blues*. New York: Macmillan, 1978.

Shaw, Arnold. *The Rockin' '50s*. New York: Hawthorne, 1974.

Shaw, Arnold. *Sinatra: Twentieth-Century Romantic*. New York: Holt, Rinehart & Winston, 1968.

Shelton, Robert. "Rock Star's Explosive Blues Have Vintage Quality." *New York Times*, December 4, 1968.

Sinatra, Nancy. *Frank Sinatra: My Father*. Garden City, NY: Doubleday, 1985.

Sinclair, Gordon. "Sinclair Says Elvis 'Fine Lad,' Hopes to Last for 40 Years." *Toronto Star*, October 29, 1956.

Smith, Billy. "The Audubon House." *The Record*, June 1979.

Stone, Harold. "Meet Mr. Rock'n'Roll." *Top Secret*, November 1956.

Sublette, Ned. *The World That Made New Orleans: From Spanish Silver to Congo Square*. Chicago: Lawrence Hill, 2008.

Tamarkin, Jeff. "Roy Orbison: An Interviewer's Dream." *Goldmine*, May 5, 1989.

Thomas, Bob. "It Looks Like Romance for Elvis Presley and Ann-Margret." *Memphis Press-Scimitar*, August 6, 1963.

Thompson, Gordon. *Please Please Me: Sixties British Pop, Inside Out*. New York: Oxford University Press, 2008.

Tindall, George Brown. *The Emergence of the New South, 1913–1945*. Baton Rouge: Louisiana State University Press, 1967.

Torgoff, Martin, ed. *The Complete Elvis*. New York: G. P. Putnam's Sons, 1982.

Tosches, Nick. *Unsung Heroes of Rock'n'Roll: The Birth of Rock in the Wild Years Before Elvis*. 3rd ed. New York: Da Capo, 1999.

Tracy, Kathleen. *Elvis Presley: A Biography*. Westport, CT: Greenwood Press, 2007.

Tucker, David M. *Lieutenant Lee of Beale Street*. Nashville: Vanderbilt University Press, 1971.

U.S. Department of Commerce. *Historical Statistics of the United States*, vol 2. Washington, DC: 1975.

Vallenga, Dick. *Elvis and the Colonel*. With Mick Farren. New York: Delacourte Press, 1988.

VanHecke, Susan. *Race with the Devil: Gene Vincent's Life in the Fast Lane*. New York: St. Martin's Press, 2000.

Vieira, Mark A. *Sin in Soft Focus: Pre-Code Hollywood*. New York: Abrams, 1999.

Von Eschen, Penny M. *Satchmo Blows up the World: Jazz Ambassadors Play the Cold War*. Cambridge, MA: Harvard University Press, 2004.

Ward, Brian. *Just My Soul Responding: Rhythm and Blues, Black Consciousness, and Race Relations*. Berkeley: University of California Press, 1998.

Ward, Ed, Geoffrey Stokes, and Ken Tucker. *Rock of Ages: The Rolling Stone History of Rock & Roll*. New York: Rolling Stone Press, 1986.

West, Red, Sonny West, and Dave Hebler. *Elvis, What Happened?* As told to Steve Dunleavy. New York: Ballantine, 1977.

White, James H. "Elvis Back in Town with Sideburns Clipped and the Army on His Mind." *Memphis Commercial-Appeal*, March 15, 1958.

Wilson, John S. "Elvis Presley: Rocking Blues Shouter." *New York Times*, January 13, 1957.

Wilson, John S. "Elvis Returns . . ." *New York Times*, May 8, 1960.

Winship, Michael. *Television*. New York: Random House, 1988.

Zmijewisky, Steven, and Boris Zmijewsky. *Elvis: The Films and Career of Elvis Presley*. Secaucus, NJ: Citadel Press, 1976.

Index

About the Authors

GLEN JEANSONNE is professor of history at the University of Wisconsin–Milwaukee, where he has taught 20th-century American history since 1978. He has also taught at Williams College, the University of Michigan, and the University of Louisiana–Lafayette. Jeansonne has authored or edited 14 books, published more than 70 articles, and won 22 grants. He is the recipient of two lifetime teaching awards and a research award at his present university.

DAVID LUHRSSEN has taught at the University of Wisconsin–Milwaukee, the Milwaukee Institute of Art and Design, and Milwaukee Area Technical College. He is coauthor of *Changing Times: The Life of Barack Obama*; *A Time of Paradox: America Since 1890*; and *Searching for Rock and Roll*. He has published articles in *Historically Speaking, History Today*, and the *Journal of American History*. Luhrssen is also the arts and entertainment editor of Milwaukee's weekly newspaper, the *Shepherd Express*, and has written about music, film, culture, and books for *Billboard, Entertainment Weekly*, and other publications.

DAN SOKOLOVIC is a writer and publisher and a PhD candidate in the history and modern studies program at the University of Wisconsin–Milwaukee. His research interests lie in cultural studies of the authenticity and continuity of 20th-century American popular music, particularly the 1960s–1980s rock period and the post-1990 alternative scenes.